Metaphors and Social Identity Formation in Paul's Letters to the Corinthians

Metaphors and Social Identity Formation in Paul's Letters to the Corinthians

KAR YONG LIM

☙PICKWICK *Publications* · Eugene, Oregon

METAPHORS AND SOCIAL IDENTITY FORMATION IN PAUL'S LETTERS TO THE CORINTHIANS

Copyright © 2017 Kar Yong Lim. All rights reserved. Except for brief quotations in critical publications or reviews, no part of this book may be reproduced in any manner without prior written permission from the publisher. Write: Permissions, Wipf and Stock Publishers, 199 W. 8th Ave., Suite 3, Eugene, OR 97401.

Pickwick Publications
An Imprint of Wipf and Stock Publishers
199 W. 8th Ave., Suite 3
Eugene, OR 97401

www.wipfandstock.com

PAPERBACK ISBN: 978-1-4982-8289-5
HARDCOVER ISBN: 978-1-4982-8291-8
EBOOK ISBN: 978-1-4982-8290-1

Cataloging-in-Publication data:

Names: Lim, Kar Yong.

Title: Metaphors and social identity formation in Paul's letters to the Corinthians / Kar Yong Lim.

Description: Eugene, OR : Pickwick Publications, 2017 | Includes bibliographical references and index.

Identifiers: ISBN 978-1-4982-8289-5 (paperback) | ISBN 978-1-4982-8291-8 (hardcover) | ISBN 978-1-4982-8290-1 (ebook)

Subjects: LCSH: Bible. Corinthians, 1st—Criticism, interpretation, etc. | Bible. Corinthians, 2nd—Criticism, interpretation, etc. | Metaphor in the Bible. | Group identity—Biblical teaching. | Identification (Religion)—Biblial teaching.

Classification: LCC BS2675.5 L4 2017 (print) | LCC BS2675.5 (ebook)

Manufactured in the U.S.A.   04/26/17

Contents

List of Tables | vi
Permissions | vii
Acknowledgments | ix
Abbreviations | x
Introduction | xv

Part I
1. Paul's Use of Metaphors in the Corinthian Letters | 3
2. Reading Paul's Metaphor through Social Identity Theory | 26

Part II
3. "My Brothers and Sisters": Sibling Metaphor | 51
4. "In Christ Jesus I became Your Father": Familial Metaphors | 93
5. "You are God's Temple": Temple Metaphor | 137
6. "You are the Body of Christ": Body Metaphor | 159

Part III
7. Paul, Metaphors, and Social Identity Formation in the Corinthian Letters | 191

Bibliography | 203
Author Index | 229
Ancient Document Index | 235

Tables

Table 1.1: Metaphors and Transference of Metaphors | 10

Table 1.2: Source and Target Domains | 20

Table 3.1: The Use of ἀδελφοί in Paul's Undisputable Letters | 53

Table 3.2: Instances where ἀδελφοί Is Not Translated as "Brothers" or "Brothers and Sisters" in the NRSV | 54

Table 4.1: Frequency of Children and Childhood-Related Terms and Expressions in Paul's Undisputed Letters Based on Aassgard's Tabulation | 97

Permissions

All Greek Scripture quotations are from Nestle-Aland, Novum Testamentum Graece, 28th Revised Edition, edited by Barbara and Kurt Aland, Johannes Karavidopoulos, Carlo M. Martini, and Bruce M. Metzger in cooperation with the Institute for New Testament Textual Research, Münster/Westphalia, © 2012 Deutsche Bibelgesellschaft, Stuttgart. Used by permission.

Unless otherwise indicated, all English Scripture quotations are from the New Revised Standard Version Bible, copyright 1989, Division of Christian Education of the National Council of the Churches of Christ in the United States of America. Used by permission. All rights reserved.

Scripture quotations marked NIV are taken from The Holy Bible, NEW INTERNATIONAL VERSION®, NIV® Copyright © 1973, 1978, 1984, 2011 by Biblica, Inc.® Used by permission. All rights reserved worldwide.

Scripture quotations marked TNIV are taken from The Holy Bible, Today's New International Version®, TNIV®. Copyright 2001, 2005 by Biblica, Inc.® Used by permission. All rights reserved worldwide.

Scripture quotations marked ESV are from the ESV® Bible (The Holy Bible, English Standard Version®), copyright © 2001 by Crossway, a publishing ministry of Good News Publishers. Used by permission. All rights reserved.

Scripture quoted by permission. Quotations designated (NET) are from the NET Bible® copyright ©1996-2016 by Biblical Studies Press, L.L.C. http://netbible.com. All rights reserved.

Portions of chapter 5 have been previously published as "Paul's Use of Temple Imagery in the Corinthian Correspondence: The Creation of Christian Identity." In *Reading Paul in Context: Explorations in Identity Formation: Essays in Honour of William S. Campbell*, edited by Kathy Ehrensperger and J. Brian Tucker, 189-205. LNTS 428. London: T. & T. Clark, 2010. Used by kind permission of Bloomsbury Publishing Plc.

Acknowledgments

WRITING A BOOK IS never a lone enterprise carried out by the author, and more so if it has taken more than eight years to complete the project. I am deeply indebted to colleagues and students at Seminari Theoloji Malaysia (Malaysia Theological Seminary) who have been a constant source of encouragement and inspiration for me. Over the years, many friends (and there are too many to name) contributed financially to this project, and this enabled me to carry out research and writing at Trinity Theological College, Singapore; Tyndale House, Cambridge; and Ridley College, Melbourne. Coming from an under-resourced country, I deeply treasure the opportunity to work in these excellent libraries where many ideas were exchanged with colleagues from all over the world. In addition, the Evangelical Free Church of Malaysia awarded a bursary for my sabbatical in 2015. The trustees of the Theological Research Scheme also approved a special grant that funded the publication of this book. Thank you for all your generosity.

A number of friends volunteered to read earlier drafts of this manuscript. In particular, I would like to thank Dorothy Teoh, Su Ming, and Dr Yvonne Foo for their labour of love. Their comments, feedback, and suggestions to improve this book are greatly appreciated. Any shortcomings in this book remain my responsibility.

Finally, without the support of my family, this book would not have been written. Thank you for all your love, encouragement, and sacrifices for me and for the work of the kingdom.

The Twelfth Sunday after Trinity, 2016
Seremban, Malaysia

Abbreviations

AB	Anchor Bible
AcBib	Academia Biblica
ACCS	Ancient Christian Commentary on Scripture
AJA	*American Journal of Archaeology*
AJPS	*Asian Journal of Pentecostal Studies*
AnBib	Analecta Biblica
ANTC	Abingdon New Testament Commentaries
ANRW	*Aufstieg und Niedergang der römischen Welt: Geschichte und Kultur Roms im Spiegel der neueren Forschung. Part 2, Principat.* Edited by Hildegard Temporini and Wolfgang Haase. Berlin: de Gruyter, 1972–
ASE	*Annalli di storia dell' esegesi*
BDAG	Danker, Frederick W., Walter Bauer, William F. Arndt, and F. Wilbur Gingrich. *Greek-English Lexicon of the New Testament and Other Early Christian Literature.* 3rd ed. Chicago, IL: University of Chicago Press, 2000.
BECNT	Baker Exegetical Commentary on the New Testament
BETL	Bibliotheca ephemeridum theologicarum lovaniensium
BiBh	*Bible Bhashyam*
BibInt	*Biblical Interpretation*
BibInt	Biblical Interpretation Series
BJSP	*British Journal of Social Psychology*
BTB	*Biblical Theology Bulletin*
BTS	Biblical Tools and Studies
BZNW	Beihefte zur Zeitschrift für die neutestamentliche Wissenschaft

CBET	Contributions to Biblical Exegesis and Theology
CBNTS	Coniectanea Biblica New Testament Series
CBQ	*Catholic Biblical Quarterly*
Colloq	*Colloquium*
ConC	Concordia Commentary
COP	Colloquium Oecumenicum Paulinum
CP	*Classical Philology*
CSPESPT	Cambridge Studies in Population, Economy and Society in Past Time
CTJ	*Calvin Theological Journal*
CTR	*Criswell Theological Review*
EC	Early Christianity
ECIHC	Early Christianity in Its Hellenistic Context.
ECL	Early Christianity and Its Literature
EJSP	*European Journal of Social Psychology*
EMSP	European Monographs in Social Psychology
ERT	Evangelical Review of Theology
ERSP	European Review of Social Psychology
EvQ	*Evangelical Quarterly*
FRLANT	Forschungen zur Religion und Literatur des Alten und Neuen Testaments
FRC	Family, Religion, and Culture
GCT	Gender, Culture, and Theory
GTR	Gender, Theory, and Religion
HBT	*Horizons in Biblical Theology*
HTR	*Harvard Theological Review*
HTS	Harvard Theological Studies
IBC	Interpretation: A Bible Commentary for Teaching and Preaching
ICC	International Critical Commentary
Int	*Interpretation*
IJIR	*International Journal of Intercultural Relation*
JAAR	*Journal of the American Academy of Religion*
JBL	*Journal of Biblical Literature*
JETS	*Journal of the Evangelical Theological Society*

JRH	*Journal of Religious History*
JSI	*Journal of Social Issues*
JSNT	*Journal for the Study of the New Testament*
JSNTSup	Journal for the Study of the New Testament Supplement Series
JTS	*Journal of Theological Studies*
LEC	Library of Early Christianity
LNTS	Library of New Testament Studies
LPS	Library of Pauline Studies
LSJ	Henry George Liddell, Robert Scott, and Henry Stuart Jones. *A Greek-English Lexicon*. 9th ed. Oxford: Clarendon, 1996.
LTQ	*Lexington Theological Quarterly*
NA28	Nestle-Aland, *Novum Testamentum Graece* 28th ed.
NCBC	New Cambridge Bible Commentary
Neot	*Neotestamentica*
NGTT	*Nederduitse gereformeerde teologiese tydskrif*
NICNT	The New International Commentary on the New Testament
NIGTC	New International Greek Testament Commentary
NovT	*Novum Testamentum*
NovTSup	Supplements to Novum Testamentum
NSBT	New Studies in Biblical Theology
NTM	New Testament Monographs
NTR	New Testament Readings
NTS	*New Testament Studies*
PAST	Pauline Studies
PBM	Paternoster Biblical Monographs
PTMS	Princeton Theological Monograph Series
PNTC	Pillar New Testament Commentary
QJS	*Quarterly Journal of Speech*
ResQ	*Restoration Quarterly*
RevExp	*Review and Expositor*
RivB	*Rivista biblica italiana*
SBEC	Studies in the Bible and Early Christianity
SBL	Studies in Biblical Literature
SBLDS	Society of Biblical Literature Dissertation Series

SBLMS	Society of Biblical Literature Monograph Series
SBLStBL	Society of Biblical Literature Studies in Biblical Literature
SBLSymS	Society of Biblical Literature Symposium Series
SIHC	Studies in the Intercultural History of Christianity
SNTSMS	Society for New Testament Studies Monograph Series
SP	Sacra Pagina
STAR	Studies in Theology and Religion
StBibLit	Studies in Biblical Literature (Lang)
TDNT	*Theological Dictionary of the New Testament.* Edited by Gerhard Kittel and Gerhard Friedrich. Translated by Geoffrey W. Bromiley. 10 vols. Grand Rapids, MI: Eerdmans, 1974–2006
TENTS	Texts and Editions for New Testament Study
TR	Theology and Religion
TynBul	*Tyndale Bulletin*
WBC	Word Biblical Commentary
WUNT	Wissenschaftliche Untersuchungen zum Neuen Testament

Introduction

> Now I appeal to you, brothers and sisters, by the name of our Lord Jesus Christ, that all of you be in agreement and that there be no divisions among you, but that you be united in the same mind and the same purpose. (1 Cor 1:10)

> And so, brothers and sisters, I could not speak to you as spiritual people, but rather as people of the flesh, as infants in Christ. I fed you with milk, not solid food, for you were not ready for solid food. (1 Cor 3:1–2a)

> Do you not know that you are God's temple and that God's Spirit dwells in you? If anyone destroys God's temple, God will destroy that person. For God's temple is holy, and you are that temple. (1 Cor 3:16–17)

> For though you might have ten thousand guardians in Christ, you do not have many fathers. Indeed, in Christ Jesus I became your father through the gospel. (1 Cor 4:15)

> For just as the body is one and has many members, and all the members of the body, though many, are one body, so it is with Christ . . . Now you are the body of Christ and individually members of it. (1 Cor 12:12, 27)

PAUL'S OCCASIONAL LETTERS WRITTEN to various Christ-communities are primarily meant to persuade, correct, and shape the thinking and behavior of his audience so that they are rooted in his understanding of the gospel. To achieve this goal, he uses a variety of means including rhetorical strategy, emotional appeals, and references to Scripture in his letters. As part of his rhetorical strategy, the use of metaphors features frequently and prominently. This can be seen from a selection of verses taken from 1 Corinthians and highlighted above. In these verses, Paul utilizes a range of metaphors drawn from different aspects of human life and experience such as fictive kinship, religious building, and the human body.

MOTIVATIONS AND AIMS OF INVESTIGATION

Paul's use of metaphors is intriguing. But this is not the only reason why I embarked on this investigation. My reasons are three-fold. First of all, I am fascinated by the literature, history, and the origins of the early Christ-movement, and the events and people that shaped it. I am intrigued by how Paul brought the gospel to the Mediterranean world and how this gospel, initially established on Jewish roots, would eventually take shape in a foreign, gentile world with a Hellenistic worldview that was markedly incompatible with the Jewish religious identity. I am also keen to examine how Paul not only proclaimed the gospel but continued to shape the gentile followers of this Christ-movement into a community of ἐκκλησία with its distinctive ethos and social identity within the Roman Empire, and how this laid the foundation for the beliefs, teachings, and ecclesiastical structures that guided subsequent followers, resulting in its growth into an established religion and institution.

Secondly, I am interested in exploring language as a means of communication. Paul's primary means of communication with the predominantly gentile communities he founded is through letter writing. As a letter writer, Paul uses various techniques and rhetoric prevalent in the Greco-Roman conventions of his day. By employing various tools of rhetoric, irony, typologies, and using appeals based on *ethos*, *pathos*, and *logos*, Paul's written communication would have impacted his audience. Of special interest in my investigation here is Paul's use of metaphors, a powerful element in linguistics and ancient rhetoric. The use of metaphors not only adds color to Paul's reasoning. It is also a powerful means to drive home what he is trying to reinforce through the teaching of his gospel and to correct the thinking of his audience—thinking that would eventually govern their behavior. This then raises a series of questions that I will attempt to address in this book: What is metaphor? Why did Paul frequently employ such a diverse range of metaphors in his letters? What was the function of metaphor in the Greco-Roman conventions of Paul's day? Did Paul randomly choose these metaphors in his letters as some sort of ornamental linguistic tool that formed part of his rhetorical strategy? Or, did he carefully and deliberately select these metaphors in order to accomplish specific goals in his communication with the Corinthians? How would the recipients of his letters have reacted to these metaphors? Did the use of metaphors shape the worldview and behavior of the recipients? What role did metaphors play in the formation of Christian social identity?

This leads me to my final motivation. I am interested in the social relations of Pauline community. What did Paul do to shape this movement in its formative years? How did the first Christ-followers perceive themselves, and how did they see themselves in relation to their contemporaries outside the ἐκκλησία? In what ways did they still share the cultural heritage of their contemporaries and social world? How would the gospel shape their social identity as followers of Christ since the ἐκκλησία comprised people from different ethnic groups? What were some of the ways and means Paul used to establish and nurture these communities so that they became, within a few decades, a fast-growing movement that transcended geographical boundaries? By using metaphors such as "brothers and sisters," "temple," and "body," how did Paul creatively shape and influence the way the recipients thought and interacted with one another as insiders, with outsiders, and in the formation of group identity?

THE STARTING POINT: PAUL'S USE OF METAPHORS AND FORMATION OF SOCIAL IDENTITY IN THE CORINTHIAN LETTERS

Of all the Christ-movements founded by Paul, the Corinthian congregation was the one that faced the most challenging issues, ranging from internal divisions, problematic behavioral traits such as sexual immorality, lawsuits among members of the community, and eating food sacrificed to idols. Other disturbing issues included abuse in the celebration of the Eucharist, chaos in the order of worship, and failed collection for the poor in Jerusalem. The Corinthian letters are, therefore, excellent candidates to examine how Paul attempted to resolve these issues and conflicts in the community.

Also, Paul probably spent the most time and energy on this Christ-movement, compared to other communities he founded. In terms of the number of visits he had with the Corinthians, there was the founding visit that lasted eighteen months (Acts 18:1); followed by the "painful visit" (2 Cor 2:1; 12:21); and potentially a third visit (2 Cor 12:14, 20–21; 13:1–2). In between these visits, there were other planned visits that did not materialize (see 1 Cor 16:2, 5 and 2 Cor 1:15–16, 23; 2:3). When it comes to Paul's correspondence with the Corinthians, we have a series of at least four, if not more, letters between them over a period of time. Unfortunately, not all these letters survived. Apart from the two canonical letters known as 1 and 2 Corinthians, it has been widely established that there could be at least two other letters that did not survive: a letter written prior to the canonical 1 Corinthians generally known as the "previous letter" (1 Cor 5:9 and 11) and a "severe letter" or "letter of tears" (2 Cor 1:23—2:11 and 7:5–16) possibly written some time in between the canonical 1 and 2 Corinthians. As such, if we take the literary integrity of 2 Corinthians,[1] we could confidently establish that there are at least four correspondences between Paul and the Corinthians in the following chronological order: "previous letter"; 1 Corinthians; "severe letter"; and 2 Corinthians.[2]

The two canonical Corinthian letters written by Paul are evidence of a church that was afflicted by conflicts and tensions internally and externally—among the members of the Christ-movement; between the members and Paul; and among the members, Paul, and external parties opposed to Paul. The extent of the conflicts and tension is striking because it is at Corinth that Paul spent the second longest span of time throughout his active missionary career after Ephesus. Within that period of eighteen months (cf. Acts 18:1), Paul would have had ample opportunities to instruct the Christ-followers in his understanding of the gospel. Yet, despite this privilege and the benefit of prolonged instruction from Paul, this recalcitrant community failed to conform to the teaching of Paul's gospel.

Another reason why I chose the Corinthian letters for my study is that Paul uses a variety of metaphors in these letters. A cursory reading of Paul's letters to the Corinthians reveals a diverse range of metaphors, as I have highlighted earlier. These metaphors are drawn from the cultural background that the predominant Greco-Roman audience of Paul's letters were familiar with. It is also significant and interesting to note that these metaphors were employed at strategic places in Paul's argument contained in these two letters as he addressed a very difficult, conflict-ridden church.

Finally, the problems and conflicts of the Corinthian Christ-movement were not so much theological or doctrinal in nature. If examined carefully, these problems directly involved social relations in the community. In light of this, Bruce Winter suggests that the problem of the Corinthian church was not so much that it was in the world, but that too much of the social life

---

1. The literary integrity of 2 Corinthians has been subjected to intense debate. Comprehensive reviews of these issues exist elsewhere (see the introductory section of most commentaries on 2 Corinthians). Whatever position one takes concerning the integrity of 2 Corinthians, there is no serious objection that this letter is written after 1 Corinthians. As I have argued elsewhere, it makes better sense to take the unity of 2 Corinthians rather than treating it as a composite of several letters. See Lim, *Sufferings of Christ*, 28–29; and Hall, *Unity of the Corinthian Correspondence*.

2. For further discussion on Paul's visits and correspondences with the Corinthians, see Harris, *Second Epistle to the Corinthians*, 1–50.

of the Roman world was found within the community.[3] If Winter is correct in his observation, then the Corinthian letters could profitably be used to examine how Paul attempted to create a distinctive social identity rooted in his gospel for the Christ-followers, by using a diverse range of metaphors in resolving the communal conflicts.

PLAN FOR THE BOOK

Part I of the book will comprise two chapters. I have already presented the issues and the motivations for my investigation in the introduction. In chapter 1 that follows, I will examine the meaning of metaphor and how it was understood in the days of Paul in terms of its function and rhetoric. By drawing insights from the Conceptual Theory of Metaphor, I will also explore how the meaning of metaphor is mirrored and embedded in Paul's letters to the Corinthians, and what Paul hopes to achieve and accomplish by employing these metaphors. A brief review on how Paul's use of metaphors has been researched and studied will also be given some attention. Moving on to chapter 2, I will briefly discuss the theory of social identity formation and explore how Paul uses these metaphors in social identity formation of the Corinthians.

Part II of the book will then examine in some depth a series of metaphors. In order to contain the size of this study, I will only consider metaphors that are used frequently throughout the Corinthian letters or that appear in high density and close proximity that are directly related to social relation and identity of the Corinthians. I will discuss metaphors related to fictive kinship in chapters 3 (sibling metaphor) and 4 (familial metaphors), temple metaphor in chapter 5, and body metaphor in Chapter 6. In these chapters, I will follow the same general procedure of discussing the usage of the metaphor in the Jewish (if relevant) and Greco-Roman contexts, the use of the metaphor by Paul and its social implication on the Corinthians, and the function of metaphors in the formation of social identity.

Finally, in Part III, I will bring together a synthesis of my findings and their implications in shaping the social identity formation of the Corinthians and our understanding of New Testament communities.

---

3. Winter, *After Paul Left Corinth*, 27–28. Winter further argues that much of the conflicts and problems in the Corinthian church were directly related to the social ethics of the social world of Corinth.

Part I

1

Paul's Use of Metaphors in the Corinthian Letters

INTRODUCTION

IN HIS LETTERS TO the Corinthians, Paul skillfully uses metaphors[1] drawn from the social reality, cultural background, and symbolic universe of his predominantly Greco-Roman audience. He also creatively employs metaphors to instruct, rebuke, and build up these communities. Not only are metaphors central to Paul's arguments, they are also a powerful tool of communication which enabled his audience to visualize things in new and different ways.

Referring to the recipients' former pagan religious practices, Paul declared: "Do you not know that you are God's temple and that God's Spirit dwells in you? If anyone destroys God's temple, God will destroy that person. For God's temple is holy, and you are that temple" (1 Cor 3:16–17).

Paul also drew on architectural terminology to express his role as an apostle to those who would have been familiar with construction, having witnessed the rebuilding of the city of Corinth since 44 BCE: "For we are God's servants, working together; you are God's field, God's building. According to the grace of God given to me, like a skilled master builder I laid

---

1. Throughout this book, I will use the terminologies of "metaphor," "imagery," and "analogy" interchangeably. No distinction is intended, and these terminologies are used simply for the sake of linguistic variety.

a foundation, and someone else is building on it. Each builder must choose with care how to build on it" (1 Cor 3:9–10).

Paul also evoked the imagery of *paterfamilias* in addressing the Corinthians: "I am not writing this to make you ashamed, but to admonish you as my beloved children. For though you might have ten thousand guardians in Christ, you do not have many fathers. Indeed, in Christ Jesus I became your father through the gospel" (1 Cor 4:14–15).

Knowing that the Corinthians were familiar with the Isthmian Games held bi-annually near Corinth, Paul employed athlete imagery in speaking to them: "Do you not know that in a race the runners all compete, but only one receives the prize? Run in such a way that you may win it. Athletes exercise self-control in all things; they do it to receive a perishable wreath, but we an imperishable one. So I do not run aimlessly, nor do I box as though beating the air; but I punish my body and enslave it, so that after proclaiming to others I myself should not be disqualified" (1 Cor 9:24–27).

The patronage system was deeply entrenched in the Greco-Roman society, and Paul drew on the social convention of using letters of recommendation in 2 Corinthians: "Are we beginning to commend ourselves again? Surely we do not need, as some do, letters of recommendation to you or from you, do we? You yourselves are our letter, written on our hearts, to be known and read by all; and you show that you are a letter of Christ, prepared by us, written not with ink but with the Spirit of the living God, not on tablets of stone but on tablets of human hearts" (2 Cor 3:1–3).

Finally, Paul also used imagery familiar to the Greco-Roman audience when he compared the Corinthian community to the function of a human body: "Indeed, the body does not consist of one member but of many. If the foot would say, 'Because I am not a hand, I do not belong to the body,' that would not make it any less a part of the body. And if the ear would say, 'Because I am not an eye, I do not belong to the body,' that would not make it any less a part of the body. If the whole body were an eye, where would the hearing be? If the whole body were hearing, where would the sense of smell be? But as it is, God arranged the members in the body, each one of them, as he chose" (1 Cor 12:14–18).

How do we make sense of these diverse metaphors that Paul used in his correspondence to the Corinthians? Are they merely random rhetorical tools he employed to drive home a point in his argument? Or was Paul's use of metaphors a very calculated and deliberate attempt to convey the truth of the gospel in a deeper manner? Was there a wider agenda in Paul's theological discourse when he used these metaphors in rebuking, exhorting, and encouraging the Christ-followers in Corinth?

Until the last decade, Paul's use of metaphors has been largely downplayed by his interpreters. This is evident when one compares the number of studies dedicated to the investigation of metaphors to those on, say, Pauline theology. Even when studies on metaphors are being carried out, they are usually from the perspective of a particular theological framework that often discounts the social reality of these metaphors. Some examples of these include election, redemption, justification, reconciliation, and adoption where Paul's theology has been largely perceived as the springboard from which to understand these metaphors. However, without a proper understanding of Paul's use of imagery, it is impossible to arrive at a complete understanding of his message to his audience. Ian Paul has underscored this serious lack of proper interpretation of metaphor, and this is puzzling as metaphor "is one of the most crucial areas on the whole of hermeneutics since so much of biblical theology hangs on metaphors."[2]

The thesis of this study is that Paul used metaphor not only to instruct, rebuke, and present a theological argument of his understanding of the various issues that confronted the community, but that his primary reason was to employ metaphor in the task of community building and social identity formation in Christ, one that was deeply rooted in the Scripture of Israel and the social conventions of the Greco-Roman world. As such, Paul's use of these metaphors goes beyond a theological treatise. Metaphors are used to convey Paul's understanding of what it means to be followers of Christ as demonstrated in the Corinthians' communal existence as the living exegesis of the gospel of Christ.

PREVIOUS STUDIES ON PAUL'S USE OF METAPHORS

An earlier study of Paul's metaphors is the 1964 publication of Herbert M. Gale.[3] Gale expresses surprise that little treatment has been given to the investigation of the analogies of Paul. This lack of attention is even more pronounced since a number of Paul's analogies "have played an extremely important role in the formulation and expression of many of the most important Christian theological ideas and doctrines."[4] As such, he sets out to explore Paul's use of metaphors in the seven undisputed letters with the aim that these analogies "can be employed justifiably as a basis for an understanding of the apostle's theological thought."[5] The primary aim of Gale's

2. Paul, "Metaphor," 507.
3. Gale, *Use of Analogy*.
4. Ibid., 7.
5. Ibid., 8. For further discussion on how Paul's use of analogies functions within his

investigation is directed at uncovering Paul's theological thought through metaphors and not how they function in the understanding of the recipients of the letters.

Subsequent works by G. B. Caird[6] and Peter W. Macky[7] deal primarily with linguistic and interpretive issues concerning metaphors, and not specifically with their function in Paul's letters. Anthony Byatt's work covers a broad range of metaphors in the New Testament arranged in a thematic order.[8] Byatt expounds on the meaning of individual figurative words or phrases found in the New Testament, and he is less concerned with how these metaphors contribute to the flow of argument within the wider discourse.

Since Gale's work, the study of Paul's use of imagery in his letters has gained significant attention and momentum, and more so in the last decade. Most of these recent studies focused on Paul's use of a particular image, either in one of his letters or throughout the Pauline corpus, as reflected in the recent works of Aasgaard, Aus, Berge, Breytenbach, Burke, Byron, Finlan, Gaventa, Goodrich, Gupta, Harris, Hogeterp, Kim, Konsmo, Lanci, McNeel, Patterson, Rosner, and Tsang, amongst others.[9] These studies, without doubt, contribute significantly to our understanding of metaphors in Paul's thought and in his letters. What remains to be explored is how a cluster of metaphors as seen in the Corinthian letters could have functioned in Paul's argument.

David J. Williams' reference-type format approach remains one of the most comprehensive studies of metaphors, and provides extensive information on the socio-historical background drawn from both Jewish and Greco-Roman sources in illuminating Paul's diverse use of metaphors.[10] However, Williams' treatment follows a thematic outline of Paul's use of metaphors. Despite many strengths of this work, such thematic treatment

theological thought, see ibid., 223–31.

6. Caird, *Language and Imagery of the Bible*.

7. Macky, *Centrality of Metaphors*.

8. Byatt, *New Testament Metaphors*.

9. Recent studies on Paul's use of imagery, amongst others, include: Aasgaard, *My Beloved Brothers and Sisters!*; Aus, *Imagery of Triumph and Rebellion*; Berge, *Language of Belonging*; Breytenbach, *Grace, Reconciliation, Concord*; Burke, *Family Matters*; Burke, *Adopted into God's Family*; Byron, *Slavery Metaphors*; Finlan, *Background and Content*; Gaventa, *Our Mother Saint Paul*; Goodrich, *Paul as an Administrator*; Gupta, *Worship that Makes Sense to Paul*; Harris, *Slave of Christ*; Hogeterp, *Paul and God's Temple*; Kim, *Significance of Clothing Imagery*; Konsmo, *Pauline Metaphors*; Lanci, *A New Temple for Corinth*; McNeel, *Paul as Infant*; Patterson, *Keeping the Feast*; Rosner, *Greed as Idolatry*; and Tsang, *From Slaves to Sons*.

10. Williams, *Paul's Metaphors*.

often suffers from a major setback, in that how these metaphors function within a particular letter is insufficiently addressed or downplayed. In addition, Williams' work is based upon the assumption that knowledge of the background sources is sufficient for interpreting the metaphors, without paying close attention to the context of Paul's letters.

It was not until the recent publication by Raymond F. Collins that a serious attempt to trace Paul's use of metaphors within his individual letters was pursued.[11] In his work, Collins investigates how Paul uses metaphors in each of the seven undisputed letters in order to "clarify the gospel for a particular audience and persuade the various churches to whom he wrote his letters of the truth of his message."[12] Collins' work is significant as it marks a departure from previous studies that focus on a singular metaphor within a letter or letters of Paul. Collins is less concerned with how the metaphor functions within Paul's theological thought. His primary aim is to see how Paul's choice of metaphor is directly related to the thrust of his argument within the individual letters and to the truth of his gospel. In this respect, Collins pays more attention to the occasional nature of Paul's letter and the social location of the respective audiences. By assigning communicative effect to the metaphors, Collins successfully brings forward the argument that there is much more coherence in Paul's diverse use of metaphors with regards to the presentation of the gospel in his individual letters. Collins' approach is useful for my investigation and fits neatly with the approach I will use in this book. However, the limited length of his work means Collins was not able to direct his attention to fuller investigation of how the metaphors function within the individual letters.

Thus far, we have seen that studies on Paul's metaphors have been largely motivated by interest in Paul's theological thought, are concentrated on social historical examination of the metaphors, and are concerned with thematic studies focusing on a particular metaphor in a letter. The focus of many of these studies has been on Paul as a strategic and theological thinker, and not so much as on him as a social agent that brings about ethical and social transformation and change. Strangely, much less space is devoted to investigating how these metaphors function within the understanding of the audience. The ethical and transformative effects of metaphors in Paul's rhetoric have received even less attention. In this respect, Gupta's work on Paul's cultic metaphor is probably one of the very few exceptions that takes into serious consideration the social dimension of Paul's community in interpreting the use of metaphors as powerful vehicles for theological

---

11. Collins, *Power of Images in Paul*.
12. Ibid., viii.

and ethical transformation and reshaping of the mind and perception of the audience.[13] Gupta's work is therefore crucial and lays a solid foundation for further study of Paul's use of metaphors.

While there has been progress seen in the study of Paul's use of imagery, what remains to be explored is how Paul's use of diverse metaphors within a particular letter functions in the formation of Christian identity in relation to cults and rituals; ethical teachings and behavioral patterns; and group dynamics and boundaries with outsiders. These concerns will be addressed in Part II of this book comprising chapters 3–6.

THE USE AND FUNCTION OF METAPHOR IN PAUL'S DAY

Metaphorical language forms part of communication in daily life; indeed the use of metaphors is indispensable in any effective communication. It is a powerful means of communication that not only enables an idea, concept, or message to be conveyed in a creative way, but also helps the audience grasp, feel, or "see" ideas differently by evoking their senses, emotions, and thinking. What is inexpressible and intangible may be made vivid and visible. With proper interpretation by the hearer, metaphor is an effective tool to marshal the points or arguments raised by the author in a very forceful and persuasive manner.

However, metaphors could also be easily misunderstood and misapplied by the audience. This is particularly so within the context of religious language. Originally designed to convey some principles of faith, the understanding of these metaphors over time and across cultures, may run the risk of ceasing to bear the same relevance or understanding as intended by the author within the original cultural context.[14] In some cases, these metaphors may even lose their identity as metaphors, and become confused with literal truths or be interpreted through a certain theological grid or framework. An example of this is the temple imagery that Paul used in 1 Cor 3:16–17 and 6:19–20. Paul was drawing on the Greco-Roman understanding of the symbolism of temple in addressing the Corinthians. However, over time, this passage has come to be popularly interpreted to mean that the church

---

13. Gupta, *Worship that Makes Sense to Paul*, 155–221. See also Wanamaker, "Metaphor and Morality," 409–33, whose work takes into account the notion of morality and metaphor in examining Paul's moral concepts, moral thinking, and moral reasoning.

14. For further investigation on the use of metaphor in religious language, see the compendium of essays in Feyaerts, *Bible through Metaphor and Translation* and Soskice, *Metaphor and Religious Language*.

has now replaced the Jerusalem Temple. In the Greco-Roman context, the notion of temple replacement is likely to have been alien to Paul's thought within the context of 1 Corinthians.[15] Thus, it is important that as we investigate Paul's use of imagery in the Corinthian correspondence, we should not be importing or imposing our twenty-first-century understanding and practices and our theological grid onto first-century usage of these metaphors.

Understanding Metaphors: The Legacy of Aristotle

The systematic study of the use of metaphors goes back to Aristotle. Aristotle (384–322 BCE) famously declared the central importance of metaphor, and was the first rhetorician to write in a concentrated way about the proper use of metaphor.[16] Considered as the "father of metaphor" in Greek literature, Aristotle's works have been frequently cited by many philosophers after him.[17]

Aristotle's classical understanding of metaphor includes its four different classes as elaborated in *Poetics* 21.7:

> Metaphor is the application of a strange term either transferred from the genus and applied to the species or from the species and applied to the genus, or from one species to another or else by analogy.[18]

Aristotle emphasized metaphor as the concept of transference of a word from one point of reference to another. He further explained the use of metaphors and it is worth quoting in full:

> An example of a term transferred from genus to species is "Here *stands* my ship." Riding at anchor is a species of standing. An example of transference from species to genus is "Indeed *ten thousand* noble things Odysseus did," for ten thousand, which is a species of many, is here used instead of the word "many."
> An example of transference from one species to another is

---

15. See chapter 5 below on the use of temple imagery for further investigation of this fascinating imagery.

16. For further discussion on Aristotle's view of metaphor, see Ricoeur, *Role of Metaphor* and Soskice, *Metaphor and Religious Language*, 1–14.

17. See van der Watt, *Family of the King*, 1–60, for further treatment on the theory of metaphor and the influence of Aristotle. See also Soskice, *Metaphor and Religious Language*, 3–10.

18. All quotations from classical sources are taken from Loeb Classical Library, Harvard University Press, Cambridge, MA.

"*Drawing off* his life with the bronze" and "*Sneering* with the tireless bronze," where "drawing off" is used for "severing" and "severing" for "drawing off," both being species of "removing."

Metaphor by analogy means this: when B is to A as D is to C, then instead of B the poet will say D and B instead of D. And sometimes they add that to which the term supplanted by the metaphor is relative. For instance, a cup is to Dionysus what a shield is to Ares; so he will call the cup "Dionysus' shield" and the shield "Ares' cup." Or old age is to life as evening is to day; so he will call the evening "day's old-age" or use Empedocles' phrase; and old age he will call "the evening of life" or "life's setting sun." Sometimes there is no word for some of the terms of the analogy but the metaphor can be used all the same. For instance, to scatter seed is to sow, but there is no word for the action of the sun in scattering its fire. Yet this has to the sunshine the same relation as sowing has to the seed, and so you have the phrase "sowing the god-created fire."

Besides this, another way of employing metaphor is to call a thing by the strange name and then to deny it some attribute of that name. For instance, suppose you call the shield not "Ares' cup" but a "wineless cup."[19]

According to Aristotle, when a metaphor is employed in place of a literal word, it also provides an avenue for an understanding or experience to be transferred from one realm to another, or from one source domain to a target domain. This can be seen in one of the examples used by Paul in 1 Cor 3:16–17 and 6:19–20 presented diagrammatically as follow:

Table 1.1: Metaphors and Transference of Metaphors

Metaphors/Source domain	Transference of Metaphors/Target domain
Ancient temple	Christ-followers
Dwelling place of deity	Dwelling place of God/Holy Sprit

In this respect, metaphors link two or more objects or things together that are not conventionally related to one another, such as the Christ-followers and an ancient temple. By doing so, metaphors invite the reader or hearer to allow this association to interact with and interpret each other and thus create a forceful meaning. In the case of the temple imagery, which may be alien to some twenty-first-century hearers not accustomed to rituals in

---

19. Aristotle, *Poet.* 21.8–16.

religious temples, one must allow the social and religious practices of the ancient world to be operative in order to understand this relationship. A temple represents the dwelling place of the deity, its power, and its popularity. Worshippers coming into a temple were expected to pay homage and worship the deity. Thus, when Paul evokes temple imagery, a process of selection and screening occurs. Some aspects of the metaphor are hidden while others are emphasized and extended. Although a temple may refer to a physical building, this aspect is not transferred to the community of Christ-followers. A temple may conjure up an image of the dwelling place of a deity, and this is emphasized when applied to a community of believers where God reigns and rules. This process of selection and screening is one that modern-day hearers of Paul's metaphors must grapple with. This process is certainly going to be more difficult the more we are temporally, geographically, and culturally removed from the expression when it was first coined and used by Paul.

Since Paul's letters are addressed to real communities in real historical situations, the use of metaphors is also intricately related to the social reality of these communities. Therefore, the importance of understanding the ancient social context cannot be downplayed. In this respect, Jan van der Watt helpfully underscores this importance:

> . . . the socio-historical framework within which a metaphor was originally created plays an important role in the continued cognitive and emotive functioning of a metaphor. When reading ancient texts, it is even more critical that one should assimilate socio-historic data when interpreting metaphors. In order to understand the intensity, intent and meaning of a metaphor in an ancient text, it is necessary to understand the socio-historical context in which it was originally used.[20]

In the following chapters, the social reality of the metaphors Paul used will be given special treatment to help us appreciate and understand how these metaphors functioned in the social identity formation of the Christ-followers.

The Function and Use of Metaphors in Communication according to Ancient Writers

Aristotle greatly promoted the use of metaphors and praised those who expertly used them in communication. He commented that "by far

20. Van der Watt, *Family of the King*, 12.

the greatest thing is the use of metaphor. That alone cannot be learnt; it is a token of genius."[21]

Aristotle further elaborated on the use of metaphor in communication.[22] Since eloquent prose requires the use of remarkable diction, he believed that the use of metaphor is the best way for a gifted communicator to achieve the next level of verbal excellence.

> For all use metaphors in conversation, as well as proper and appropriate words; wherefore it is clear that, if a speaker manages well, there will be something "foreign" about his speech, while possibly the art may not be detected, and his meaning will be clear. And this . . . is the chief merit of rhetorical language.[23]

Aristotle encouraged the use of variety in metaphors that appeal to all senses, in particular the use of sight and sound.[24] If used appropriately, metaphors can be tools that convey clarity and accuracy in speech in which it will be able to impress the audience.

According to Aristotle, the most valuable element of proportional metaphors is the intellectual and sensual pleasure derived from them. Properly proportional metaphors help the learning process of the reader while a disproportional metaphor hinders the learning process. Aristotle said, "Of the four kinds of metaphor, the most popular are those based on proportion."[25] He further elaborated:

> Easy learning is naturally pleasant to all, and words mean something, so that all words which make us learn something are most pleasant. Now we do not know the meaning of strange words, and proper terms we know already. It is metaphor, therefore, that above all produces this effect.[26]

For Aristotle, each writer and reader has a role to play in the learning process. By using an original metaphor, the writer is able to open up a new perspective in recognizing truth. Words, to Aristotle, "are popular if they contain metaphor, provided it be neither strange, for then it is difficult to take it at a glance, nor superficial, for them it does not impress the hearer."[27] Hence it is important to strike a balance in using metaphor.

21. Aristotle, *Poet.* 22.16–17.
22. Aristotle, *Rhet.* 3.2.6–15.
23. Ibid., 3.2.6–7. See also ibid., 3.2.8–9.
24. Ibid., 3.2.13.
25. Ibid., 3.10.7.
26. Ibid., 3.10.2.
27. Ibid., 3.10.6.

While the use of metaphor is important and can be a powerful tool in rhetoric, Aristotle also warned that care must be exercised in its use. He issued several warnings concerning the use of metaphors. First, the choice of metaphor must suit the context in which it is being used. "We must consider, as a red cloak suits a young man, what suits an old one; for the same garment is not suitable for both. And if we wish to ornament our subject, we must derive our metaphor from the better species under the same genus; if to depreciate it, from the worse."[28] Aristotle then proceeded to give numerous examples of how this can be achieved:

> Thus, to say (for you have two opposites belonging to the same genus) that the man who begs prays, or that the man who prays begs (for both are forms of asking) is an instance of doing this; as, when Iphicrates called Callias a mendicant priest instead of a torch-bearer, Callias replied that Iphicrates himself could not be initiated, otherwise he would not have called him mendicant priest but torch-bearer; both titles indeed have to do with a divinity, but the one is honourable, the other dishonourable. And some call actors flatterers of Dionysus, whereas they call themselves "artists." Both these names are metaphors, but the one is a term of abuse, the other the contrary. Similarly, pirates now call themselves purveyors; and so it is allowable to say that the man who has committed a crime has "made a mistake," that the man who has "made a mistake" is "guilty of crime," and that one who has committed a theft has either "taken" or "ravaged."[29]

Secondly, Aristotle also cautioned against their improper use that would lead to failure to produce persuasion in rhetoric:

> . . . for metaphors are also inappropriate, some because they are ridiculous—for the comic poets also employ them—others because they are too dignified and somewhat tragic; and if they are farfetched, they are obscure, as when Gorgias says: "Affairs pale and bloodless"; "you have sown shame and reaped misfortune"; for this is too much like poetry. And as Alcidamas calls philosophy "a bulwark of the laws," and the *Odessey* "a beautiful mirror of human life," and "introducing no such plaything in poetry." All these expressions fail to produce persuasion, for the reasons stated. As for what Gorgias said to the swallow which, flying over his head, let fall her droppings upon him, it was in the best tragic style. He exclaimed, "Fie, for shame, Philomela!";

28. Ibid., 3.2.9–10.

29. Ibid., 3.2.10. For Aristotle's further treatment on this matter, see his *Rhet.* 3.3.3–4; 3.4.1; 3.10.7; 3.11.5.

for there would have been nothing in this act disgraceful for a bird, whereas it would have been for a young lady. The reproach therefore was appropriate, addressing her as she was, not as she is.[30]

Aristotle also warned that the use of metaphors must be appropriate to the subject. Metaphors are to persuade. If a writer uses far-fetched metaphors, it loses its appeal to persuade. If it loses its appeal, then a metaphor may have lost its power to instruct. "Further, metaphors must not be far-fetched, but we must give names to things that have none by deriving the metaphor from what is akin and of the same kind."[31]

Aristotle's concept of metaphor became the benchmark from which further theories and usage of metaphors were subsequently developed. The Athenian Peripatetic, Demetrius of Phaleron, built on the work of Aristotle in presenting the approach to metaphor. According to Demetrius, metaphors should be employed in elevated style of writing:

> Metaphors must be used; for they impart a special charm and grandeur to prose style. They should not, however, be crowded together, or we shall find ourselves writing dithyrambic poetry in place of prose. Nor yet should they be far-fetched, but natural and based on a true analogy.[32]

In suggesting that metaphors are a necessary part of diction and cautioning that they should not be overused, Demetrius followed closely after the principle laid down by Aristotle.

However, Demetrius brought the discussion further by insisting that the use of metaphors promotes clarity of thought through economy of words that literal language sometimes lacks.

> Some things are, however, expressed with greater clearness and precision by means of metaphors than by means of the precise terms themselves: as "the battle shuddered." No change of phrase could, by the employment of precise terms, convey the meaning with greater truth or clearness. The poet has given the designation of "shuddering battle" to the clash of spears and the low and continuous sound which these makes. In so doing, he has seized upon the aforesaid "active" metaphor and has represented the battle as "shuddering" like a living thing.[33]

---

30. Ibid., 3.3.4. See also 3.4.1.
31. Ibid., 3.2.12.
32. Demetrius, *Eloc.* 2.78.
33. Ibid., 2.82. For further discussion on the use of metaphor according to

Several Roman authors also further developed the thinking on metaphor. One example is Cicero (106–43BCE). He defined metaphor as "a short form of simile, contracted into one word; this word is put in a position not belonging to it as if it were its own place, and if it is recognizable it gives pleasure, but if it contains no similarity it is rejected."[34]

Cicero revealed the standardization of the use of metaphor less than a century before Paul. Metaphors essentially enrich words, minimize the number of words needed to explain a concept, and result in a pleasurable learning experience which Cicero described as "entertaining quality."[35] In fact, the use of metaphor is one of the three rules to be applied in oratory apart from the use of rare words and new coinage of words.[36] He further elaborated:

> The explanation is that when something that can scarcely be conveyed by the proper term is expressed metaphorically, the meaning we desire to convey is made clear by the resemblance of the things that we have expressed by the word that does not belong...Consequently the metaphors in which you take what you have not got from somewhere else are a sort of borrowing; but there is another somewhat bolder kind ... that convey some degree of brilliance to the style.[37]

For Cicero, the use of metaphors makes meaning clear or better conveys the whole meaning of the matter, whether it consists in an action or a thought and also serves to achieve brevity. Even in cases where "there are plenty of specific words available, metaphorical terms give people much more pleasure, if the metaphor is a good one."[38] Cicero further commented:

> I suppose the cause of this is either that it is a mark of cleverness of a kind to jump over things that are obvious and choose other things that are far-fetched; or because the hearer's thoughts are led to something else and yet without going astray, which is a very great pleasure; or because a single word in each case suggests the thing and a picture of the whole; or because every metaphor, provided it be a good one, has a direct appeal to the senses, especially the sense of sight, which is the keenness: for while the rest of the senses supply such metaphors as "the

Demetrius, see 2.78–90.

34. Cicero, *De Or.* 3.157.
35. Ibid., 3.155.
36. Ibid., 3.155. See also 3.152–55.
37. Ibid., 3.156.
38. Ibid., 3.159.

fragrance of good manners," "the softness of a humane spirit," "the roar of the waves," "a sweet style of speaking," the metaphors drawn from the sense of sight are much more vivid, virtually placing within the range of our mental vision objects not actually visible to our sight.[39]

And, in prose, if metaphors can be used, it will give "brilliance to the style."[40] Hence Cicero stated that "everyone derives more pleasure from words used metaphorically and not in their proper sense than from the proper names belonging to the objects."[41]

Cicero also lay down some rules for the use of metaphors:[42]

1) There must be real resemblance.

2) The resemblance is not too far-fetched.

3) Since metaphors directly hit our senses, one should avoid all unseemliness in the things to which the comparison will lead the hearer's mind.

4) One should avoid metaphors in which the resemblance contains an ugly idea that exaggerates or understates the literal and proper words.

5) One should also avoid metaphors that are too harsh, and if used should be softened with proper introduction.

Quintilian, a first-century Roman expert and teacher of rhetoric (35–96CE), a contemporary of Paul, suggested that the commonest and by far the most beautiful of *tropes*[43] is metaphor. Metaphor is not "merely so natural a turn of speech that it is often employed unconsciously or by uneducated persons, but it is in itself so attractive and elegant that however distinguished the language in which it is embedded it shines forth with a light that is all its own."[44] Quintilian further agreed with Aristotle that metaphor is the tool of a gifted rhetorician and enhances the language. If metaphor is "correctly and appropriately applied, it is quite impossible for its effect to be commonplace, mean or unpleasing. It adds to the copiousness of language by the interchange of words and by borrowing, and finally succeeds in accomplishing the supremely difficult task of providing a name for

---

39. Ibid., 3.160–61.
40. Ibid., 3.161.
41. Ibid., 3.159.
42. Ibid., 3.162–66.
43. Quintilian, *Inst.* 8.6.1: "By *trope* is meant the artistic alteration of a word or phrase from its proper meaning to another."
44. Ibid., 8.6.4.

everything."⁴⁵ In this respect, metaphor is able to make a concept clear and to ornament it. Quintilian further elaborated:

> A noun or a verb is transferred from the place to which it properly belongs to another where there is either no *literal* term or the *transferred* is better than the *literal*. We do this either because it is necessary or to make our meaning clearer or, as I have already said, to produce a decorative effect. When it secures none of these results, our metaphor will be out of place.⁴⁶

Metaphor is not only able to produce decorative effect, it is also "designed to move the feelings, give special distinction to things and place them vividly before the eye."⁴⁷ As such, when used properly, "effects of extraordinary sublimity are produced when the theme is exalted by a bold and almost hazardous metaphor and inanimate objects are given life and action."⁴⁸

For Quintilian, there are four classes of metaphors: "In the first we substitute one living thing for another . . . Secondly, inanimate things may be substituted for inanimate . . . or inanimate may be substituted for animate . . . or animate for inanimate."⁴⁹

Quintilian also warned about the need for careful usage of metaphors. The metaphorical use of words cannot be recommended except in connected discourse.⁵⁰ Overuse of metaphors is to be avoided, as it will "obscure our language and weary our audience . . . our language will become allegorical and enigmatic."⁵¹ Furthermore, excessive use of metaphor is described as "a fault, more especially if they are of the same species."⁵² The choice of metaphor should be given careful consideration. If a wrong choice of metaphor is used, they may sound "harsh, that is, far-fetched."⁵³ Finally, Quintilian also cautioned that metaphor "should always either occupy a place already vacant, or if it fills the room of something else, should be more impressive than that which it displaces."⁵⁴

Thus far, drawing on ancient writers, I have noted that metaphors predominantly function as transference of substitutionary devices, replacing

45. Ibid., 8.6.5.
46. Ibid., 8.6.5–6.
47. Ibid., 8.6.19.
48. Ibid., 8.6.11.
49. Ibid., 8.6.9–10.
50. Ibid., 8.3.38.
51. Ibid., 8.6.14.
52. Ibid., 8.6.16.
53. Ibid., 8.6.17.
54. Ibid., 8.8.18.

one concept or idea with another, or saying what can be said literally in a more decorative and illustrative way. Metaphors have been regarded as having ornamental effects on language, as a poetic way of illustrating or creating variety in literary form. Used wisely, a metaphor is a powerful tool to enhance the status of the orator and influence the attitude and actions of the hearers. There are also instances where metaphors should be avoided. Hence authors hoping to drive home their point should adopt the use of metaphor in their communication in order to evoke the appropriate and desired response from the audience.

THE MODERN CONCEPTUAL THEORY OF METAPHOR

Although Aristotle considered metaphor as more than a mere rhetorical device, for a long time metaphor had been seen as no more than just that. It is only in the last century that metaphor has been regarded not simply as a trope but also as a cognitive device. In his 1936 publication, I. A. Richards argued that a metaphor is composed of two thoughts that he labels as *tenor* and *vehicle*.[55] The *tenor* is the subject while the *vehicle* is the figurative language that illuminates the *tenor*. According to Richards, these two thoughts of different things are active together and they are supported by a single word, or phrase, whose meaning is the resultant of their interaction.[56] This interaction model was further developed by Max Black in 1962.[57] According to Black, when a metaphor with two thoughts interacts, it produces a meaning that goes beyond any literal meaning could express, thus producing new meaning out of the interaction. In this case, the hearers are compelled to connect two ideas in a way they would never have thought of without the metaphor. In doing so, the reader should be familiar with the ideas to be connected. Black provides an example of "man is a wolf" in which the idea of "man" interacts with the idea of "wolf" in order to communicate new meaning about "man." Black suggests that "wolf" evokes the attributes of the source domain: wolves are fierce, hungry, carnivorous, and treacherous, and these attributes that are compatible with "man" will be brought to the forefront when one thinks of "man is a wolf" while those that are inconsistent will be filtered out and pushed to the background.[58] As a result, metaphor

---

55. See Richards, *Philosophy of Rhetoric*.
56. Ibid., 93.
57. Black, *Models and Metaphors*.
58. Ibid., 40–41.

"*organizes* our view of man."⁵⁹ Based on this, Black argues that metaphor has the power to change how one sees the subject and one's attitudes towards it.

Apart from viewing them as merely ornamental decorative objects, poetic imaginative devices, or rhetorical enhancement tools, metaphors also inform and govern our thought and action. This theory, generally known as Conceptual Metaphor Theory or Cognitive Metaphor Theory, is championed by George Lakoff and Mark Johnson.⁶⁰ Moving away from the traditional understanding of metaphor, Lakoff and Johnson state that metaphor is "understanding and experiencing one kind of thing in terms of another."⁶¹ They further suggest that we basically use three kinds of metaphors to structure reality:

1) Orientational metaphors—this involves descriptive language that depicts spatial movement in a particular direction, whether it be up-down, front-back, center-periphery, or near-far orientation. For example, "I feel uplifted" is used to describe one's feelings.⁶² There is a tendency to describe something positive in an upward manner and negative in a downward manner.

2) Ontological metaphors—these function by way of entities and substances related to the ways of viewing events, activities, emotions, and ideas. For example, one may say that he is in love, or we are the body of Christ.⁶³

3) Structural metaphors—this category of metaphors structures one concept in terms of another. For example, when someone says, "time is money," time is associated with money, a precious commodity.⁶⁴

More than any other kind of metaphors, structural metaphors are deeply rooted in the cultural and social reality from which they are drawn. These metaphors are important because they are drawn from social life that defines the existence and experiences of the listeners and offer rich and creative potential for elaboration. Most of Paul's metaphors belong to this category.

Lakoff and Johnson also state that metaphor is not only central to the thought process at the cognitive level, they are also pervasive in everyday

---

59. Ibid., 41, emphasis his.
60. Lakoff and Johnson, *Metaphors We Live By*.
61. Ibid., 5.
62. Ibid., 14–21.
63. Ibid., 25–32.
64. Ibid., 61–68.

life, especially in our actions and how we relate to others.[65] They label this as mapping—understanding one mental domain in terms of another. To illustrate how an understanding or experience could be transferred from one area to another, Lakoff and Johnson speak of source domain and target domain. The world of figurative imagery is considered as source domain and the target domain is what needs to be illuminated or understood by analogy. For example, when we conceive of arguments in terms of war, we will devise strategies, defend our positions, and demolish propositions by others in order to win the argument. Lakoff and Johnson point out that this is not merely a fancy way of talking about argument, but how we conceive our arguments. Therefore, metaphor influences not only our words but also our behavior, actions, and emotions when we are involved in an argument. Other examples of how both the source and target domains work are seen in the following Table 1.2.

Table 1.2: Source and Target Domains

Source domain	Target domain
Family in antiquity	Church as a family governing Christian relations with one another within the church where adherents are called "brothers and sisters."
Temple in antiquity	Christ-followers as temple of God in which God dwells and this shapes how one should live one's life worthy for a dwelling place of God.

Metaphors are also capable of giving new understanding of our experiences that relate to our past, our daily activities, and to what we know and believe.[66] The fact that metaphors have the power to create new reality could also lead to cultural changes.[67] Lakoff and Johnson give an example of the introduction of "time is money" into different cultures leading to the Westernization of cultures throughout the world.[68] The notion of "time is money" is then able to govern our thinking and behavior, and how we perceive reality. We may then talk about time management in the way we spend our time. We describe time in the language of investment, such as "investing your time in something worthwhile." We talk about "wasting our time" in carrying out efforts that do not achieve our desired goals. The use of metaphor is thus able to shape the way we think about time that leads to

65. Ibid., 3.
66. Ibid., 139.
67. Ibid., 145.
68. Ibid.

the way we use our time. However, this metaphor would not have worked in some rural parts of the Majority World where life takes on a much slower pace. The population may not necessarily associate time with a previous commodity. In fact, time is often "wasted" in order to strengthen familial bonds and relationships with others where meetings and encounters are often carried out unhurriedly. This insight is particularly useful in the investigation of metaphors used by Paul. In the following chapters, I will demonstrate how Paul uses metaphors frequently to introduce new social realities in his communities.

According to Lakoff and Johnson, metaphors also allow things that are otherwise not measureable to be measured. For example, one may use the ontological metaphor to measure love, as in "a lot of love." In the case of familial metaphors, they can be extremely powerful and influential linguistic elements in communicating and characterizing relations with one another within the family of Christ-followers. The use of this fictive kinship metaphor goes beyond linguistic or ornamental description of the social reality—the metaphor becomes the social reality and governs the way Christian social relations function, not as a mere gathering of individuals and strangers, but as a family that defines how one member relates to another.

At the same time, metaphors can also vary in terms of quality. They can be graded from "dead" to "alive." What makes a metaphor dead is its overly popular usage. These metaphors have already gained cultural acceptance to the extent that they almost lose their significance as metaphors. Demetrius warned that metaphors can lose their effect. "Metaphors have in some cases been so well established by usage that we no longer require the literal expressions, but the metaphor has definitely usurped the place of the literal term."[69] This is so true with many of the Pauline metaphors. For example, the language of justification and grace contains strong theological connotations to the extent that they almost lose their original effect as metaphors. However, dead or dormant metaphors can be reawakened. Fresh meanings can be attributed to dead metaphors by an original usage from an ingenious analogy. Dead metaphors can also be used in combination with other metaphors, resulting in some new usage. Another way they can be awakened is to use them under extraordinary circumstances. This new usage could bring new imaginative and figurative meaning to the metaphors.

To sum up, the Conceptual Theory of Metaphor promoted by Lakoff and Johnson argues that metaphor is not only a helpful tool, but it is inherent in how we perceive reality. In fact, metaphors are capable of shaping new realities by inspiring and transforming our way of thinking, behavior, and

---

69. Demetrius, *Eloc.* 2.86–87.

the way we live. They are what Lakoff and Johnson describe as "metaphors we live by."[70] Metaphors are a powerful tool that could potentially elucidate how Paul's letters functioned persuasively by lodging in the imagination of the listeners, even long after they were heard, and how they subsequently shaped the listeners' thinking and affected their actions.

As a result of the development of the theory of metaphor, metaphors can no longer be perceived as merely a function of language in saying what could be said literally in some decorative, poetic, or creative way. The use of metaphors goes beyond that to encapsulate the cognitive, emotive, and evaluative aspects of the hearers. Since metaphors are grounded in our human experience, they not only inform, but also govern our understanding, actions, and the way we live. Used creatively, metaphors have the capacity to construct new realities. In other words, a metaphor could be a powerful tool used to shock the hearers if they take time to ponder over it, challenging the hearers to appropriate and corrective actions, provided they are obedient to the truth expressed by a metaphor, and construct a social identity rooted in the fresh meanings conveyed.

A QUESTION OF METHOD

While studies on Paul's use of metaphor have been gaining momentum in recent years, it is strange that a systematic methodology in identifying and interpreting the metaphors used by Paul has not been fully developed.[71] It was not until fairly recently that Nijay Gupta took up the challenge to develop hermeneutical principles in interpreting Pauline metaphors by giving due consideration to three interconnected disciplines: Conceptual Theory of Metaphor, biblical semantics, and the study of biblical intertexuality.[72] Gupta outlines seven principles involved in identifying and interpreting metaphors:

1) Figurativeness. The first step is to determine whether the word or idea can be taken literally as opposed to figuratively or symbolically, by taking into account the linguistic, historical, and rhetorical features.

---

70. Lakoff and Johnson, *Metaphors We Live By*, 53–55.

71. Byatt, *New Testament Metaphors*, xxi–xxv, comes close to drawing up some ground rules for interpreting metaphors, but it could hardly be considered as a well drawn-up methodology.

72. See Gupta, "Towards a Set of Principles," 169–81; and his *Worship that Makes Sense to Paul*, 46–51.

2) Quality. This involves determining how frequently the metaphor is being used—the higher the frequency, the more it will lead to widespread recognition and to common usage.

3) Exposure. This principle raises the question to what extent was the author exposed to or in contact with the source domain? It is increasingly plausible to imagine that as a traveling apostle, Paul would have been exposed to the varied culture and customs of the Greco-Roman world.

4) Contextual coherence. This principle involves finding a thematic thread that establishes the metaphor within its literary context taking into account the sentences, paragraphs, and chapters surrounding it. Is the source domain made prominent elsewhere in the discourse?

5) Analogy. Is the metaphorical term or phrase used in similar ways elsewhere in the test? Or, if the word is rare, is the target domain related to the hypothetical source domain in other contemporaneous texts with a similar context?

6) History of interpretation. Gupta has noted that the study of biblical metaphors is a recent enterprise, and studies of Pauline metaphor before the twentieth century are uncommon. As such, another route to studying the interpretation of Paul's metaphors is through early translations, giving careful attention to the way a particular metaphor was translated into another language.

7) Intertextual influence. This principle is to be applied to those terms and concepts embedded within an intertextual dimension. If there is a metaphorical idea that stands within an allusion to the Jewish scriptures, the source may shed light on the source domain of the metaphor.

In addition to the comprehensive methodology laid out by Gupta, I propose that several additional critical factors need to be taken into consideration in interpreting Paul's use of metaphors.

1) Social reality. As I suggested earlier, one of the major pitfalls in the study of Paul's use of metaphor is the immediate theologizing and application of his ideas before a critical analysis of the literary, rhetorical, social, and historical factors affecting the interpretation of the metaphor. A good example is attributing theological argument to the imagery of justification, or adopting a temple replacement ideology in reading Paul's use of temple imagery. This task of theologizing prior to careful treatment of the text should be avoided as it distorts what Paul is saying to his recipients. If Paul wished to persuade and

convince his gentile audience effectively, it was only natural for him to use metaphors drawn primarily from the social rules and values of the community. As such, for metaphors to operate at a cognitive level to influence the way one thinks and acts, the social and historical realities of the metaphors cannot be ignored.

In light of this, bringing archaeological evidence into interaction with biblical texts is also of paramount significance. From here, one may take into consideration the relationship of the world, customs, and culture of the audience in close dialogue and interaction with the biblical text. Archaeological evidence should not be investigated in isolation of the text, or vice versa. It is unfortunate that significant archaeological evidence has often been relegated to the periphery in most commentaries, or received only some reviews and brief analysis in the introductory chapter but was not critically interacted or referred to in subsequent pages. Temples, coins, paintings, statues, monuments, buildings, and biblical texts are not only the products of a particular culture but also part of the production of meaning.

2) Familiarity. Gupta's methodology, while comprehensive, remains firmly focused on the world of the author and how Paul used and understood metaphor. As I argued earlier, in order for metaphor to influence both the author and audience, both parties must be familiar with it. Furthermore, if metaphor is a means of communication, then both the author and audience participate in the communication process. This is even more so as Paul's writing is not detached from the life of his audience. Neither does he write as an armchair apostle or missionary who is confined within his ivory tower, completely detached from the reality of the world of his audience. Therefore, what is equally important is not how the author perceives the metaphor, but also how the audience hear and understand it and how its usage impacts them.

In this respect, the semantic range of the usage at the time the metaphor is coined, selected, or emphasized is to be understood by both the author and intended audience. This is necessary to know which part of the metaphorical identification belongs to the original social reality and which belongs to our modern construct. For example, to be spiritually hot or cold or lukewarm in first-century Laodicea meant something quite different from the common and popular contemporary usage today.

If Paul wanted to win the new Christ-followers over, it is not inconceivable that he would speak to them using their own idiom and metaphors drawn from their social reality that they were familiar with.

3) Suppression and addition. The act of selecting and using the metaphor is in itself an act of interpreting, in which attention to certain aspects of reality are being drawn. At the same time, inevitable that during this process, some aspects of the source domain are necessarily hidden or ignored, while others are highlighted or emphasized. As I suggested earlier, with the use of temple imagery, the physical building from the source domain is suppressed while the notion of the temple as a dwelling place of God is transferred to the target domain when applied to the gathering of Christ-followers as a temple of God. If the source domain can be sensitively discerned, it could unearth insightful themes in Paul's letter that help us further unpack his understanding of his gospel and identity formation of the Christ-followers.

Metaphors can also be open and ambiguous. In this instance, metaphors can be extended, and take on new meaning. This happens when the metaphor highlights uncommon aspects of the source domain or attracts new aspects from other source domains or metaphors. An example is the manner in which Paul applies the metaphor of a nursing mother (1 Cor 3:2) to himself. It is highly unusual for a man in the Greco-Roman world to use a feminine imagery to himself as this was tantamount to questioning his own masculinity. In light of this, a closer examination of how this use of metaphor would have impacted the audience should be carried out.[73]

SUMMARY

In this chapter, I argued that as a linguistic tool, metaphors add color to the language and provide aesthetic value to the listener. They also serve as a rhetorical tool in the art of persuasion. Metaphors elicit an emotional response, cause the audience to see things from a different perspective by creating associations between two previously unrelated objects. Metaphors operate not only at a verbal or linguistic level but also at the cognitive level. According to the Conceptual Theory of Metaphor, metaphors have the power to shape the way we think and to govern our behavior.

The use of metaphors is also culturally inherent. One cannot detach the meaning of the metaphor from the author's or the audience's symbolic universe. In addition, one also needs to examine the textual context and consider how by using metaphor, it would take on new or refreshed meaning and experience in the lives of the recipients.

---

73. For further discussion, see chapter 4 below.

2

Reading Paul's Metaphor through Social Identity Theory

IN THE PREVIOUS CHAPTER, I argued that metaphors shape the way one thinks and acts. Accordingly, how are metaphors used by Paul to shape the social identity of the Christ-followers? Before I could address this question, I will provide a brief evaluation of Social Identity Theory (SIT) as a method in examining how Paul's use of metaphors contributes to the process of social identity formation.

SOCIAL SCIENCES IN NEW TESTAMENT STUDIES

Three decades ago, Wayne Meeks in his groundbreaking work on the social description of early Christianity, analyzed the factors that contributed to Pauline churches' sense of belonging to a distinct group and the ways in which these communities distinguished themselves from their social environment.[1] In the chapter on "The Formation of the EKKLESIA," Meeks lists various factors in the formation of Christian identity in Pauline community.[2]

---

1. Meeks, *First Urban Christians*. See also Malina, *New Testament World*. The contribution of Meeks' work is significant and his work continues to influence social-scientific approaches to Paul and the early Christ-movement until today. This is reflected in the twenty-fifth anniversary edition examining the influence of social-scientific approaches to Pauline Studies. See Still and Horrell, *After the First Urban Christians*.

2. Meeks, *First Urban Christians*, 74–110.

This is further developed in subsequent chapters in his work. First, in order for a group to persist, Meeks contends that it must have social boundaries, maintain stability as well as flexibility, and create a unique culture. This is achieved through aspects of language of belonging and separation, practice and expressed sentiments, and attitudes that promote group cohesion articulated through purity and boundaries.[3] Next, there must be leadership structure that deals with allocation of power, the differentiation of roles, and management of conflict.[4] There are also rituals such as baptisms and the celebration of the Eucharist that promote group solidarity.[5] Finally, there are patterns of belief and life that not only define the ethos of the group but also govern group behavior.[6] All these factors work together in constructing a new identity for the Pauline community where "their ideas, their images of God, their way of organizing life, their rituals, would become part of a massive transformation, in ways they could not have foreseen, of the culture of the Mediterranean basin and of Europe."[7]

Since the publication of Meeks' work, studies focusing on the formation of Christian identity employing social-scientific approaches have gained accelerated momentum and made further significant progress.[8] This has a huge impact on our understanding of Paul's relationship with the Christ-community he founded and the social and cultural milieu of Pauline Christianity. The primary concern of most of these studies is how much cultural overlap between the Pauline community and its surrounding Greco-Roman environment is to be allowed, what constitutes the identity markers that distinguish the Pauline community from its environment, and how Paul creates a distinct sense of Christian identity. I will not be providing

---

3. Ibid., 85–110.

4. Ibid., 111–39.

5. Ibid., 140–63.

6. Ibid., 164–92.

7. Ibid., 192.

8. For example, see Horrell, *Social Ethos*; Tucker, *You Belong to Christ*; Tucker, *Remain in Your Calling*; Finney, *Honour and Conflict*; Nguyen, *Christian Identity in Corinth*; Hansen, *All of You are One*; Campbell, *Paul and the Creation of Christian Identity*; Hodge, *If Sons, Then Heirs*; and Tellbe, *Christ-Believers in Ephesus*. See also the collection of Edwin Judge's earlier works now published in a single volume in Judge and Scholer, *Social Distinctives*; Holmberg, *Exploring Early Christian Identity*; Holmberg and Winninge, *Identity Formation in the New Testament*; Blasi et al., *Handbook of Early Christianity*; and the Festschrift for Wayne Meeks edited by White and Yarbrough, *Social World of the First Christians*; and the recent compendium of essays celebrating the twenty-fifth anniversary of *First Urban Christian* edited by Still and Horrell, *After the First Urban Christians*.

detailed reviews of these works here as they exist elsewhere,⁹ but I will draw on some of these studies and make appropriate comments and reviews in later chapters in this book. This surge of interest in identity studies leads David Horrell to state: "Identity has become something of a buzz-word in recent social science and in studies in early Christianity."[10]

PERSONAL IDENTITY AND SOCIAL IDENTITY: MOVING FROM "I" TO "WE"

How does one perceive identity? The self-concept of identity has two components, namely social identity and personal identity. There are a number of identifications under each of the components. For social identity, the identifications are derived from those belonging to the group, such as nationality, ethnicity, religion, occupation, and gender; while personal identity revolves around personal attributes that are generally cemented in relationships with specific individuals or objects, such as a son, daughter, cousin, wife, and partner of someone.

In some cultures, social identity is more salient than personal identity in self-concept. In other words, when an individual sees himself or herself as a group member, he or she tends to depersonalize self. This person will then experience self as similar to the group he or she belongs to. As a result, the norms and interests of the group take priority and become the norms and interest of the individual.

As Bruce Malina has pointed out, ancient Mediterranean culture did not share the Western idea of the individual or individualism. Contemporary Western understanding of identity focuses on the self rather than the group, and the autonomous individual is held in high esteem when it comes to defining self. Malina believes that people in the ancient Mediterranean world had dyadic personality or collectivistic personality in which people were corporately defined in relation to other groups of people, rather than through self-assessment.[11] They were group-embedded and group-oriented people—a person in such a community needed another in order to know who he or she really was. They perceived themselves and formed their self-concept in terms of how others perceived them. They thought of themselves

---

9. See Tucker, *You Belong to Christ*, 1–34, 61–88; and Tucker, *Remain in Your Calling*, 1–29.

10. Horrell, *Solidarity and Difference*, 91. See also Horrell, *Becoming Christian*.

11. Malina, *New Testament World*, 61–62. See his further discussion on first-century personality in ibid., 58–80. See also Malina, "Collectivism in Mediterranean Culture," 17–28.

as interrelated to others both horizontally (with those who shared the same social status) and vertically (with those who were above and below them in social rank).[12] If the Western ideal of individualism believes that each person is unique within a group setting, then first-century people perceived themselves unique as a group because they belonged to a distinctive group that set their community apart from others. If we can think of our Western understanding of individualistic identity as moving from "we" to "I," then dyadic identity moves from "I" to "we."

For the first-century community, the integrity of the group was far more important than individuals. Loyalty to family, clan, village, and religious group was fundamental to one's identity. Individuals were identified by their family and specifically, in relation to the male head of the household, *paterfamilias*. In this respect, people were governed by what others thought of them and identity was understood in relational or social terms. In this kind of relationship, what was pivotal for group identity of ethnic origin, family, clan, or tribe was the value of honor and, conversely, of shame, and this value determined how people defined themselves and how they belonged to groups. Furthermore, boundaries were often established based on group identity. Shared past and common values were held in high esteem and often reinforced within group dynamics. For example, in the ancient Mediterranean culture, honor was typically given to individuals who advanced the cause of the group to the extent that they excelled in the expectations of the social category they belonged to, while shame was typically accorded to the opposite. At the same time, individuals belonging to the group also accepted their roles in relation to others within the group, typically in a hierarchical fashion. They obeyed authority, and were willing to sacrifice for the sake of maintaining group integrity. For example, within a household, the roles of master and slaves were clearly defined. Judith Lieu summarizes it well: "Awareness of sameness and of difference, of a shared past and agreed values, of continuities and of boundaries, whether physical or behavioural, were all present, either implicitly or explicitly, as Greeks and Romans viewed themselves and others."[13]

To a certain extent, while the dyadic personality may seem alien in the Western context, it is not so in many parts of Asia where group-oriented social identity remains more salient than personal identity, and where group norms or behavior often define the identity of the group. For example, in the Malaysian society where I come from, ethnic boundaries, culture, language, and even religious beliefs are intricately interconnected in the formation of

12. Malina, *New Testament World*, 62.
13. Lieu, *Christian Identity*, 17.

identity of a community. Any threat affecting an individual that appears to challenge the cohesiveness of the community will attract serious negative consequences from the entire community. An ethnic Malay who belongs to the dominant group which constitutes 60 percent of the population is defined, according to Article 160(2) of the Federal Constitution of Malaysia, as "a person who professes the religion of Islam, habitually speaks the Malay language, (and) conforms to Malay custom." This definition clearly reflects the dyadic personality of an ethnic group, and one can understand that in the event there is a religious conversion of a person who is ethnically Malay out of Islam, that person is often labeled as a traitor to his or her ethnic group and religion, and this would attract strong negative reaction from the community.[14] Similarly, many other ethnic groups in Malaysia such as those of Chinese and Indian descent, also exhibit dyadic group personality. Honoring and worshipping ancestors, forming clan associations based on the family name or dialect group, and establishing associations based on one's trade or skills are examples of social cohesiveness of the Chinese community in Malaysia. As a Malaysian of Chinese descent, I will be bringing some of my own background—of being rooted in a community with strong dyadic personality—to the reading of Paul's letters where emphasis on group norms, conformity, personal sacrifices, and authority and hierarchical structures all point to a collectivist nature. This same background provides me with sensitivities that are attuned to Paul's quest of building communities whose identity is now rooted in Christ, communities that are distinct and unique in their respective environment.

SOCIAL IDENTITY THEORY

The term "identity" is essentially a social concept. Identities are shaped and formed in relation to other individuals and groups within a society. In light of this, any study of identity formation of the Pauline community must not only take into account the dyadic nature of personality, but also consider a methodological approach that embraces and incorporates such personality. In this study, I will employ Social Identity Theory (SIT) as part of the interpretative framework in investigating Paul's use of metaphor in the Corinthian correspondence.

SIT, developed by Henri Tajfel, is based on his studies of group dynamics utilizing the minimum group paradigm. In an essay published in 1972, he proposes that in order to provide members within a group with positive

---

14. For example, see the case of Lina Joy, a female Malay converted out of Islam to Christianity in Lee, *Freedom of Religion in Malaysia*, 85–88.

social identity, this group needs to establish a positively valued distinctiveness from other groups.[15] Tajfel further argues that seeing oneself differently constitutes a significant part of one's identity formation. We are what we are because they are not what we are.

Tajfel defines social identity as "that *part* of an individual's self-concept which derives from his knowledge of his membership of a social group (or groups) together with the value and emotional significance attached to that membership."[16] Another helpful definition of social identity is further provided by Richard Jenkins: "Social identity is our understanding of who we are and of who other people are, and reciprocally, other people's understanding of themselves and of others (which includes us)."[17]

Central to Tajfel's research is his understanding of a group as a collection of individuals who perceive themselves to be members of the same social category, share some emotional involvement in this common definition of themselves, and achieve some degree of social consensus about the evaluation of their group and their membership of it.[18] As such, the uniqueness of SIT is that belonging to a group is largely a psychological state which is distinct from that of being a unique individual, which is the dominant understanding of individual identity today in the Western context. This psychological state confers upon the group a social identity, a shared representation of who one is, and how one should behave and regard others.

In this respect, comparison with others becomes a key factor in the formation of group identity, especially what distinguishes one group from another in terms of gender, family, occupation, socio-economic status, ethnicity, nationality, religion, sports, etc. Once these social dimensions have been established, they will determine the behavior and interaction of members with other groups. For example, a football team compares itself with another in terms of skills or scores, and this will determine how a match is to be played on the field. Likewise, supporters of both teams will react differently when the team they support wins or loses the match. In other words, members are not evaluated on the basis of their personal attributes, but on the basis of what the group stands for. It is when people share a strong common social identity that social relations within the group are enhanced to reflect cohesiveness, behavioral pattern transformed to display

---

15. Tajfel, "La catégorisation sociale," 272–302. See also Dominic and Hogg, *Social Identity Theory* and Dominic and Hogg, *Social Identity and Social Cognition.*

16. Tajfel, "Social Categorization," 63, emphasis his.

17. Jenkins, *Social Identity*, 5.

18. Tajfel and Turner, "An Integrative Theory of Group Conflict," 40.

the norms of the group, and a strong sense of belonging emerges to enable members to work together in a trusting and supporting environment.

PROCESS OF SOCIAL IDENTITY FORMATION AND THE CORINTHIAN CHRIST-COMMUNITY

According to Tajfel and Turner, the process of social identity formation involves three concepts:[19]

1) Social Categorization

2) Social Identification

3) Social Comparison

Social Categorization

Social categorization involves the idea that in order to understand groups, people are placed into various categories within the social context. Individuals will naturally find out things about themselves as long as they have the ability to understand the boundaries, behaviors, or norms of various groups and define who belong to the different groups. When people are categorized into groups, they will begin to cultivate the same interests, ideas, and behaviors that are reflective of the belief, ideology, and norms of the group they belong to. Once a sense of belonging has been developed, they will also compare themselves with others in order to seek positive distinctiveness. This process keeps the group members together and forms cohesiveness among the members, thus creating a deep sense of belonging that will ultimately make them different from those outside the group.

Within the Corinthian community, various groups formed along the lines of certain personalities. One group aligned itself with Cephas, one of the original Twelve; another with Apollos, an excellent orator; still another with Paul, the founder of the community; and others with Christ (1 Cor 1:11–12). These groups are further divided along social status—the rich and poor, and the "strong" and "weak."

19. Ibid., 33–47.

Social Identification

The second concept is social, or group identification. Members identify with groups to which they belong. Once they have categorized themselves, they will be able to identify themselves with certain characteristics in the group that reinforce their sense of belonging. Tajfel develops his theory that social identity process primarily involves three dimensions in establishing the ethos, values, status, and boundaries for a particular group as against other groups in a society—the cognitive, emotional, and evaluative dimensions.[20] Tajfel further argues:

> The number and variety of social situations which an individual will perceive as being relevant in some ways to his group membership will increase as a function of: (1) the clarity of his awareness that he is a member of a certain group; (2) the extent of the positive and negative evaluations associated with this membership; (3) the extent of the emotional investment in the awareness and the evaluations.[21]

The cognitive dimension provides the group members with a strong sense of belonging and distinctiveness as compared to other groups. The emotional dimension brings various rituals and practices to enhance the emotional ties in group dynamics in order to establish a strong sense of solidarity, identity, and belonging to the group. The evaluative dimension deals with how the members within the group rate themselves in relation to other groups. Here, self-definition of one's values, status, and ethos as against other groups come into play.

Ultimately, social identity formation is particularly concerned with how members of one group seek to differentiate themselves from other groups so as to achieve a positive social identity. This process eventually leads to ingroup (us) and outgroup (them). Belonging to a group confers upon this group social identity, and this identity is a shared/collective representation of who one is and how one should behave. For example, in the early Pauline communities, rituals including baptism and the Eucharist are introduced to distinguish themselves from other groups.

---

20. Tajfel, *Differentiation between Social Groups*, 28.
21. Ibid., 39.

Social Comparison

The final concept is known as social comparison. The process of defining "us" also inevitably involves defining "others" as well. In the process of defining these boundaries, differences and similarities will constantly be emphasized in order to create a unique self-identity for the group. Members of the group will accentuate their similarities and those factors that bind them together. At the same time the sharp differences with others will also be highlighted to draw the group into closer cohesion. As such, the process of identity formation implies the drawing up of boundary lines between the group and others. It is through these boundaries that one discovers what one is and what one is not. In fact, the group can understand itself better in terms of "others," by insisting on what it is not. This is often achieved by the process of self-categorization based on stereotyping or prejudice, whether positively of "insiders" or negatively of "outsiders."[22] For example, "Cretans are always liars, vicious brutes, lazy gluttons" (Titus 1:12).

Group members will gain a certain amount of self-esteem if they feel superior about themselves when they compare themselves with inferior groups. However, the positive perception may be lost when they compare themselves with outgroups that exhibit superior traits. In this instance, there could be a shift of loyalty from the members to identify with the other groups, or it could motivate the group to change its behavior.

Social comparison was clearly seen in the first-century Mediterranean world. For example, the Romans maintained their identity through a process of social comparison with others who were considered uncivilized. In the Corinthian context, Paul's opponents caused some conflicts within the community by painting a very negative picture of the apostle (2 Cor 10:10), in order to gain control or secure the loyalty of members who were originally aligned with him. Another example is the reference to the unusual generosity of the Macedonian churches to shame the Corinthians, and move them to contribute to Paul's Jerusalem collection project (2 Cor 8:1–5). In another instance, Paul described the Corinthians as behaving worse than the pagans when they tolerated someone who was "having his father's wife" (1 Cor 5:1–2).

---

22. For Self-Categorization Theory, see Turner et al., *Rediscovering the Social Group*. See also Turner, "Social Categorization and the Self-Concept," 77–122.

TEMPORAL ASPECTS OF SOCIAL IDENTITY FORMATION

While Tajfel has suggested that groups must be understood as an on-going process, the temporal aspects of SIT have been largely ignored, as noted by Susan Condor.[23] She highlights one major weakness in Tajfel's work, and that is where the issues he sought to address such as prejudice, intergroup differentiation, intergroup conflict, social movements and so forth, are assumed to be relatively enduring over time.[24] This can be seen in Tajfel's methodology that is based on laboratory experiments relying on minimum group paradigm studies. In his research, investigation is carried out based on minimum conditions required for discrimination to occur between groups. For example, Tajfel's first experiment among English schoolboys in the early 1970s showed that discrimination existed based on a very flimsy and objectively irrelevant sense of group membership, against a perceived outgroup. Typically, a number of assumptions such as concepts, values, or practices were accepted as static to allow a better view of reality in relation to the onset of human group formation. However, this methodology is limited in its ability to illuminate diachronic processes, especially those taking place over an extended period of time. It is especially true that in reality, social relations are realized and developed over time; they form a temporal trajectory rather than a static set of positions. How intra- and inter-group processes may unfold and transform over time remains to be fully explored in social identity and self-categorization theories. This is seen when theories such as the minimum group paradigm studies are carried out; they are attempts to explain social activity in terms of a local cause-and-effect sequence, which often entail a consideration of the motives of the groups involved. Based on Tajfel's experiment, once it was established that the schoolboys were complying with general cultural norms of group behaviors resulting in competition between social groups and that they behaved as they did in order to achieve their social identity, the story ended there. The experiment was terminated, and what happened next was never further explored. The way group interaction in competition or cooperation develops over time has largely been neglected. Brown and Ross have noted

---

23. Condor, "Social Identity and Time," 285–315. See also Cinnirella, "Exploring Temporal Aspects," 227–48, in which possible social identities, which represent individual and shared cognitions about possible past group memberships, possible future group memberships, and perceptions of the possible past and future for current group memberships, are explored. See also Lim, "If Anyone is in Christ," 289–310, for examining temporal aspects of social identity formation in the Pauline communities.

24. Condor, "Social Identity and Time," 290.

this and offered their critique of SIT in which the focus is on "structure and the expense of process."[25] This is where Condor suggests that in the absence of a clear understanding of social groups as serial processes, group behavior can only be built upon static constructions.[26]

Recognizing the weakness of the lack of temporal consideration in SIT, Condor suggests employing "temporal comparison" as a possible approach that could profitably be used to address issues of temporality in social identity tradition. According to Condor, temporal comparison can be defined as "the process of judging the present status of an object, individual or group against its own past."[27] While this approach was originally developed in work on personal identity, it has been used in a number of studies involving intergroup contexts, and what emerges is a profitable approach to examining social identity that could be articulated in relation to notions of time and history.[28]

The lack of temporal consideration in social identity formation as observed by Condor is crucial in this study. I will demonstrate that temporal comparison could profitably be used in the investigation of the social identity formation of the Corinthians. As observed by Condor,[29] it could also be used in both positive and negative cognitive and evaluative judgments in the social identity formation of the Corinthians.

EFFECTS OF INTERGROUP/INTRAGROUP CONTACT AND CONFLICTS

One stimuli for SIT in the evaluative criteria is the positive group identity maintained by the ingroups through a process of comparison and evaluation against the outgroups. This evaluative aspect, while ascribing positive characteristics to the ingroup, does not necessarily translate into hatred for the outgroup. However, extended ingroup favoritism and outgroup discrimination could potentially be a fertile ground for conflict and social tension. Many forms of discrimination, bias, and prejudices may develop

---

25. Brown and Ross, "The Battle for Acceptance," 155–78, quotation from 155.

26. Condor, "Social Identity and Time," 296.

27. Condor, "Temporality and Collectivity," 660–61.

28. For example, see the empirical studies by Mummendey et al., "Nationalism and Patriotism," 159–72.

29. For further discussion, see Condor, "Temporality and Collectivity," 657–61. See also Condor, "Having History," 213–53, where she examines the ways Anglo-Britons may use and make sense of the stereotypes of their nation's history in both positive and negative ways.

as a consequence, leading the ingroups to categorize the outgroups that are evaluated unfavorably as inferior. This unequal group status is particularly potent and is often drawn along the lines of wealth, power, honor, social status, etc. Furthermore, the need to justify ingroup values in the form of moral superiority, and the demand of loyalty to the group may lead to disdain and hostility toward outgroups that are viewed as inferior. This phenomenon of the creation of ingroup bias and outgroup derogation could potentially result in identity-based conflicts.[30]

In order to reduce conflicts arising from group contact, several strategies have been proposed.[31]

1) Recategorization. This strategy involves the use of cross-cutting evaluative criteria to diffuse or prevent any potential, perceived or real ingroup-outgroup differentiation and intergroup comparison. It presupposes that individuals belong to different ingroups across different domains of social life. A member who is ingroup according to a set of evaluative criteria may be evaluated as outgroup based on a different set of criteria. For example, a Christ-follower in Corinth may not share the same social status with another Christ-follower. In order to diffuse the conflict based on social status, this strategy would employ evaluative criteria that avoid contested identity boundaries and structure a definition of group categorization in ways that reduce intergroup bias and conflict. This can be done by personalizing the intergroup situation or finding additional categorical dimensions that cut across the original ones in order to make the ingroup bias less likely.[32] In this case, the emphasis on social status will not be used as an evaluative criterion.

2) Superordinate identity. Instead of attempting to remove categorization from the evaluative criteria, this approach seeks to incorporate any outgroups into a new and larger superordinate identity. This results in the outgroup members now sharing a common ingroup identity as the ingroup with the hope that they will become a cohesive group by reducing intergroup discrimination and bias.[33] According to this approach, the ethnic identity of both the Jewish and gentile Christ-followers is no longer an evaluative criterion, and ethnic identity is now subsumed in their Christ identity.

---

30. For further discussion, see Brewer, "Psychology of Prejudice," 429–44.
31. See Brown, "Social Identity Theory," 745–78.
32. See Brewer and Miller, "Beyond the Contact Hypothesis," 281–302.
33. See Gaertner et al., "Common Ingroup Identity Model," 1–26.

3) Superordinate identity with ongoing subgroup salience. Both the above models—decategorization and common ingroup identity—involve the elimination of category boundaries and the abandonment of subgroup identities. In real life entities, this would be hard to achieve because the subgroups may resist any attempts to assimilate them into a dominant cultural identity or may oppose any negotiation perceived as detrimental to their inherent values or identity. Another avenue for considering intergroup conflict reduction is the creation of new superordinate identities that do not obliterate or eliminate subgroup salience, but rather affirm the existing distinct subgroup identities.[34] According to this model, both the Jewish and gentile ethnic identities and the economic status of the rich and poor are maintained as both groups negotiate the process of identity formation as Christ-followers.

SIT also provides insight into the workings of intragroup behavior by focusing on what is required to maintain group cohesiveness, stability, and sense of identity. If a group lacks salient identity or a clear sense of communal belonging, this will lead to problems and conflicts within the group.[35] Conflicts exist among the Corinthian Christ-followers as evidenced by Paul's letters to them. These ranges from divisions in the assembly to civil litigation, sexual immorality, and worship chaos, amongst others. I will be considering how Paul's use of metaphors constitutes one of the strategies for conflict resolution.

IMAGERY, TEXT, AND IDENTITY IN CONCERT: READING PAUL'S METAPHORS THOUGH THE LENS OF SOCIAL IDENTITY THEORY

In the previous chapter, I highlighted that metaphors function not merely as a tool of communication, but also shape the way one thinks and acts. Metaphors function as a mapping from a source domain to a target domain. More often than not, the metaphors used by Paul were not some abstract concepts but were drawn from the daily reality of his audience. These metaphors conjured up images operative in the minds of the Christ-followers and this subsequently shaped the way they thought and acted. In this chapter, I have also reviewed SIT as a framework to understand identity formation.

---

34. See Hewtone and Brown, "Contact Is Not Enough," 1–44; van Oudenhouven, Groenewoud, and Hewstone, "Co-operation," 649–62; and Brewer, "When Contact Is Not Enough," 291–303.

35. See Tucker, *You Belong to* Christ, 152–80, for a discussion on the lack of salient "in Christ" social identity in Corinth leading to the problems in the Christ-movement.

This will be the lens used to read Paul's letters to the Corinthians in the formation of Pauline community.

Philip Esler debuted the use of SIT in New Testament studies in 1994,[36] and this is now widely used in Pauline studies.[37] By paying attention to social identity, these studies help us understand how Paul sought to inculcate the value of collective forms of identity in the self-concept of the individual Christ-followers. Before we proceed to examine the metaphors Paul used in the Corinthian letters, I will now consider the question on how the power of metaphor as visual imagery works together in concert through the text in the formation of social identity.

Imagery, Text, and Identity in the Greco-Roman World

During the Roman Empire, Caesar Augustus created an identity that was centered on his image and person as the emperor. This example shows how an individual with sufficient power and authority was able to converge the identity of the group with his own person thereby constructing an identity that crossed the boundaries of other groups. Members of the Empire were constantly reminded of their sense of belonging through concrete visuals found in Roman cities depicted through arches, coins, temples of imperial cult, and statues of Caesar himself. Other images also included works of art, poetry, religious rituals, state ceremonies, triumphal processions, and the emperor's clothing, conduct, and forms of social interaction. By doing do, Augustus portrayed and promoted values for group membership and identity.

Zanker has argued that visual imagery often "reflects a society's inner life and gives insight into people's values and imagination that often cannot be apprehended in literary sources."[38] He also puts forward the

---

36. Esler develops the use of SIT in Pauline studies as seen in his publications: *First Christians in Their Social Worlds*; *Galatians*; and *Conflict and Identity in Romans*. See also his edited volume, *Modelling Early Christianity*.

37. For example, see Barentsen, *Emerging Leadership in the Pauline Mission*; Esler, *Conflict and Identity in Romans*; May, *The Body for the Lord*; Darko, *No Longer Living as the Gentiles*; and Tucker, *You Belong to Christ*. See also Baker, *Identity, Memory and Narrative in Early Christianity*. For reviews of recent scholarship on social identity in Pauline studies, see Tucker, *You Belong to Christ*, 87–124. For various approaches in exploring Christian identity, see the collected essays in Holmberg, *Exploring Early Christian Identity*; and Barclay, *Pauline Churches and Diaspora Jews*. See also Nyugen, *Christian Identity in Corinth*, 1–2, who dismisses social identity as a "modern model" and sets out to construct an ancient model or grid for identity in his work. Nyugen's swift dismissal appears to be premature and unwarranted.

38. Zanker, *Power of Images*, 3.

argument that it was during the reign of Augustus (27 BCE–14 CE) that visual communication took a decisive turning point in all forms of art and architecture. Augustus recognized the potential for constructing identity through images so that new rituals of power and a new mythology of Rome and the emperor could be created systematically. As such, these visual imageries were strategically placed at the center of social and public life: in the agora, baths, gymnasia, theaters, and places where people gathered for social and commercial activities.

After the assassination of Julius Caesar in 44 BCE, the struggle for sole power lasted for thirteen years, and it was during this period that art and architecture played a considerable role. In his will, Julius Caesar named his great-nephew Gaius Octavius or Octavian as his heir. Octavian, who took the name Augustus, capitalized on the status of his great-uncle and adoptive father, Julius Caesar, by using visual imagery from honorific statues to promote a new identity for himself that included a new image, a new name, and a new title.

Augustus used the appearance of a comet as a sign of Caesar's apotheosis, and put the symbol of the star on Caesar's head in coins and statues. Soon, the star appeared as a symbol of hope on coins, rings, and seals. In 42 BCE, Octavian deified Julius Caesar into a state cult and the worship of a new god in the Roman Empire began. From then on, Octavian was known as *divi filius*, son of the deified Caesar, and he laid claim to the divine and heroic ancestors from the Julian ancestry. This title of *divi filius* subsequently appeared in coins, an effective use of visual representation of the new title. Zanker argues that the "meaningful use and repetition of images and messages was a new phenomenon, particularly when one considers that coin types of the previous decades had seldom aimed at such effects."[39]

Apart from coins, Augustus also ensured public acknowledgement of his new identity through honorific statues erected under official auspices. Portraits of a new image of Augustus emerged, marked by a harmony of proportion, demonstrating timeless dignity.[40] In later years, statues of Augustus wearing a toga with veiled head appeared, showing him to be a priest offering sacrifice or prayer. This was for the entire Empire to see that Augustus considered the performance of his religious duties his greatest responsibility and highest honor.[41] This pious portrait of Augustus earned him honor and subsequent worship as one with divine powers.

---

39. Ibid., 37. For further discussion, see 33–65.
40. See ibid., 98–100.
41. Ibid., 127. See his wider discussion in 118–35.

Buildings and architecture such as temples and the Roman Forum triumphal arches also took on a grandeur, more elaborate design. Augustus even had his own imposing Mausoleum built.[42] Strabo described the Mausoleum soon after its completion:

> Most worth seeing is the so-called Mausoleion, a large mound set upon a tall socle by the river. It is planted with evergreen trees up to the top. Above stands the bronze statue of the Emperor Augustus. Within the mound are the graves intended for him, his relatives, and friends. Behind there is a large grove with splendid walks, in the midst of which is an elevated place, where Augustus's corpse was burnt.[43]

The *Res Gestae Divi Augusti*, the funerary inscription of Augustus, showcased that his deeds were nothing but glamorous and extraordinary. The *Res Gestae* was significant because it gave insight into the image Augustus portrayed to the Roman people, and this was further reflected in the coins minted containing references to the *Res Gestae*.

Through art and architecture, Augustus succeeded in using visual language—the deliberate and meaningful use and repetition of images and messages—to transform Roman society during his reign. The use of these visual representations was not only an effective means of communication, but was also a powerful instrument for propaganda.

Augustus' deliberate and systematic means of constructing identity through visual language was well developed by the first century CE, and certainly by the time of Paul. The employment of visual imagery through metaphorical transfer from visual materials to the text as a means of constructing identity has received some attention in recent years. In an edited volume on *Picturing the New Testament*, various contributors examined ancient artifacts that were familiar at the time of the New Testament in dialogue with the text.[44] Images and texts played a crucial role in the production and reception of early Christian ideas. These were part of the culture and symbolic world that the early Christ-followers sought to have people understand. Two essays written by Philip Esler and Harry Maier from this volume are noteworthy.[45] In Esler's article, he argues that Paul used athlete metaphor to assist him in constructing the social world and group identity of

---

42. For further discussion, see ibid., 72–77.

43. Strabo, *Geogr.* 5.3.9.

44. Weissenrieder et al., *Picturing the New Testament*. See also Maier, *Picturing Paul in Empire*.

45. Esler, "Paul and the *Agon*," 356–84 and Maier, "Barbarians, Scythians and Imperial Iconography," 385–406.

the Christ-followers. Esler examines the Greek games in their social context as illuminated in ancient visual representations and how this understanding is able to throw light on how Paul used the athlete motif in his letters. For example, Paul used images of victorious athletes scripted in honor discourse and also in visual representations of events at the games in painted images to construct reality.

Similarly, Maier reads Colossians in the light of imperial politics and especially imperial iconography. He attempts to bring visual representation and literary texts into dialogue with each other as a means of understanding the formation of social identity. Imperial iconography includes "architecture, the imagery of imperial coins, clothing strategic deployment of images of the emperor and the symbols associated with his reign and ritualized state ceremony."[46] By exploring imperial iconography, Maier sees parallels in the understanding of enthronement language in Colossians and its relation to the military language of triumph. Christ is depicted as enthroned in the heavens, with the world's peoples and powers being subjected to his rule. This Colossian representation of Christ drawn from imperial language also celebrates ethnic diversity in unity under the lordship of Christ.

Two recent monographs drawing on visual representation of Roman imperial ideology to engage in a re-imagination of Paul, his writings, and his world are also worth mentioning. Davina Lopez, using a gender critical re-imagination of Paul, engages the visual representation of Roman imperial ideology in re-imagining Paul as an apostle to the conquered in her reading of Galatians.[47] Lopez seeks to examine what Paul meant by identifying himself as an apostle to the nations. Lopez finds her answer through the way the Roman Empire depicted the relationship between the conquering and conquered peoples in visual representation such as inscriptions, statues, and reliefs. Based on her findings, Lopez argues that Roman power was often depicted as aggressive and masculine while those who were conquered were represented by images of helpless women. By using a gender-critical examination, Lopez traces the theme of conquest and domination, and concludes that the language of "nations" would have been heard by his contemporaries as defeated nations positioned as those destined to serve Rome. As an apostle to the conquered, Paul expressed his solidarity with those who were defeated, and this mission to the nations, according to Lopez, was "a transformative humanizing project that seeks to render the

---

46. Maier, "Barbarians, Scythians and Imperial Iconography," 385.
47. Lopez, *Apostle to the Conquered*.

rejected stones—the female personifications pinned underneath the heft of male penetrative conquest—into cornerstones."[48]

The other monograph by Brigitte Kahl attempts to re-imagine Galatians by examining the interaction with Roman Imperial ideology.[49] By using critical re-imagination, Kahl draws on "images and other visual or written sources—including spaces, buildings, performances, and rituals—to deconstruct and reconstruct our perception of the ancient world in its interaction with the 'word(s)' of the text."[50] Kahl bases her reading of Galatians by relating it to the depiction of Gauls in the Roman Empire. The Gauls, portrayed as the conquered and lawless barbarians placed under the rule of Rome, were often depicted as Titans and Giants. This description ideologically sets the subjugation of the Gauls against the backdrop of Gigantomarchy. As a result, Kahl finds the Great Altar at Pergamon to be relevant for Galatians because the defeat of the Giants was a depiction of Rome's defeat of the Gauls. Thus, reading through the visual textuality of the Great Altar at Pergamon and biblical narratives of Exodus and Deuteronomy, Kahl's interpretation of Galatians results in a passionate plea by Paul, writing to a vanquished people under Rome "to resist the idolatrous lure of imperial religion and social ordering."[51]

Thus far, we have seen how visual imagery is a powerful tool used to evoke the imagination of the intended audience. By using metaphors that conjure up powerful imageries, they lead to certain cognitive processes in hearers/readers that govern their thoughts and actions. These thoughts and actions resulted in constructing the social world and identity of the hearers/readers.

Imagery, Text, and Social Identity in Pauline Studies

Rosemary Canavan argues that visual imagery is a powerful tool used in the construction of identity by bringing the metaphors of the text into dialogue with the visual images drawn from the world of the hearers.[52] This employment of visual imagery as a means of construction of social identity

---

48. Ibid., 173.
49. Kahl, *Galatians Re-imagined*.
50. Ibid., 27.
51. Ibid., 287.
52. Canavan, *Clothing the Body of Christ*. While Colossians has been often identified as belonging to the Deutero-Pauline corpus, the influence of Paul is widely acknowledged. See Canavan's further discussion in 24–30.

is labeled as "visual construction of identity."[53] By using metaphors of clothing and body in Col 3:1–17, Canavan argues that the author of the letter offered a means of understanding the ongoing transformation of becoming the body of Christ. The notion of changing clothes as reflected in the language of "putting off" and "putting on" is used three times in Col 3:8, 9, and 10, 12. This change of clothes indicates a change of identity exemplified through the removing of the old self (Col 3:9) and the putting on of the new self (Col 3:10). Canavan examines the depiction of clothing and body based on statues, *stelae*, funerary monuments, and coins to build a mural of images that shaped the identity of those who lived in the Lycus Valley, and particularly Colossae, in the first century CE.[54] By comparing and constructing these images, Canavan investigates how they were understood in the first century CE and applied in the context of Col 3:1–17.[55] In doing so, Canavan develops a dialogue between the text and image where they not only paralleled each other but also critiqued a systematic visual construction of identity at Colossae. She develops three correlations between the text and image that juxtaposed against Caesar and Christ, namely, focus identity, clothing imagery, and body as representative of a group.[56] For focus identity, instead of Caesar as god, Christ is the head of every ruler and authority. For clothing imagery, Caesar was portrayed in specific styles of clothing to portray his divine authority; the Christ-followers in Colossae were to put off all vices and clothe themselves with virtue and love in Christ. For body imagery, Caesar was the personification of Rome and representative of the body of Rome while Christ is the head of the body. Based on this dialogue, Canavan concludes that the careful use of clothing and body imagery in Col 3:1–17 illustrates a way "to critique the current power structures and to give the Christ followers a recognizable means of living their identity in Christ."[57]

Another recent monograph that has also helped us understand the dialogue between metaphor and identity is the work of Jennifer Houston McNeel.[58] Drawing from Cognitive Metaphor Theory and SIT, McNeel focuses on the use of infant and nursing mother metaphors in 1 Thess 2:5–8. She argues that when Paul, a male Jew in the patriarchal first-century soci-

---

53. Ibid., 5–6, 54–56. For further discussion, see Hölscher, *Language of Images* and Zanker, *Power of Images*.

54. Canavan, *Clothing the Body of Christ*, 67–133.

55. See the summary chart in ibid., 183–84.

56. Ibid., 179–90.

57. Ibid., 193.

58. McNeel, *Paul as Infant and Nursing Mother*.

ety, described himself as a helpless infant and a breastfeeding woman, these metaphors powerfully and vividly conveyed his understanding of the countercultural, humble, and intimate nature of his apostleship and the gospel. By describing himself as an infant, Paul indicated to the Thessalonians his transparency and innocence as he dealt with the Christ-followers. Casting himself as a wet-nurse, he demonstrated his intimacy and affection for the Thessalonians in caring and nourishing them. By using these kinship metaphors, Paul drove home the point that the Thessalonians were siblings. This kinship relationship bound them more closely to one another and to Paul than to their own countrymen (cf. 1 Thess 2:14), thus constructing and cementing their Christian identity.

Thus far, we have explored how images, metaphor, and the construction of identity formation interacted through the text. Engaging in textual analysis requires that both the readers and recipients understand each other's symbolic universe, culture, values, and ideology. How can texts like Paul's letters written to a fledgling Christ-community shape and form identity? How can these texts function to build identity when many of these Christ-followers still maintained their previous identity rooted in Roman civic identity?

Judith Lieu argues that texts play "a central part not just in the documentation of what it meant to be Christian, but in actually shaping Christianity"[59] and it is through this "remarkable literary creativity and productivity that a multifaceted self-conscious identity was produced."[60] Following this, there are several key characteristics to be observed as we examine the letters of Paul in shaping identity:[61]

1) How is the audience being addressed? How would this naming exercise reinforce positive group identity among members of the Christ-community and yet separate them from others?

2) Who is the central figure that holds the group together?

3) What is the focus of this community?

4) What is the teaching/instruction/forms of beliefs that characterize this community and sets it apart from others?

5) What are the rituals that would forge the cohesiveness of the community?

---

59. Lieu, *Christian Identity*, 40.

60. Ibid., 41. See also her wider discussion found in the chapter on "Text and Identity," 27–61.

61. Modified from Carter, *Matthew and the Margins*, 9–14. See also Tucker, *You Belong to Christ*, 31–35.

6) Who are the leaders of the community and how does social organization promote the welfare of the community?

7) What are some of the factors that contributed to community development?

8) How does this community treat the less fortunate and marginalized?

9) How does this community deal with opposition that comes from both internal and external forces?

10) Is there any community development that is well defined by its origins, governance and practices, and pattern of lifestyle?

11) What could be the history and tradition, shared past, agreed values, continuities and boundaries safeguarding the identity of the community against contamination, invasion, and embodiment of others that ensure continuity of the community over time?

These questions further allow me to examine Paul's use of metaphor in the Corinthian letters and how the power of imagery can be used to construct identity. In this respect, Paul's use of familiar metaphors such as siblings, body, and temple not only in some ways parallels the style of visual construction of identity, but also in the construction of a unique social identity that is rooted in Christ.

Applying SIT to the study of metaphors in the letters to the Corinthians also involves all the three concepts of categorization, identification, and comparison. I will be investigating how Paul, in creating a positive and unique identity, attempts to propose a distinctive sense of belonging to members of the Christ-movement regardless of ethnicity, and to distinguish it from other groups existing in the Roman city of Corinth. I will also be examining how Paul is concerned with maintaining the distinctive group identity of the Corinthians in relation to the outgroups. Finally, I will be looking at how Paul defends the distinctiveness of the Corinthians by reminding them of their membership within the group. He does this by developing the evaluative dimension, drawing out positive values and distinctiveness of the group based on the gospel he proclaims. In other words, I am keen to unearth the unique kind of identity that Paul was proposing to members of this Christ-believing community, demonstrating that Paul's choice of metaphors is not merely a rhetorical device, but constitutes a deliberate and calculated selection in the construction of Christian identity.

SOME CONCERNS

Can one use contemporary approaches to interpret ancient Pauline texts? On the surface, doing so ignores the historical context of the text, resulting in ahistorical reading. This has been highlighted in Edwin Judge's pioneering work, which used social history to read ancient texts. For Judge, the concern is that modern social-scientific approaches were developed much later and in a context alien to the Roman Empire.[62] Those who employ these methods are alleged by Judge to engage in "the sociological fallacy."[63] For Judge, any social historical examination of ancient cultures and contexts should rely on papyrological, textual, and inscriptional evidence rather than modern approaches.[64] Similar concerns have also been raised by Andrew Clarke and Henri Nguyen.[65] Rather than dismissing completely the use of contemporary social-scientific approaches in reading Pauline texts, a dialogical approach combining social theory and historical-critical methods in the context of exegetical investigation of the texts would be more profitable.[66] In doing so, one needs to bear in mind that theories cannot substitute evidence, and the text must be allowed first to speak to the interpreter. As Kathy Ehresperger rightly summarizes, "Contemporary theories can provide an illuminating perspective and shed light on aspects of the fragmentary discourse of the Pauline epistolary conversation which would otherwise go unnoticed."[67] Similarly, for Kahl, the task for her is not so much exegetical but rather seeking a critical re-imagination that "seeks to recover the previous seeds of an alternate meaning that never took root within the dominant history of occidental Pauline interpretation."[68] Certainly there is room where historical-critical tools and social scientific analyses could collide to aid us in understanding more clearly group dynamics and the social implications of Paul's letters, as eloquently demonstrated by Tucker.[69]

---

62. Judge, "Social Identity of the First Christians," 201–17, especially 210–17 for his discussion.

63. Ibid., 210.

64. Ibid.

65. Clarke, *Secular and Christian Leadership in Corinth*, 3–7 and Nguyen, *Christian Identity in Corinth*, 10–51. For limitation and discussion on the critique of applying SIT to Pauline community, see Nebreda, *Christ Identity*, 46–51.

66. See Tucker, *You Belong to Christ*, 4–14. Tucker's work exemplifies the dialogically approach using contemporary theories with rigorous historical-critical methods.

67. Ehresperger, *Paul and the Dynamics of Power*, 3.

68. Kahl, *Galatians Re-imagined*, 4.

69. Tucker, *You Belong to Christ*, 5.

The use of SIT as a heuristic device for reading Pauline texts may be supported by the following reasons. First of all, in the Corinthians letters, Paul was dealing with a shift from a referent group that was rooted in Roman civic identity to one that was now in Christ. This shift of allegiance and group identification from the Roman social identity and Imperial ideology to one that was in Christ, informed by the Scripture of Israel, required transformation of cognitive understanding of one's identity. Secondly, Paul was dealing with group related issues, conflicts, and concerns in his letters. In this respect, the use of SIT that is fundamentally rooted in the studies of group membership, social relationship, and group behavior can be substantiated and will provide insights into how Paul negotiated the formation of social identity rooted in the gospel he proclaimed. This approach will not only help us gain a better understanding of how the Corinthians understood each other but also how they viewed others, especially the outgroups.[70] As Paul's letters form one of the earliest canonical writings of the New Testament, it is crucial to examine how the early Christ-movement navigated the process of identity formation.

SUMMARY

If metaphors are part of how we think and understand reality, then they are part of how we understand ourselves and relate to others. In this respect, metaphors play a significant role in the formation of social identity. In his letters, Paul uses metaphors to persuade the Corinthians to view their relationship with one another, with him, and with those outside the community. He presents to the Corinthians a social reality that is rooted in his gospel, and invites them to share his view. While we may not know exactly how the Corinthians responded to Paul, through the use of metaphor we may see how Paul attempted to inspire a change of thinking and behavior that would lead to the formation of a new social identity that was rooted in Christ.

---

70. See Tajfel, "Social Categorization," 63.

Part II

3

"My Brothers and Sisters"
Sibling Metaphor

INTRODUCTION

IN CHAPTER 1, I established that metaphors are not merely rhetorical devices to enhance communication but are also cognitive tools used to shape the way one thinks and acts. I also made the point that metaphors cannot be understood apart from the cultural context in which both speaker and hearer share a common understanding of the target and source domains. As such, I will examine these metaphors predominantly from the Greco-Roman context, the milieu for the major part of Paul's audience.

Paul used a diverse range of familial metaphors encompassing sibling, father, mother, and child to shape the thinking of his audience and propel them to action. I will examine sibling metaphors in this chapter and focus on the remaining familial metaphors in the following chapter 4. But before I do so, it would be helpful to map Paul's use of familial language in the Corinthian letters.

MAPPING PAUL'S USE OF FAMILIAL LANGUAGE IN THE CORINTHIAN LETTERS

Many studies focusing on family in the Pauline corpus are dominated by those related to the Household Codes and, to a lesser extent, the connection between the social institution of the family in antiquity and the notion of fictive-kinship in the Pauline community.¹ This is strange since Paul's letters contain a high number of familial terminologies. For example, in 1 Corinthians, kinship language features frequently, and is used in varied ways. Paul used the identity of God as the father of the community to address the Corinthians (1 Cor 8:6; 15:24; 2 Cor 1:2–3; 6:16–18; 11:31). He also likened himself to a father who begat the Corinthians and who disciplined his children (1 Cor 4:14–17; 2 Cor 6:13). Paul also reminded the Corinthians that he was also a responsible father who provided for his children (2 Cor 12:15). He asked them to imitate him (1 Cor 4:16; 11:1), a language rooted in the familial values of imitating the father's lifestyle and religious behavior. Timothy, a co-sender of the letter, was described as Paul's beloved and faithful child and also an older sibling to the Corinthians (1 Cor 4:17). Maternal imagery also features in 1 Corinthians, with Paul declaring himself as feeding the Corinthians with milk (1 Cor 3:2). He also dealt with the relationship between husbands and wives (1 Cor 7:1–16; 11:2–16); meals taken at home (1 Cor 11:22); and believers in households (1 Cor 1:16; 16:5) amongst others. From this sample, it is clear that the use of familial imagery is widespread in the Corinthians correspondence.

However, Paul's favorite and most frequently used familial imagery is that of ἀδελφοί,² sibling, or "brothers and sisters." This sibling address appears a total of 113 times in Paul's undisputable letters as depicted in the following Table 3.1. Out of these, ἀδελφοί echoes fifty one times throughout the Corinthians letters—thirty nine times in 1 Corinthians and twelve times in 2 Corinthians— representing an impressive 45 percent of overall usage. With the exception of 1 Cor 9:5 where the reference is to the brothers of Jesus, the term is used for surrogate family throughout 1 Corinthians.

---

1. For a sample of some of these studies, see Crouch, *Origin and Intention*; Balch, *Let Wives be Submissive*; and Hering, *Colossian and Ephesian Haustafeln*. See also studies on family in the New Testament: Osiek and Balch, *Families in the New Testament World*; Balch and Osiek, *Early Christian Families in Context*; Balla, *Child-Parent Relationship*; Moxnes, ed., *Constructing Early Christian Families*; and van Henten and Brenner, *Families and Family Relations*. See also Rawson, "'The Roman Family' in Recent Research," 119–38.

2. While it is masculine, the use of ἀδελφοί is intended to be inclusive, and better translated as "brothers and sisters." See BDAG s.v. and LSJ, s.v. See also Trebilco, *Self-designations and Group Identity*, 24–25 and Aasgaard, *My Brothers and Sisters*, 7–8. Contra, Fatum, "Brotherhood in Christ," 192–94. In the undisputed letters of Paul, ἀδελφή, a female sibling terminology, only appears twice in 1 Cor in 7:15 and 9:5, and three times elsewhere in Rom 16:1, 15 and Phlm 2. In these occurrences, the addresses are clearly female.

Table 3.1: The Use of ἀδελφοί in Paul's Undisputable Letters

Letters	Frequency of ἀδελφοί	Percentage of Use
Romans	19	16.8%
1 Corinthians	39	34.5%
2 Corinthians	12	10.6%
Galatians	11	9.7%
Philippians	9	8.0%
1 Thessalonians	19	16.8%
Philemon	4	3.5%
Total	113	100%

Paul also emphasized the relationship between himself and the Corinthians by adding the personal possessive pronoun "my" or "my beloved" to "brothers and sisters," as seen in 1 Cor 1:11 and 15:58 respectively. This underscores Paul's deep concern and love for a community that was divided. The use of kinship language and terms of endearment is an effective rhetorical tool in calling this community to the unity that should characterize their membership within the family of Christ (1 Cor 1:10).

Unfortunately, the emphasis on Paul's use of sibling language is somewhat misplaced in some modern English translations. For example, a comparison between the NA28 and the NRSV reveals that ἀδελφοί is arbitrarily translated as "believers," "friends," or as pronouns such as "one or another." At times, ἀδελφοί is not even translated at all. Of the fifty one times where ἀδελφοί is used in the Corinthian letters, it is translated other than "brothers" or "brothers and sisters" a total of fourteen times in the NRSV, as highlighted in Table 3.2 below.[3]

---

3. In the NIV2011, there are five instances in the Corinthian letters where ἀδελφοί is not translated as "brother/brothers" or "brothers and sisters." See 1 Cor 5:11; 7:14; 8:1, 12; 15:31. The ESV does better by faithfully translating all the occurrences of ἀδελφοί as "brother" or "brothers" except for 1 Cor 7:14 which is translated as "husband." Note that the ESV is not a gender inclusive translation.

Metaphors and Social Identity Formation

Table 3.2: Instances where ἀδελφοί Is Not Translated as "Brothers" or "Brothers and Sisters" in the NRSV

Passage	NA-28	NRSV
1 Cor 6:5–6	πρὸς ἐντροπὴν ὑμῖν λέγω. οὕτως οὐκ ἔνι ἐν ὑμῖν οὐδεὶς σοφός, ὃς δυνήσεται διακρῖναι ἀνὰ μέσον τοῦ ἀδελφοῦ αὐτοῦ; ἀλλὰ ἀδελφὸς μετὰ ἀδελφοῦ κρίνεται καὶ τοῦτο ἐπὶ ἀπίστων;	I say this to your shame. Can it be that there is no one among you wise enough to decide between one *believer* and another, but a *believer* goes to court against a *believer*—and before unbelievers at that?
1 Cor 6:8	ἀλλὰ ὑμεῖς ἀδικεῖτε καὶ ἀποστερεῖτε, καὶ τοῦτο ἀδελφούς.	But you yourselves wrong and defraud—and *believers* at that.
1 Cor 7:12	Τοῖς δὲ λοιποῖς λέγω ἐγὼ οὐχ ὁ κύριος· εἴ τις ἀδελφὸς γυναῖκα ἔχει ἄπιστον καὶ αὕτη συνευδοκεῖ οἰκεῖν μετ' αὐτοῦ, μὴ ἀφιέτω αὐτήν·	To the rest I say—I and not the Lord—that if any *believer* has a wife who is an unbeliever, and she consents to live with him, he should not divorce her.
1 Cor 7:14	ἡγίασται γὰρ ὁ ἀνὴρ ὁ ἄπιστος ἐν τῇ γυναικὶ καὶ ἡγίασται ἡ γυνὴ ἡ ἄπιστος ἐν τῷ ἀδελφῷ· ἐπεὶ ἄρα τὰ τέκνα ὑμῶν ἀκάθαρτά ἐστιν, νῦν δὲ ἅγιά ἐστιν.	For the unbelieving husband is made holy through his wife, and the unbelieving wife is made holy through her *husband*. Otherwise, your children would be unclean, but as it is, they are holy.
1 Cor 8:11–13	ἀπόλλυται γὰρ ὁ ἀσθενῶν ἐν τῇ σῇ γνώσει, ὁ ἀδελφὸς δι' ὃν Χριστὸς ἀπέθανεν. οὕτως δὲ ἁμαρτάνοντες εἰς τοὺς ἀδελφοὺς καὶ τύπτοντες αὐτῶν τὴν συνείδησιν ἀσθενοῦσαν εἰς Χριστὸν ἁμαρτάνετε. διόπερ εἰ βρῶμα σκανδαλίζει τὸν ἀδελφόν μου, οὐ μὴ φάγω κρέα εἰς τὸν αἰῶνα, ἵνα μὴ τὸν ἀδελφόν μου σκανδαλίσω.	So by your knowledge those weak *believers* for whom Christ died are destroyed. But when you thus sin against *members of your family*, and wound their conscience when it is weak, you sin against Christ. Therefore, if food is a cause of *their* falling, I will never eat meat, so that I may not cause *one of them* to fall.

Passage	NA-28	NRSV
1 Cor 14:26	Τί οὖν ἐστιν, ἀδελφοί; ὅταν συνέρχησθε, ἕκαστος ψαλμὸν ἔχει, διδαχὴν ἔχει, ἀποκάλυψιν ἔχει, γλῶσσαν ἔχει, ἑρμηνείαν ἔχει· πάντα πρὸς οἰκοδομὴν γινέσθω.	What should be done then, my *friends*? When you come together, each one has a hymn, a lesson, a revelation, a tongue, or an interpretation. Let all things be done for building up.
1 Cor 14:39	Ὥστε, ἀδελφοί [μου], ζηλοῦτε τὸ προφητεύειν καὶ τὸ λαλεῖν μὴ κωλύετε γλώσσαις·	So, my *friends*, be eager to prophesy, and do not forbid speaking in tongues;
1 Cor 15:58	Ὥστε, ἀδελφοί μου ἀγαπητοί, ἑδραῖοι γίνεσθε, ἀμετακίνητοι, περισσεύοντες ἐν τῷ ἔργῳ τοῦ κυρίου πάντοτε, εἰδότες ὅτι ὁ κόπος ὑμῶν οὐκ ἔστιν κενὸς ἐν κυρίῳ.	Therefore, my beloved,[A] be steadfast, immovable, always excelling in the work of the Lord, because you know that in the Lord your labor is not in vain.
2 Cor 11:9	καὶ παρὼν πρὸς ὑμᾶς καὶ ὑστερηθεὶς οὐ κατενάρκησα οὐθενός· τὸ γὰρ ὑστέρημά μου προσανεπλήρωσαν οἱ ἀδελφοὶ ἐλθόντες ἀπὸ Μακεδονίας, καὶ ἐν παντὶ ἀβαρῆ ἐμαυτὸν ὑμῖν ἐτήρησα καὶ τηρήσω.	And when I was with you and was in need, I did not burden anyone, for my needs were supplied by the *friends* who came from Macedonia. So I refrained and will continue to refrain from burdening you in any way.

A. Note that ἀδελφοί is left out in the translation.

As depicted in Table 3.2 above, when some occurrences of ἀδελφοί are not translated literally, readers reading the English translation may miss the significance of this metaphor.

The Use of ἀδελφοί: Divisions and Conflicts of an Unprecedented Nature

One of Paul's biggest challenges was dealing with church divisions and conflicts in 1 Corinthians. After his customary greetings and thanksgiving (1 Cor 1:1–9), Paul immediately launched into addressing the divisions among the Corinthians based on the oral report he had received from members of Chloe's household. He was informed that there were "quarrels" (ἔριδες) in the Christ-community (1 Cor 1:11) with different parties taking sides with different leaders (1 Cor 1:12). Paul returned to the same issue in 1 Cor 3:3 where he noted, "there is jealousy and quarreling among you" (ἐν ὑμῖν ζῆλος καὶ ἔρις), and again in 1 Cor 11:18–19 where "there are divisions among you . . . there have to be factions among you" (σχίσματα ἐν ὑμῖν ὑπάρχειν . . . αἱρέσεις ἐν ὑμῖν εἶναι). When there was discord and disunity with various groups fighting over the nature of leadership,[4] Paul responded by using sibling language: "I appeal to you, brothers and sisters (ἀδελφοί), by the name of our Lord Jesus Christ, that all of you agree, and that there be no divisions (σχίσματα) among you, but that you be united in the same mind and the same judgment" (1 Cor 1:10).

In 1 Cor 1—4, Paul used ἀδελφοί a total of six times in addressing the issue of divisions. By appealing to the Corinthians as siblings, Paul sought to remind them of their identity as belonging to one family.

Apart from divisions over the nature of leadership, there were also legal disputes between members in the ἐκκλησία. When the disputes turned ugly, Paul forcefully confronted them, again by appealing to sibling imagery: "I say this to shame you. Is it possible that there is nobody among you wise enough to settle a dispute between the brothers? But instead, one brother goes to law against another brother—and this in front of unbelievers! The very fact that you have lawsuits among you means you have been completely defeated already. Why not rather be wronged? Why not rather be cheated? Instead, you yourselves cheat and do wrong, and you do this to your brothers" (1 Cor 5:5–8).[5]

In the Corinthian setting, some held that it was permissible to eat meat that had been sacrificed to idols while others were against it. As in 1 Cor 5:5–8, the word ἀδελφός appears often, a total of four times within three verses in 1 Cor 8:11–13. In using sibling imagery, Paul was not only

---

4. I have argued elsewhere that the problems of discord and disunity in the Corinthian church were not necessarily due to the presence of these leaders in their midst but over the nature of leadership, reflecting some forms of social divisions and factionalism resulting from the manner in which leaders were evaluated based on the prevailing Greco-Roman conventions. Neither was it due to some competing mission activities of Peter and Paul as argued by Goulder, *Paul and the Competing Mission in Corinth*. For further discussion, see my *Sufferings of Christ*, 158–96, 198. Cf. Savage, *Power through Weakness*; Clarke, *Secular and Christian Leadership in Corinth*, 2nd ed.; Winter, *After Paul Left Corinth*, 31–43; and Nguyen, *Christian Identity in Corinth*. See also Finney, *Honour and Conflict in the Ancient World*, 69–109. On the use of the word σχίσματα describing the divisions in Corinth, see Mitchell, *Paul and the Rhetoric of Reconciliation*, 71–80. Mitchell concludes that this word is a fitting term to refer to "political or social division and factionalism" (73) among the Corinthians, and does not refer to some specific theological or doctrinal positions.

5. As I pointed out, most English translations miss out the force of Paul's argument here by either translating ἀδελφός as believer or some other pronoun as seen in the NRSV and the NIV 2011. I have modified the NRSV to reflect Paul's use of sibling language here.

defending the weaker brothers but also reminding the stronger brothers of their role and responsibility to care, honor, and respect the weaker brothers: "Therefore, if food makes my brother or sister to stumble, I will never eat meat, lest I make my brother stumble" (1 Cor 8:13). The ethical dimension of the sibling imagery is clear here: The stronger brothers had to think beyond their selfish interest and consider how their actions might have affected others. If they continued in their eating habit, Paul described this action as destroying the weaker brothers and sisters (1 Cor 8:11).

The most striking use of sibling imagery is in 1 Cor 11:33–34 where Paul dealt with the abuse of the Lord's Supper. Here, Paul wanted the Corinthians to celebrate the Eucharist as a family meal instead of letting class distinctions rule and divide them (1 Cor 11:20–22). In order to correct their behavior, Paul addressed the elites or wealthy members[6] as ἀδελφοί μου, "my brothers and sisters": "So then, my brothers and sisters, when you come together to eat, wait for one another—if anyone is hungry, let him eat at home—so that when you come together it will not be for judgment" (1 Cor 11:33–34).

6. Although Paul seemed to name a few Christ-followers who appear to be relatively wealthy (for examples, Gaius, Erastus, and Phoebe from Cenchrea), it is unlikely that they belonged to the noble lineage or the aristocratic elites of the city. See the works of Meggitt, *Paul, Poverty and Survival*; Friesen, "Poverty in Pauline Studies," 323–61; Friesen, "Prospects for a Demography," 352–70; Barclay, "Poverty in Pauline Studies," 363–66; and Longenecker, "Exposing the Economic Middle," 243–78. Jongkind, "Corinth in the First Century A.D.," 139–48, proposes the possibility of a "middle class" in ancient Corinth. Cf. Pogoloff, *Logos and Sophia*, 210–11, who suggests that "even the highest status Corinthians are only of middling status . . . (and) must cope with their relative *lack* of status rather than their relative *boast* of status" (emphasis his). See also Finney, *Honour and Conflict*, 94–100; and Gill, "In Search of the Social Elite," 323–37. Social stratification within the Roman Empire is difficult to ascertain with concrete evidence (See Theissen, *Social Setting of Pauline Christianity*, 69–119). Based on numerous studies, conclusions are generally tentative and qualified. Meeks typifies most of the works in this area when he concludes that "the evidence we have is fragmentary, random and often unclear. We cannot draw up a statistical profile of the Pauline communities nor fully describe the social level of a single Pauline Christian" (Meeks, *First Urban Christians*, 72). See also Theissen, *Social Setting of Pauline Christianity*, 73. Although in popular literature, the discovery of the Erastus inscription has often been used as evidence for the elite status of Erastus, a member of Pauline community in Corinth (see Rom 16:23), it has been fraught with difficulties as demonstrated by Friesen, "Prospects for a Demography," 369; and Friesen, "Wrong Erastus," 231–56. See also Clarke, "Another Corinthian Erastus Inscription," 146–51; Gill, "Erastus the Aedile," 293–300; Goodrich, "Erastus, Quaestor of Corinth," 90–115; Goodrich, "Erastus of Corinth (Rom 16.23)," 583–593; and Meggitt, "Social Status of Erastus," 218–23. Nevertheless, there is no denying that there were among the Corinthians some who were relatively wealthy compared to the rest of the Christ-followers. In this respect, I will continue to use the word "elite" not necessarily referring to those from the aristocratic elite, but simply to underscore the presence of those who were regarded as relatively wealthy in Corinth.

In the use of spiritual gifts when the Corinthians gathered for worship, some quarters placed more importance on the gifts of speaking in tongues than other gifts (1 Cor 14:6). In addressing this issue, Paul again evoked sibling imagery: "Now concerning spiritual gifts, brothers and sisters, I do not want you to be uninformed" (1 Cor 12:1). He underscored the need for siblings to build up one another instead of causing chaos and confusion: "What should be done then, my brothers and sisters? When you come together, each one has a hymn, a lesson, a revelation, a tongue, or an interpretation. Let all things be done for building up" (1 Cor 14:26).

To promote group cohesiveness, Paul also used sibling language in 1 Cor 15:58: "Therefore, my beloved brothers and sisters, be steadfast, immovable, always excelling in the work of the Lord, because you know that in the Lord your labor is not in vain." Similarly in 2 Cor 13:11, Paul exhorted the Corinthians, as brothers and sisters, to "put things in order, listen to my appeal, agree with one another, live in peace; and the God of love and peace will be with you." Mutual agreement and harmony were hallmarks of siblings in a family.

In 2 Corinthians, more than half the usage of ἀδελφοί occurs within the context of Paul's appeal to the Corinthians concerning the monetary collection for Jerusalem (2 Cor 8–9). As siblings, they were to share financial recourses with one another, especially with those who were in need.[7]

From this cursory survey, it is clear that the use of sibling imagery features prominently in the Corinthian letters. I will now proceed to review previous research on Paul's use of sibling imagery, followed by an examination of how sibling relations were understood in Paul's time.

BRIEF SURVEY OF CURRENT RESEARCH INTO PAUL'S USE OF FAMILIAL METAPHORS

Robert Banks's *Paul's Idea of Community* is probably one of the earliest studies that examined Paul's use of familial metaphors.[8] Banks laments that familial metaphor "has all too often been overlooked or only mentioned in passing."[9] In Banks's view, the frequency of the use of this metaphor should

---

7. Out of the twelve times where ἀδελφός or ἀδελφοί appears in 2 Corinthians, seven times are directly related to the sharing of financial resources: six times are found in 2 Cor 8–9 dealing with the collection for Jerusalem (see 2 Cor 8:1, 18, 22 (2x); 9:3, 5) and once in 2 Cor 11:9. For further treatment on Paul's understanding of generosity as the motivation behind the collection for Jerusalem, see Lim, "Generosity from Pauline Perspective," 20–33; and Lim, "Paul the Economist?" 19–31.

8. Banks, *Paul's Idea of Community*, 52–61.

9. Ibid., 53. Similarly, S. Scott Bartchy, echoes Banks's lament: "the widespread

rightly be regarded as the most significant metaphorical usage of all. More than any other imagery used by Paul, familial metaphor revealed the essence of his thinking about community.[10]

Banks's lament has been picked up in subsequent studies that incorporate the application of social sciences to biblical studies.[11] Karl O. Sandnes, by employing insights from social cultural anthropology, argues that the ἐκκλησία functioned as an alternative family for the Christ-believers.[12] He draws on his findings from East Asian ancestral worship and filial piety to bring out the significance of religious conversion in early Christianity. In the Confucian-based society where ancestral worship is expected to be carried out by the children of the deceased, it is not surprising that Christians find themselves torn between loyalty to Christ and loyalty to parents. As such, the ἐκκλησία as a family of brothers and sisters becomes an alternative family for these new converts who may be perceived as challenging the Confucian values of continuity, loyalty, and harmony within the family. Sandnes' thesis is that the ideal environment where new converts can be nurtured and grow is a family-like congregation that compensates for the loss of the old family ties that may have been severed when they moved to a new family.[13]

Sandnes raises a very pertinent question on the need for a new or alternative family to compensate for the loss of previous family ties. His research, carried out in the collectivistic context of Asia may very well raise similar questions as to whether this was the norm within Pauline communities. It is very plausible that those from the lower strata of the Greco-Roman society, such as slaves, may have found new identity, significance, and meaning in an intimate, more egalitarian, and new close-knit fictive family structures where everyone was treated as "brothers and sisters."

---

ignoring of the significance of Paul's use of kinship terminology make(s) it clear that some extensive work needs to be done if the social and cultural context of this root metaphor in Paul's language is to be taken seriously by scholars and their readers." See Bartchy, "Undermining Ancient Patriarchy," 68–78; quotation from 70.

10. Banks, *Paul's Idea of Community*, 53.

11. See my previous chapter where I reviewed the application of the social sciences in the investigation of early Pauline community in the last three decades, particularly the works of Edwin Judge and Wayne Meeks. Meeks argues that the language of belonging such as "brothers and sisters" is used as one of the means on how Pauline community identified themselves as a movement in the formation of the ἐκκλησία. For further discussion, see Meeks, *First Urban Christians*, 85.

12. Sandnes, *A New Family*.

13. Ibid., 82. See also Sandnes' subsequent publication, "Equality within Patriarchal Structures," 150–65.

S. Scott Bartchy takes Sandnes argument further by stating that Paul, following the example of Jesus, attempted to undermine the authority and social cohesiveness of the institution of the family rooted in patriarchal domination by offering an alternative family structure made up of fictive "brothers and sisters." In doing so, Bartchy argues that Paul's goal was not to create an egalitarian community in the political sense, but a well-functioning family in the kinship sense. For Bartchy, Paul's vision of a family was one where the "strong" would use their strength not for themselves but to empower the "weak" as brothers and sisters.[14] Bartchy's observation will be further built upon in my discussion below.

How does familial social relationship work in a family? In his work, Joseph Hellerman seeks to construct a model of the ancient Mediterranean family and employs it to understand a broad sampling of conceptions of Christian community from the time of Jesus to the mid-third century CE.[15] Following Bartchy, Hellerman sees the importance of siblingship within the patrilineal kinship structure prevailing in the Mediterranean world. He argues that the sibling relationship had priority over other kind of social relations, even marital bonds, and outlines several characteristics of sibling relations such as sibling loyalty, dealing with divided loyalty, protection of honor, sharing of resources, veneration of ancestors, and preoccupation with family inheritance.[16] Based on this understanding, Hellerman argues that the earliest churches around the Mediterranean reflected this ancient family structure as closely knit family groups.[17] The social matrix most central to this early conception of community was the surrogate kinship group of siblings who saw themselves as brothers and sisters. In this respect, Hellerman views members of this familial community who put sibling metaphor into practice as those who exercised genuine concern to preserve the honor of their local church communities and to meet the material needs of the group's individual members. In addition, this sibling imagery also demanded a high degree of loyalty from the members of the community. As such, sibling imagery bound those who lived the ideals of the imagery together, and marginalized those who were perceived to be betrayers of this brotherhood.[18]

14. Bartchy, "Undermining Ancient Patriarchy," 68–78. See also Meeks, *The First Urban Christians*, 85, who suggests that Paul's fictive kinship language like "brothers and sisters" promotes egalitarian structures compared to the structured hierarchical Mediterranean society.

15. Hellerman, *Ancient Church as Family*.

16. Ibid., 27–58.

17. Ibid., 225.

18. Ibid., 215–16.

Is the use of familial metaphors to describe the ἐκκλησία as an alternative family, as proposed by Sandnes and Meeks, one that is intended to be without hierarchy? Trevor Burke argues otherwise in his investigation based on familial language in 1 Thessalonians.[19] Burke believes that something far more radical and fundamental is at work in Paul's use of familial metaphors and this is reflected in describing the ethical conduct of the Christ-followers towards one another and those who were considered outsiders by the community.[20] According to Burke, Paul's use of kinship language records the highest ratio in terms of the use of the metaphor to the number of verses in 1 Thessalonians. By narrowing down to a single letter (unlike previous studies that focused on the use of familial language in the wider Pauline corpus), Burke is able to examine in greater depth all the familial terms used by Paul, particularly the paternal and sibling metaphors. By using both the imagery of "father" and "nursing mother," Burke demonstrates Paul's heavy responsibility in teaching and instructing the Thessalonians and his deep affection in nurturing them. He further examines Paul's use of sibling metaphor in addressing two main contentious issues in the Thessalonian community, namely, sexual morality/business (1 Thess 4:3–8) and ethical working practices (1 Thess 4:9–12; 5:12–15). Based on his exegesis, Burke argues that there are four main ideals highlighted by Paul in regulating the community: peace/harmony; brotherly love; honor/respect in relation to the brotherhood and to outsiders; and status. Burke also argues that in conformity with the norms and conventional attitudes of brothers in the ancient world, Paul recognized that there was a hierarchy or difference in status/seniority between brothers. Paul specifically exhorted senior or leading brothers to exercise their authoritative duty of admonishing the rest in his absence to ensure that no brother retaliated against another brother or against outsiders. This finding of Burke argues against those who believe that the early Christian communities started as non-hierarchical structures only to degenerate into hierarchical structures through the passage of time.[21] Similarly, Horrell, in outlining the use of sibling and household language from Paul to the Pastoral Epistles, also holds that while Paul was aiming for equality in his use of sibling language, he also used hierarchical terminology such as father-children language.[22]

19. Burke, *Family Matters*.

20. See also Aasgaard, "Role Ethics in Paul," 513–30.

21. For example, see Schüssler Fiorenza, *In Memory of Her*, 279, who argues that the Pastoral Epistles are example of the beginning of patriarchalization of the church.

22. Horrell, "From ἀδελφοί to οἶκος θεοῦ," 83–114. See also Sandnes, "Equality within Patriarchal Structures," 150–65, where he argues that egalitarianism emerged within inherited structures of patriarchal system by examining Paul's letter to Philemon. By

Mary Katherine Birge explores how Paul uses the kinship and household language in addressing disharmony and divisions in 1 Corinthians.[23] She first attempts to unpack the use of familial kinship language in 1 Cor 3–6 by drawing from the rhetorical convention of his day. Birge argues that Paul used kinship imagery as part of his rhetorical strategy to correct the divisions among the Corinthians. While Birge finds that Paul's use of images of household and familial kinship in these four chapters was coherent and consistent in addressing divisions in the community, she wonders if the same could be said in 1 Cor 12–14 where similar issues dealing with conflicts and divisions in the community were being dealt with. Birge then sets out to test her thesis by examining 1 Cor 12–14. She argues that the same language and imagery of familial kinship is also used by Paul to promote unity and argue against thoughts, words, and actions that divide the community. Birge concludes that the imagery of kinship is a significant interpretive lens to read and understand 1 Corinthians.

Now the question is this: What was the source of such kinship and household language? Birge argues that the initial source was found in Paul's religious history as a Jew and the cultural setting of Paul's days. She assigns weight to Jewish literature such as Sirach, Wisdom of Solomon, *Testaments of the Twelve Patriarchs*, Philo, Josephus and *The Rule of the Community* and *Damascus Document* from the Qumran community as primary sources for Paul's understanding of household and kinship imagery. Her reference to Greco-Roman conventions is only limited to the practice of rhetoric, rather than the Greco-Roman understanding of family and kinship. Birge then argues that the notion of being "in Christ" dissolved all boundaries of status and privilege that Greco-Roman society had established among people who were not "kin" to one another. Birge's work is useful because she argues that the repeated use of similar imagery of kinship and household in 1 Cor 3–6 and 12–14 underscores the fact that the divisive nature of the Corinthian community was not compatible with their new kinship that was now rooted in Christ.

Thus far, we have seen that although there has been a keen interest in the study of Paul's use of sibling imagery in the last couple of decades, a number of these studies subsume siblingship under family without distinguishing them. While there is benefit to this treatment of Paul's use of familial imagery, it does not distinguish between the relations of siblings

---

calling both Philemon and Onesimus as brothers, the master and his slave were now ascribed a new status and identity in Christ on an equal footing, but that does not mean within this relationship there was no hierarchical relationship between master and slave. See also Punt, "He is Heavy," 153–71.

23. Birge, *Language of Belonging*.

within the family. Undoubtedly, Paul's use of familial imagery is varied and incorporates household behavior, household codes, parent-child relationship, disciplinary father, and nursing mother amongst others. However, the most dominant familial language used in the Corinthian letters is that of sibling imagery. What is clearly needed is a comprehensive treatment of the use of sibling imagery.

Probably the most detailed study of Paul's use of sibling imagery is the work by Reidar Aasgaard.[24] Rather than seeing the metaphor as drawn primarily from the Jewish context as Birge did, Aasgaard argues that the sibling imagery derives its meaning predominantly from the socio-historical context of family in antiquity. The strength of Aasgaard's work is his extensive investigation of the meaning and function of the fictive kinship terms of brother and sister drawing on primary sources of the Greco-Roman world, particularly Plutarch's treatise *De Fraterno Amore*, or *On Brotherly Love*.[25] With an informed understanding of family in antiquity, Aasgaard investigates a series of passages in the Pauline corpus that deals with sibling imagery, namely, Rom 8:29; 1 Thess 4:9–12/Rom 12:9–13; 1 Cor 8:11/Rom 14:15; 1 Cor 6:1–11; and Philemon to demonstrate how the sibling metaphor functions in these passages. Unlike Sandnes, Aasgaard argues that Paul did not use sibling language to compensate for the loss of old familial ties, but adapted the notion of social siblingship in the Greco-Roman world to that of Christian family. For Aasgaard, Paul was in "dialogue with the family of Antiquity."[26] Paul seemed to use the sibling metaphor as one of the strategies for "Christian infiltration" into the network of the family, which was the basic social network of antiquity.[27] As such, Paul used imagery of siblingship in the shaping of Christian self-understanding, both among Christians and those in the outside world. By calling Christians siblings, Paul provided them with a strong sense of identity and belonging that characterized such relationships, and these included honoring one another and keeping concord and harmony with one another.[28]

SIBLINGSHIP IN ANTIQUITY

Family is an important institution in antiquity, as declared by Cicero:

24. Aasgaard, *My Beloved Brothers and Sisters*. See also his "Brotherhood in Plutarch and Paul," 166–82.
25. Aasgaard, *My Beloved Brothers and Sisters*, 34–116.
26. Ibid., 346.
27. Ibid.
28. Ibid., 306–7.

> ... the first bond of union is that between husband and wife; the next, that between parents and children; then we find one home, with everything in common ... Then follows the bond between brothers and sisters, and next those of first and then of second cousins; and when they can no longer be sheltered under one roof, they go out into other homes, as into colonies. ... The bonds of common blood hold men fast through good-will and affection; for it means much to share in common the same family traditions, the same forms of domestic worship, and the same ancestral tombs.[29]

Within family institution, the sibling relationship is central, and Cicero placed it after the union between husband and wife, and parents and children. However, Aristotle placed the sibling relationship next to the parent/child relationship and ahead of the relationship between spouses.[30]

Sibling Relationship

One of the most important texts on sibling relationship in antiquity is that of L Mestrius Plutarchus' *De Fraterno Amore* (*On Brotherly Love*), a treatise written in the late nineties CE. This significant source of writing is unique because it is probably the only complete treatise from antiquity bequeathed for us that has brotherly relations as its central focus.[31]

Siblingship and Family

Plutarch positioned the sibling relationship within the framework of the family. Like many of his contemporaries, Plutarch perceived the institution of family to be in a state of crisis and decline. He observed at the introduction of his treatise, "brotherly love (φιλαδελδίαν) is as rare in our days as brotherly hatred (μισαδελφίαν) was among men of old."[32] This is tragic as the closeness of siblings is reflected in a common biological origin:

> Nature (φύσις) from one seed (σπέρματος) and one source (ἀρχῆς) has created two brothers (ἀδελφοὺς), or three, or more,

29. Cicero, *Off.* 1.17.54–55.
30. Aristotle, *Eth. Nic.* 8.12.1–6.
31. For further discussion on treatment on Plutarch's work *On Brotherly Love*, see Aasgaard, "My Beloved Brothers and Sisters!" 93–106. See also Aasgaard, "Brotherhood in Plutarch and Paul," 166–82; Burke, *Family Matters*, 98–110; and Klauck, "Brotherly Love," 144–56.
32. Plutarch, *Frat. amor.* 478C.

not for difference (διαφοράν) and opposition (ἀντίταρξιν) to each other, but that by being separate they might the more readily co-operate (σθωεργῶσιν) with one another.³³

Because of this closeness of sharing the same origin, harmonious relationship with one another is to be upheld where a home is not simply a dwelling place but a place to share common thinking or way of living: ". . . so through the concord (ὁμοφροσύνη) of brothers both family and household are sound and flourish, and friends and intimates, like an harmonious choir, neither do nor say, nor think, anything discordant (ἐναντίον)."³⁴ Plutarch further said that if slander or suspicion is spoken against one another, this is tantamount to courting with evil and inviting evil to fill the void left behind by concord and harmonious relationship.³⁵

Plutarch aimed in this treatise to restore family life and sibling relations so that family honor would once again emerge as of central value in the family and also in sibling relations. Any form of conflict, hatred and mistrust among siblings should be replaced with brotherly love, φιλαδελφία.

Solidarity among Siblings and Family Honor

Plutarch considered φιλαδελφία an important element within the family framework. He placed much emphasis on the relationship between siblings and also between siblings and other members of the family. If closeness is the paramount ideal of siblingship, what then is the nature of the relationship among siblings? How would the relationship between siblings affect the family?

Plutarch believed that human beings are social by nature and they are supposed to live in close social relationship with one another. This closeness is best seen within the family unit as exemplified by the sibling relationship.

---

33. Ibid., 478D. Cf. Hierocles, a contemporary of Epictetus, whose work, "Concerning Brotherly Love," is most useful. References to his work quoted here are according to the Stobaeus referencing. According to Hierocles, all is born "from parents and in conjunction with brother, kindred, and other members of the household" (Stob. 4.27.20).

34. Plutarch, *Frat. amor.* 479A.

35. Ibid., 479B. Hierocles also echoed similar thoughts where he believed that brothers share same origin, hence "the man who is considering how to treat his brother need to begin with no other presupposition than promptly to assume their natural sameness" (Stob. 4.27.20). Therefore, "it is pure madness to wish to form friendship with people who have no natural affection for us, voluntarily to form the most intimate relationships with them possible, and yet to neglect those ready helpers and allies who are supplied by nature itself, who happen to be brothers" (Stob. 4.27.20).

Plutarch spoke against siblings living in isolation without honoring and cherishing one another. For Plutarch, siblings provided not only friendship but support as well:

> Indeed it is our very need, which welcomes and seeks friendship and comradeship (φιλίαν καὶ ὁμιλίαν), that teaches us to honour and cherish (τιμᾶν καὶ περιέπειν) and keep our kin, since we are unable and unfitted by Nature to live friendless, unsocial, hermit's (ἀφίλους καὶ ἀμίκτους καὶ διαφυλάττειν) lives.[36]

This closeness goes beyond lip service and needs to be demonstrated in one's life. Plutarch further said that "what sort of man is he who addresses his comrade as 'brother' in salutations and letters, but does not care even to walk with his own brother when they are going the same way?"[37]

Brotherly love among siblings not only demonstrates closeness and solidarity, it also brings honor to the family, particularly the parents. Plutarch illustrated that "when . . . brothers love and feel affection for each other, and . . . they become united in their ambitions and actions, and share with each other their studies and recreations and games, then they have made their brotherly love (φιλαδελφίαν) a sweet and blessed 'sustainer of old age' for their parents."[38] It is also the greatest honor for a father to see his sons loving one another and this is far greater honor than seeing the children becoming the greatest orator or acquiring wealth or gaining success in life.[39] To underscore the fact that the unity and solidarity of sibling is crucial in honoring parents, Plutarch quoted Euripides, "For cruel are the wars of brothers," and further related the story of Artaxerxes who, when he perceived that his son Ochus had plotted against his brother, despaired and subsequently died.[40]

---

36. Plutarch, *Frat. amor.* 479C.

37. Ibid., 479D. Hierocles reflected the Golden Rule when he commented that a brother should treat his brother just the way he wishes to be treated: "Treat anybody whatsoever as though you supposed that he were you and you he. For someone would treat even a servant well if he pondered how he would want to be treated if the slave were the master and he the slave . . . Let this . . . be the first admonition, that a man should deal with his brother in the same way he would expect his brother to deal with him" (Stob. 4.27.20).

38. Plutarch, *Frat. amor.* 480B–C. Plutarch also said, "Hence what deed or favour or disposition, which children may show toward their parents, can give more pleasure than steadfast goodwill and friendship toward a brother?" (*Frat. amor.* 480A).

39. Ibid., 480C.

40. Ibid., 480D.

Siblings and Other Relations

How would brothers relate to those outside the families? Plutarch saw the relationship between siblings as unique. He compared the sibling relationship to friendship and considered siblingship as superior to friendship.

> For most friendships (αἱ πολλαὶ φιλίαι) are in reality shadows and imitations and images (σκιαὶ . . . καὶ μιμήματα καὶ εἴδωλα) of that first friendship which Nature implanted in children towards parents and in brothers toward brothers; and as for the man who does not reverence or honour this friendship, can he give any pledge of goodwill to strangers?[41]

Plutarch also strongly emphasized the difference between the sibling relationship and friendship. One may choose who to befriend, but not so for brothers who are born into a family and therefore obligated to love one another. Friendships are developed over time while siblingship is given by Nature.[42] When it comes to competing loyalties and in giving honor, siblings should always be given priority over friends even if one feels equal affection for a friend.[43] Since friends could bring the bonds of siblings together and also draw siblings away from one another, Plutarch warned against maintaining associations with friends that pulled brothers apart.[44]

Relations among Siblings

How do brothers relate to one another? What are the rights and obligations of siblings, especially when hierarchy and different social status exist among them? In this respect, Plutarch provided helpful advice for siblings. He warned brothers who are better or superior against looking down on siblings who are inferior. Instead, a superior brother should seek to honor his inferior brothers, especially in matters where he is supposedly superior.[45] If a brother is superior in rhetoric, he is to make his eloquence available for

---

41. Ibid., 479D.
42. Ibid., 481C–D.
43. Ibid., 491B.
44. Ibid., 490E; 491A–B.
45. Ibid., 485C. Epictetus also warned against speaking ill against one's sibling: "If you go off and speak ill of your brother, I say to you, 'You have forgotten who you are and what your designation is' . . . if you forget the brother you are, and become an enemy instead of a brother, will you seem to yourself to have exchanged nothing for nothing? And if, instead of being a man, a gentle and social being, you have become a wild beast, a mischievous, treacherous, biting animal, have you lost nothing?" (*Diatr.* 2.10.12–14).

his other siblings too "as though it were no less theirs than his."[46] Plutarch suggested that the inferior brother "must reflect that his brother is not the only one who is richer or more learned or more famous than himself, but that he is frequently inferior to many others."[47]

Another area where hierarchy exists is the distinction of age. In this respect, an older brother is exhorted not to conduct himself along paternalistic lines but to behave in a thoughtful and charitable manner. Likewise, the younger brother should not enter into competition with or struggle to surpass his older brother but should treat him with respect. Younger brothers are not to become fractious, and not make it their practice to despise and belittle an older brother.[48] They must also render obedience, considered as the highest honor to their older brothers.[49] Should the younger brothers be more successful, the older brother should rejoice with them, imitate them, and should not allow rivalry to exist.[50] The older brother is also exhorted to shows spirit of willingness to help and kindness of heart.[51] Where there exists any hint of rivalry or competition or superiority, every effort is to be made to guard against dissonance and jealousy, and to ensure that no vicious practice of offending and exasperating one another is carried out.[52] Plutarch summed it up beautifully by stating that "brothers walking together should not let a stone come between them."[53]

Conflicts among Siblings

Plutarch acknowledged that conflicts among siblings are inevitable. In circumstances like these, brothers must resist the spirit of contentiousness and jealousy among them. Instead they should practice mutual concessions, and learn to take defeat and take pleasure in indulging brothers rather than in

---

46. Plutarch, *Frat. amor.* 484D.

47. Ibid., 485C. Epictetus also commented along similar lines. In describing the duties of a man in relation to his sibling, Epictetus commented that for brothers, there is "incumbent deference, obedience, kindly speech, never to claim as against your brother any of the things that lie outside the realm of your free moral choice, but to cheerfully give them up, so that in the things that do lie within the realm of your free moral choice you may have the best of it" (*Diatr.* 2.10.8).

48. Plutarch, *Frat. amor.* 486F–487A.

49. Ibid., 487B.

50. Ibid.

51. Ibid.

52. Ibid., 487F.

53. Ibid., 490D.

winning victories over them.[54] Plutarch recognized that any hatred between siblings is tantamount to blaming the parents for bearing them a brother.[55] As such, any hatred between brothers should be dealt with immediately, as it is "both an evil sustainer of parents in their old age and a worse nurturer of children in their youth."[56] If divisions among siblings are allowed to continue, it would be extremely difficult for them to be reconciled later and even if they did, "their reconciliation bears with it a filthy hidden sore of suspicion."[57] If enmity continues to exist, it "keeps the painful situation ever before our eyes, and . . . the sweetest countenance of the nearest kinsman becomes the most frowning and angry to look upon, and that voice which has been beloved and familiar from boyhood most dreadful to hear."[58]

Plutarch also warned siblings against taking sides with those outside the family. A brother who does so in a conflict "appears to be doing nothing but cutting off voluntarily a limb of his own flesh and blood, and taking to himself and joining to his body an extraneous member."[59] Plutarch even criticized those who are more forgiving and tolerable towards outsiders who have faults but could not endure their own brothers' shortcomings.[60] He exhorted brothers not to pay back wrong for wrong, but to forgive.[61] If one cannot live in peace with his siblings, he will lose credibility in exhorting

---

54. Ibid., 488A.

55. Ibid., 480D.

56. Ibid., 481B.

57. Ibid., 481C. Epictetus also commented that if there is conflict among siblings, time should be allowed for the wounds to heal (*Diatr.* 1.15.6–8).

58. Plutarch, *Frat. amor.* 481D. Epictetus also advised that for conflict resolution, one's common status has priority over actions: "Everything has two handles, by one of which it ought to be carried and by the other not. If your brother wrongs you, do not lay hold of the matter by the handle of the wrong that he is doing, because this is the handle by which the matter ought not to be carried; but rather by the other handle—that he is your brother that you were brought up together, and then you will be laying hold of the matter by the handle by which it ought to be carried" (*Ench.* 43). Similarly, Hierocles also suggested the need to pacify an angry brother and be a friend to him (Stob. 4.27.20). Hierocles went even further by suggesting that wild animals can be domesticated and "will not the man who is the brother, or even someone who is in no way related, who in every respect deserves attention much more, not change to a milder disposition, even if he should not completely forsake his excessive roughness?" (Stob. 4.27.20).

59. Plutarch, *Frat. amor.* 478B–C. Cf. Epictetus who also advised that if there is tension, family members ought "to give way to our paltry body, to give way when it comes to our property, to our children, parents, brothers, to retire from everything, let everything go, then except only our judgements and it was the will of Zeus that these should be each man's special possessions" (*Diatr.* 4.7.33–47).

60. Plutarch, *Frat. amor.* 482A–C.

61. Ibid., 489C–D.

others to live in peace, and to be an agent of reconciliation.[62] When there is conflict between a sibling and the parents, Plutarch encouraged a brother to stand in as a mediator, and to rebuke his brother who is at fault.[63]

Plutarch also drew a distinction between internal and external conflict. He believed that if there is conflict caused by outsiders, this is because brothers do not treat one another properly and show hatred to one another, resulting in others taking advantage of the animosity.[64]

Plutarch dealt at length with conflicts between siblings in the area of wealth distribution and inheritance.[65] Brothers should settle conflict—especially in this area—internally, and not wash dirty linen in public. In this respect, Plutarch gives some practical advice to avoid conflict.[66] In the event that conflict could not be settled internally, arbitrators may be appointed among common friends.[67] The ultimate goal is unity and harmony among siblings.

Sibling Language and Imagery

Peter Arzt-Grabner, in examining the use of sibling language in Greek papyri, namely *BGU* VIII 1874; *POxy* VII 2148l; *SB* V 7661; *POxy* XLII 3057; and *SB* XIV 11644, concludes that the use of ἀδελφός suggests a close relationship between the sender and receiver. Usage of the term was a standard feature only if a specific social relationship existed or if there were a specific causal relationship between one group to another. The term ἀδελφός was used to express closeness, solidarity, and some kind of bond of engagement between business partners, officials, and close friends.[68]

Similarly, Philip A. Harland also argues that the term sibling had been widely used in the Greco-Roman world, based on his examination of archaeological, epigraphic, and papyrological evidence.[69] Harland examines evidence and significance of fictive kinship language used within associa-

---

62. Ibid., 481A.

63. Ibid., 483A–E. Cf. Dionysius of Halicarnassus, *Ant. rom.* 7.66.5. In exhorting the virtue that Roman citizens should be able to resolve great civil strife among classes without recourse to violence, Dionysius likened it to the ideal behaviour of a well-governed family in which siblings resolve conflicts without discord.

64. Plutarch, *Frat. amor.* 481C–E.

65. Ibid., 478 C–D; 482D–E.

66. Ibid., 483E–484F.

67. Ibid., 483D.

68. Arzt-Grabner, "'Brothers' and 'Sisters,'" 185–204.

69. Harland, "Familial Dimensions of Group Identity," 491–513.

tions and organizations, including ethnic, cultic, occupational, gymnastic, civic, and other groups in the Greco-Roman world. Based on evidence drawn from inscriptions found in Greece, Asia Minor, and Greek cities of the Danube and Bosporus, as well as papyri from Egypt, Harland suggests that familial language was used in a variety of small-group settings to refer to fellow members as "brothers" or (less often) "sisters," as well as to leaders as "mothers," "fathers," or "papas." When a member of a guild addressed another person as a brother, it was expressing solidarity, affection, or friendship, indicating close ties within a group and signifying that the association was a second home.[70] As such, Harland argues that the use of sibling language was not particularly unique in Pauline circles. Based on these visual imagery contained in inscriptions,[71] the Corinthians would have been familiar with the sibling imagery used by Paul when he addressed them as "brother and sisters."

SIBLINGSHIP AND SOCIAL IDENTITY FORMATION

Of the many metaphors available, why did Paul specifically use ἀδελφοί in addressing conflicts in the church? Why did he not use paternal or maternal imagery,[72] or appeal to apostolic authority as he did elsewhere in Gal 1–2?

In order to address these questions, I will begin by examining the differences between Pauline communities and voluntary associations that existed in the Mediterranean world. This will be followed, in greater depth, by how Paul used sibling imagery in addressing three issues relating to social identity formation: lawsuits (1 Cor 6:1–11); the abuse of the Lord's Supper (1 Cor 11:17–34); and the sharing of resources (1 Cor 16:1–4; 2 Cor 8–9).

Ἐκκλησία as an Alternative to Voluntary Associations?

Although Meeks in comparing Paul's formation of ἐκκλησία to the social groups that bore some resemblance to a family in the Greco-Roman world

---

70. Ibid., 500.

71. See my discussion on visual imagery in chapter 2.

72. At a number of places in the correspondence, Paul uses both the paternal and maternal imagery in addressing the Corinthians. For example, see 1 Cor 3:1–3, 4:14–21; and 2 Cor 12:14 amongst others. However, these are not as frequently repeated throughout the letters. For further treatment on Paul's use of paternal and maternal imageries, see Gaventa, *Our Mother Saint Paul*; Yarbrough, "Parents and Children in the Letters of Paul," 126–41; Balla, *Child-Parent Relationship*, 157–201; and Burke, *Family Matters*, 130–62.

(such as Roman household, voluntary association, Jewish synagogue, and philosophical or rhetorical school) concluded that none of the models captured the whole of Pauline ἐκκλησία, the closest model other than the Roman household that spoke of a strong sense of belonging were the voluntary associations.[73] Voluntary associations involved groupings of people into extended families for purposes such as athletics, trade, cults, and religious activities. Membership in such voluntary associations often ranged from thirty to forty members, rarely exceeding one hundred.[74] John Kloppenborg argues that voluntary associations were a common feature and forming such associations was a regular activity in Mediterranean societies.[75] In this respect, Pauline communities were often regarded as a variant of voluntary associations since they shared many common features, as Meeks has demonstrated. This included membership by free decision rather than birth, the emphasis on belonging to a group, common meals, and other fraternal activities.[76]

While there were some parallels, there were also distinctive differences. This is where the Pauline community as a closely-knit kinship family stood in sharp contrast with other social groups in the Greco-Roman world. Voluntary associations focused on social relationship and fellowship, but the ἐκκλησία went beyond that by incorporating its claim to salvation. McCready postulates that there is no evidence that clubs and associations took on exclusive epithets such as "holy," "called," or "beloved of God" that characterized references to Pauline ἐκκλησία.[77] Furthermore, the inclusivity of the ἐκκλησία which incorporated the gentiles went beyond the Jewish "boundary markers" (such as circumcision, Sabbath observance, and dietary laws) and social class distinctions in Mediterranean society. This set it clearly apart from the voluntary associations. The voluntary associations were more concerned with homogeneous membership influenced by common trades, but this was not the case for the ἐκκλησία. Pauline communities were not only inclusive and transcended social boundaries, they also celebrated diversity while focusing on unity and equality. There was also a high degree of intimacy among members of Pauline communities, compared to the voluntary associations. The imagery of "brothers and sisters" as the predominant language of belonging that emphasized close personal ties reinforced the sense of a close-knit family. Hellerman argues that familial ties

---

73. Meeks, *First Urban Christians*, 75–84.
74. McCready, "EKKLEĒSIA and Voluntary Associations," 61.
75. Kloppenborg, "Edwin Hatch," 213.
76. Meeks, *First Urban Christians*, 77–80.
77. McCready, "EKKLEĒSIA and Voluntary Associations," 62.

received their strongest emphasis in the ἐκκλησία, highlighting the internal cohesiveness of the group.[78] Furthermore, this intimacy and language of belonging is not only limited or confined within the local ἐκκλησία, but also included others in a wider geographical settings. These trans-geographical references united all the Pauline communities in solidarity and gave them a universal nature. This distinctive feature becomes even more pronounced if the Greco-Roman individual voluntary associations did not have links with members of similar associations even if they were located in the same city or worshipped the same deity. In contrast, Pauline communities took an interest in issues and concerns of other churches, such as when they made monetary contributions to the Jerusalem church. The generosity of the Macedonian church was another example of a community that took an interest in the concerns and welfare of others beyond local boundaries (2 Cor 8:1–5). The social mobility of the apostles and certain members of the communities and the exchange of letters between Pauline communities also contributed to the sense of solidarity among these communities (see Col 4:16). The language here further reinforces the familial structure of the ἐκκλησία and emphasizes the significance of the "household" as a basic social component of the early church.[79]

By integrating both Jews and gentiles, rich and poor into this community, Paul created a movement that was clearly distinct from the society around him. Margaret E. Thrall argues that it was precisely the similarity and yet the distinctive differences that set the Pauline community apart. This distinctiveness translated into an initial attraction for the gentiles to be part of the Pauline community, and thereby contributing to the success of Paul's mission in Corinth.[80] There are two major reasons for this phenomenon. Religious motivations may have resulted in the conversion of the Corinthians who were keenly interested in religious cults. The other predominant reason was sociological—the promotion of equality and solidarity among members of the community was an attractive notion. Collectively, these two reasons emphasized the nature of kinship and loyalty expected from the members of the ἐκκλησία. Thrall also argues that the "familial language used in the church may have been an incentive to conversion and likewise the promise of economic help in time of need."[81] This intimacy of member-

---

78. Hellerman, *Ancient Church as Family*, 6. See also the discussion in 4–25. Walter Burkett, in his investigation on cult groups, suggests that members of these groups continued to live as "autonomous, detached individuals with private interests, occupations and property." See Burkett, *Ancient Mystery Cults*, 44.

79. See Banks, *Paul's Idea of Community*, 33–42.

80. Thrall, "The Initial Attraction of Paul's Mission in Corinth," 59–73.

81. Ibid., 72.

ship combined powerfully with a universal vision of the drama of salvation of God, and led to the emergence of this new religious movement with a distinct Christian self-identity. Furthermore, the use of sibling language in the Pauline community is even more significant considering the fact that such language was only used among social equals in Roman groups, as argued by Hellerman.[82] Now that the rich and poor, master and slave, and Jews and gentiles—even though they were not social equals—were all addressed as "brothers and sisters" suggests that Paul deliberately used sibling imagery to create and affirm a social group that was markedly different from other groups in the Roman Empire.[83]

The Cognitive Recognition of Group Identity and Belonging: The Ugly Lawsuit

Lawsuits in the Greco-Roman World

One of the major issues confronting the Corinthians was lawsuits among them. The tone of 1 Cor 6:1–11 is one of intense indignation (1 Cor 6:1, 6), biting sarcasm (1 Cor 6:2, 5), and solemn threat (1 Cor 6:8–11). Paul used rhetorical questions such as the three "Do you not know" (οὐκ οἴδατε) statements[84] to convey his frustration with the Corinthians for failing to understand their identity in Christ, thereby exposing the community to censure in the eyes of the pagans.

Paul was silent on the nature of the problem that led to the civil litigation. The emphasis on greed, cheating, and inheritance in 1 Cor 6:7–10 seems to suggest that it was related to a business dealing that had turned sour, inheritance issues, or financial disputes.[85] Beyond that, any further

---

82. Hellerman, *Ancient Church as Family*, 22–23. See Hellerman's table in page 6 listing the characteristics of the various voluntary associations in the Greco-Roman world, comparing the ἐκκλησία with professional associations, domestic associations, cult associations, philosophical school and Jewish synagogues. Hellerman lists ten characteristics: voluntary in nature, religious orientation, common meals, trans-local in nature, socially inclusive, structurally egalitarian, focus on study, opposed dominant culture, exclusive allegiance and familial emphasis. Among all these, the ἐκκλησία stood out in terms of being trans-local in nature, socially inclusive, structurally egalitarian, focus on study, and opposed dominant culture.

83. For further discussion, see Bossman, "Paul's Fictive Kinship Movement," 163–71.

84. See 1 Cor 6:2, 3, and 9.

85. See Peppard, "Brother against Brother," 179–92; Chow, *Patronage and Power*,

observations would be speculative and would not make any significant contribution to the issue at hand. But what is clear is that the issues were "trivial" in nature (1 Cor 6:2) according to Paul.

Paul's exasperation with the litigious believers could have been further amplified by how justice was dispensed in those times. In an illuminating study, Bruce Winter supplies a wealth of information about the operation of the Roman courts to the situation in Corinth.[86] According to Winter, there were many reasons why litigation took place in the Greco-Roman world, among them, settling scores with political opponents; retaliation for breaches of relationships of trust and obligation; jealousy of a young rising star in civic life; and undermining the power base secured by one's clients by attacking them. Lawsuits were more of an arena for the battle of personalities and selfish interests where unfair advantage over the opponents was often sought. Winter highlights that in Roman society, many found the civil courts to be a useful instrument for pursuing grievances and assaulting an opponent's character among the elite members in public forums.

The right to prosecute was not automatically granted to everyone in Roman Corinth.[87] Generally, lawsuits were conducted between social equals from the elites of the city, or by a plaintiff of superior social status against someone socially inferior. Those of lower social status could not bring charges against their social superiors. Such discriminatory rules were justified by the rationale that members of higher social orders should not be publicly shamed or shown lack of respect.

So seeking justice was hardly the reason a case was brought to the civil court. The social, political, and economic elites had the upper hand in the courts because they could capitalize on their influence and wealth. They could also enhance their own reputation by injuring their opponent's character and reputation. As such, the wealthy were able to take unfair advantage of the judicial system. If both the plaintiff and defendant were of equal status, the law was an arena for a battle of the elites to outdo one another.[88]

This kind of unfair advantage also extended to the choice of prosecutor. A prosecutor of humble status might be rejected merely because of the higher status of his opponents. Even the practice of juror selection in the Greco-Roman world favored the rich and elites. Jurors were selected from the highest census group of men with wealth as a primary indicator. The

123–43; and Mitchell, "Rich and Poor," 562–86.

86. Winter, "Civil Litigation," 559–72.

87. For further discussion, see ibid., 561–62, and Winter, *After Paul Left Corinth*, 58–75.

88. See also the discussion on the process of civil litigation in the Greco-Roman world in Mitchell, "Rich and Poor," 562–86.

minimum wealth indicator was 7,500 denarii—twenty five times more than what the average annual income then.[89] Furthermore, if social standing and status were not enough to tip the scales of justice, bribery could easily do so.[90]

"Brother against Brother": Paul Addressed the Church

Paul did not identify the "brother" involved in the lawsuit. If this case were a reflection of the prevailing social convention, the plaintiff most likely possessed some form of significant financial resources, elite status, and social standing in the civic community. He would have taken his peer or a member with lower rank or status to court, possibly not for the pursuit of justice but to enhance his own status and reputation.[91] Given that these civil suits involved ugly rivalry for the pursuit of honor within the community, it was likely that the defendant was shamed and victimized by the corrupt court system. Not withstanding the outcome of the cases, the entire process would have aggravated further tensions and divisions in the community. In this respect, Paul's outrage becomes even more understandable.

This explains why Paul used the sibling language repeatedly in 1 Cor 6:5–8:

> I say this to your shame. Can it be that there is no one among you wise enough to decide between one brother and another (τοῦ ἀδελφοῦ αὐτοῦ), but a brother goes to court against a brother (ἀδελφὸς μετὰ ἀδελφοῦ)—and before unbelievers at that? In fact, to have lawsuits at all with one another is already a defeat

---

89. For further discussion, see Winter, "Civil Litigation," 564–66.

90. The fact that the civil courts were less than impartial and that substantial corruption existed is well documented. For example, Cicero opened his speech to the jury and judges in the prosecution of Verres, a notorious Roman magistrate known for his mismanagement of Sicily, by citing the well known fact that the courts would never convict any man, however guilty, if he had money. He also declared that there were three major hindrances in civil litigation, namely excessive favor, possession of resources, and bribery (see Cicero, *Caecin.* 73). Seneca related a case of a rich and powerful man daring a poor man to institute proceedings against him. The poor man answered that he could not do so because of his inferior position. The rich man exclaimed, "What would I not be ready to do to you if you impeached me, I who saw to the death of a man who merely engaged in litigation with me?" (Seneca, *Contr.* 10.1.2, 7). The city of Corinth was no different. Dio Chrysostom spoke of "lawyers innumerable perverting justice" in Corinth (Dio Chrysostom, *Or.* 8.9). Apuleius, the second-century CE Latin writer, also commented, "all our judges nowadays sell their judgement for money" (Apuleius, *Metam.* 9.33).

91. Finney, *Honour and Conflict*, 125. See also Clarke, *Secular and Christian Leadership in Corinth*, 59.

for you. Why not rather be wronged? Why not rather be defrauded? But you yourselves wrong and defraud—and brothers (ἀδελφούς) at that.⁹²

Interestingly, Paul did not merely address the ἀδελφὸς who took each other to court, but took the entire family—the church—to task. The fact that the family had allowed civil litigation to take place without mediating or preventing it from happening suggested the break-down of family relations, more so in that the matters involving litigation were described sarcastically by Paul as mere trivial matters. The church is a family. It would have been unheard of in the Greco-Roman world for its members to be involved in litigation. Cicero, in relation to a dispute involving property, stated, "Do not allow brothers (*fratres*) to engage in litigation and to settle their differences in a proceeding involving charges of scandalous conduct."⁹³

In an environment where lawsuits were threatening this familial bond, Paul specifically used language of kinship and endearment to encourage and rebuke the Corinthians. He recognized that the real threat to this community came from within the community, and not without. As such, he admonished the ἐκκλησία for failing to exercise arbitration among its members. Bringing disputes to the civil courts would not only widen the divisions within the ἐκκλησία, but would also damage its reputation in the eyes of the unbelievers. In addition, it would render any subsequent reconciliation efforts difficult if not almost impossible since civil litigation was a reflection of discord and enmity within the community. Worse, this lawsuit was another sign that the values of the surrounding culture were still deeply ingrained in the Corinthian assembly.

To resolve this issue, Paul insisted that disputes must be settled within the ἐκκλησία. His reference to the appointment of someone from within the family as an arbitrator also echoed Plutarch.⁹⁴ In reinforcing "Why not rather be wronged? Why not rather be defrauded?" (1 Cor 6:7), Paul was expressing similar views to Plutarch whereby siblings should practice mutual concessions, learn to take defeat graciously, and take pleasure in indulging brothers rather than in winning victories over them.⁹⁵ For Paul, the real defeat of a brother was not losing a case in court but getting involved in a

---

92. The NRSV does not translate the ἀδελφὸς language literally but instead, uses "one believer and another," "believer," and "believers" in this passage. I have made the necessary correction here to reflect Paul's use of sibling metaphor.

93. Cicero, *Fam.* 9.25.3. Alan C. Mitchell has also analyzed 1 Cor 6:1–11 in terms of philosophy and rhetoric about friendship. Even friends should not wrong one another. See his "Friends Do Not Wrong Friends," 134–44.

94. Plutarch, *Frat. amor.* 483D.

95. Ibid., 488A.

lawsuit with another brother. This defeat was "worse than suffering injustice or being defrauded."⁹⁶ By prohibiting civil litigation, Paul also removed the advantage that the elites enjoyed in the courts. Dale Martin comments that by doing so, "Paul destabilizes the power of the Strong and, at the same time, underscores the differences between the body of Christ and the cosmos 'out there.'"⁹⁷ Paul had to "deconstruct status difference and reverse normal power and hierarchy. . .and maintain firm communal boundaries."⁹⁸ In 1 Cor 6, Paul clearly drew the boundary between outsiders (ἄδικοι in 6:1, 9 and ἄπιστοι in 6:6) and insiders (οἱ ἅγιοι in 1 Cor 6:1, 2 and ἀδελφὸς in 1 Cor 6:5, 6, 8),⁹⁹ stressing that the Corinthians were violating familial harmony.

Finally, in 1 Cor 6:5, Paul also wanted to shame the Corinthians for failing to live up to their calling as siblings (πρὸς ἐντροπὴν ὑμῖν λέγω). He said the same thing later in 1 Cor 15:34 (πρὸς ἐντροπὴν ὑμῖν λαλῶ) where there was drunkenness among some in the ἐκκλησία. It is clear from 1 Cor 6:1–8 that the Corinthians failed to understand the seriousness of their offence in openly parading their status and power in the civic community. For Paul, this is "a parody of the gospel and must be abjured by the community."¹⁰⁰ It is interesting that in his admonition on other matters of church divisions, Paul never explicitly shamed them but, at most, admonished them as his beloved children (1 Cor 4:14). This underscored the seriousness of civil litigation where it involved outsiders, the unbelievers, as judges. In 1 Cor 6:7–11, Paul also reminded the Corinthians that as siblings, if they wronged one another without forgiveness and reconciliation, they were like those wrongdoers who rightfully belonged to the outgroup that would not inherit the kingdom of God. To drive home his point, Paul made a reference to their past where some were "fornicators, idolaters, adulterers, male prostitutes, sodomites, thieves, the greedy, drunkards, revilers, robbers" (1 Cor 6:9–10). But they had now been forgiven and reconciled with God.

To sum up, Paul used strong language to rebuke the Corinthians and insisted that they must live up to the expectation of Christian siblingship. In doing so, Paul hoped to shape the way the Corinthians thought of themselves, and moved them to resolve whatever conflicts they might have as true brothers in the family of God.

---

96. Orr and Walter, *1 Corinthians*, 197.

97. Martin, *Corinthian Body*, 78–79.

98. Ibid., 79.

99. Mitchell, *Paul and the Rhetoric of Reconciliation*, 116 n. 311, describes the use of οἱ ἅγιοι in 6:1, 2 as "the term par excellence for an 'insider' in the Christian community."

100. Finney, *Honour and Conflict*, 126.

Honor the Weaker Brother in the Family: The Abuse of the Lord's Supper

According to 1 Cor 11:17–34, divisions (σχίσματα) and factions (αἱρέσεις) marked the celebration of the Lord's Supper in the Corinthian congregation. This was also not the first time Paul mentioned divisions (σχίσματα) in the church (see 1 Cor 1:10). In this passage, Paul's emphasis was not so much on the fact that σχίσματα existed but that σχίσματα were clear evidence when they gathered together[101] for the Lord's Supper. The divisions went against the unity that the partaking of bread was intended to proclaim and affirm, as earlier alluded to in 1 Cor 10:17 where Paul reminded the Corinthians that "there is one bread" and they "all partake of the one bread" since they "who are many are one body."

The exact nature of the σχίσματα has been generally agreed to be along socio-economic lines.[102] When the Corinthians came together, they were not coming together as a family but as divided groups where those of a lower social and economic rungs were humiliated. In this respect, their coming together was not for the better but for the worse (1 Cor 11:17). This was reflected in situations where some wealthier members of the community arrived for the meal earlier than the rest, devouring the food and drink,[103] and shaming the poor who could only arrive, presumably at the end of the day's work. This can be seen in Paul's admonition:

> When you come together, it is not really to eat the Lord's Supper. For when the time comes to eat, each of you goes ahead with your own supper, and one goes hungry and another becomes drunk. What! Do you not have homes to eat and drink in? Or do you show contempt for the church of God and humiliate those who have nothing? What should I say to you? Should I commend you? In this matter I do not commend you! (1 Cor 11:20–22).

The contrast between "the Lord's supper" (κυριακὸν δεῖπνον) and "your own supper" (τὸ ἴδιον δεῖπνον) in 1 Cor 11:20–21 indicates that all were not eating together or eating the same food, or, at least the same amount of

---

101. The word, συνέρχομαι, appears a total of five times in 1 Cor 11:17, 18, 20, 33 and 34.

102. For example, see Fee, *First Epistle to the Corinthians*, 587–91 and Ciampa and Rosner, *First Letter to the Corinthians*, 541–43. Martin also sees class divisions as central to the divisions in Corinth. See Martin, *Corinthian Body*, xv–xvi. See also Henderson, "'If Anyone Hungers,'" 295–308.

103. See Winter, *After Paul Left Corinth*, 142–63.

food.[104] It is clear that Paul was rebuking the elites or wealthy here—those who had their private meals without considering or sharing the food with others,[105] those who got drunk, those who had homes to eat and drink in, and those who despised the church and humiliated others who had nothing. The works of Gerd Theissen and others have argued that these factions resulted from the practice of the Lord's Supper were consistent with the practices and values of the Greco-Roman patronage system.[106] Within such a setting, close associates of the patrons received choice wine and food and the most honored seats in the dining area, whereas the patron's client and those who were poor received lesser treatment and most likely, dined separately in the courtyard of the house. Such behavior is succinctly summarized by Theissen:

> It can be assumed that the conflict over the Lord's Supper is a conflict between poor and rich Christians. The cause of this conflict was a particular habit of the rich. They took part in the congregational meal which they themselves had made possible, but they did so by themselves—possibly physically separated from the others and at their own table.[107]

Theissen continues:

> The core of the problem was that the wealthier Christians made it plain to all just how much the rest were dependent on them, dependent on the generosity of those who were better off. Differences in menu are a relatively timeless symbol of status and wealth, and those not so well off came face to face with their own social inferiority at a most basic level. It is made plain to them that they stand on the lower rungs of the social ladder.[108]

---

104. On the differences emphasized by Paul concerning eating of meals in individual homes (οἶκος) and eating as a church (ἐκκλησία), see Barton, "Paul's Sense of Place," 234–42.

105. The NIV 1984 translates 1 Cor 11:21 as "each of you goes ahead without waiting for anybody else" but has been corrected in the NIV 2011 as "some of you go ahead with your own private suppers," a better translation of ἕκαστος γὰρ τὸ ἴδιον δεῖπνον προλαμβάνει. See Fee, *First Epistle to the Corinthians*, 598–99, and Winter, *After Paul Left Corinth*, 142–58.

106. See Theissen, *Social Setting of Pauline Christianity*, 145–74 and Murphy-O'Conner, *St Paul's Corinth*, 178–85. See also Winter, *After Paul Left Corinth*, 142–63; Fee, *First Epistle to the Corinthians*, 598–601; Jamir, *Exclusion and Judgment*, 62–113; and Walters, "Paul and the Politics," 354–59.

107. See Theissen, *Social Setting of Pauline Christianity*, 151.

108. Ibid., 160.

Because meals were a tangible platform where differences in status would be clearly distinguished simply by invitation, posture, seating location, type and amount of food served, etc, they became the means for showing honor and competing for honor.[109] In his study on Greco-Roman meal conventions, Smith notes that specific rules were put in place to regulate the behavior of association members in their dining to ensure that group concord was maintained.[110] Similar behavior was exhibited in the Corinthian meal setting.

The primary reason why Paul instructed the Corinthians on proper observance of the Lord's Supper was the disregard for the poor shown by the wealthy Corinthians. Some in the congregation had food, and some did not. Paul refused to commend the Corinthians for this practice. It is unfortunate that in examining 1 Cor 11:17–34, much concentration has been placed on the history and theological meaning of the ritual;[111] the study of the possible layout of the home of the wealthy who hosted the meal;[112] and the study of social status[113] leading to the so-called "new consensus" among New Testament scholars that regarded Pauline communities as comprising a cross section of society. While these studies certainly enrich our understanding of the social world of Paul's congregation, the focus on the poor has been

---

109. See Smith, *From Symposium to Eucharist*, 42–46. For the notion of competing for honor in the Greco-Roman world, see Finney, *Honour and Conflict*.

110. Smith, *Meals and Morality*, 323.

111. See Conzelmann, *1 Corinthians*, 192–203.

112. See Theissen, *Social Setting of Pauline Christianity*, 145–68 and Murphy-O'Connor, *St Paul's Corinth,* 178–85. Murphy-O'Connor's reconstruction of what could be a possible setting for the Lord's Supper based on typical Roman villas in the Mediterranean world is influential. He considers the Villa of Anaploga as a typical house where the Christ-followers had their meeting. Horrell acknowledges the influential suggestion of Murphy-O'Connor and cites Peter Lampe, Corolyn Osiek and David Balch, Gordon Fee, and Anthony Thiselton as those who build upon the work of Murphy-O'Connor. However, he questions the speculation of connecting the assemblies of Christ-followers in particular spaces or rooms based on a typical Roman villa. For further discussion, see Horrell, "Domestic Space," 349–69; and Schowalter, "Seeking Shelter," 327–41. See also Adams, *Earliest Christian Meeting Places*, who argues for a variety of spaces that could be used for the meetings of the early Christians. In other words, Roman villas, as suggested by Murphy-O'Connor, were not the only exclusive spaces used for such meetings. Other locations such as shops and workshops, barns, rented dining rooms, amongst others could be possible spaces for the meeting of the Christ-community, as suggested by Adams, *Earliest Christian Meeting Places*, 203–206. See also Balch, "Rich Pompeiian Houses," 28 and Oakes, *Reading Romans in Pompeii*. Yet, what remains important to note is that whether the communal meal is held within a house or elsewhere, the social class discrimination remains undisputed, as argued by Coutsoumpos, *Paul and the Lord's Supper,* 51–53, 103–30.

113. Meeks, *First Urban Christians*, 51–73.

largely ignored. Richard Hays highlights this irony and observes that without the public humiliation of the poor in Corinth, we would probably have no idea how Paul instructed the congregation to observe the Lord's Supper.[114] It is only in recent years that this deficiency has been corrected by Steven Friesen and others who rightly put the poor back into focus in the reading of this text.[115]

From 1 Cor 11:17–34, it seemed that those who had food not only disregarded the poor, but also refused to share it with them.[116] This refusal to share food violated Paul's understanding of the Lord's Supper. The hunger and humiliation experienced by the poor was a clear denial of the character of what a Pauline community should look like. Most of all, it discredited the gospel that Paul preached. As such, Paul's assault on social class structure of Roman society came to the fore as he challenged the rich to wait for everyone to be present before eating the meal together (1 Cor. 11:33).

To counter the wealthy Corinthians' unbecoming behavior, Paul first rebuked them. Their coming together as a church "is not for the better but for the worse" (οὐκ εἰς τὸ κρεῖσσον ἀλλὰ εἰς τὸ ἧσσον) (1 Cor 11:17). What should have been a gathering of believers to encourage and build one another up had become an avenue to humiliate and disgrace one another, particularly those from the lower strata of the community.

Secondly, Paul reminded the Corinthians that the celebration of the Lord's Supper was rooted in the narrative of Jesus' self-giving of himself for the benefit of others. It was when this meal was celebrated during which the poor were not disadvantaged that they proclaimed the self-giving death of Jesus for others until he comes again. Paul also warned the Corinthians that

---

114. Hays, *First Corinthians*, 203.

115. Friesen, "Poverty in Pauline Studies," 323–61; Meggit, *Paul, Poverty and Survival*; and Longenecker, *Remembering the Poor*. Meggit suggests that one strategy to alleviate the poor among Pauline community is "mutualism." The essence of Meggit's argument is that it is unlikely that Pauline community would have drawn on the generosity of the social elite class as they were relatively few in this Christ-believing community that would even be considered moderately wealthy. But this argument misses the point. The fact remains that social class distinction existed in Pauline community, whether the "rich" or "elite" were considered wealthy or moderately wealthy. Paul's appeal to those who were relatively richer in his community to give proper recognition to the poor remains unchallenged.

116. On Greco-Roman convention on meals, see Smith, *From Symposium to Eucharist*, 13–46, and 173–217, where the existence of social class distinction was common; and Jamir, *Exclusion and Judgment*, 69–76. See also Sandnes, *Belly and Body*, 187–91, who goes as far as suggesting that the Lord's Supper in the Corinthian context was an avenue where the wealthy stuffed themselves in excessive eating and drinking instead of sharing with others.

judgment awaited those who ate and drank without discerning the body of believers (1 Cor. 11:27–32).

The ritual of the Lord's Supper was meant to be a remembrance of Jesus, particularly his death.[117] This act of remembering was not just a recollection, but a living out of the very identification with the Christ who denied himself for the sake of others. It was a participation and identification with the crucified Christ. This forced the community to remember that Jesus was also a victim of extreme shame and humiliation. In other words, one could not come to the Eucharist yet forget other members of the community, particularly those who had nothing. Failure to "remember" others was tantamount to participating in the Eucharist in an unworthy manner. In light of this tradition, Paul admonished the wealthy Corinthians' behavior of despising the poor in their midst as one that stood in sharp contradiction to the very essence of the death of Jesus and the gospel he proclaimed— "Jesus Christ and him crucified" (1 Cor 2:2). The Lord's Supper was a meal to which all were welcome on an equal footing to share in the meal and to remember the death and the future coming of Christ. Rituals should be the means of uniting the community, as attested in antiquity.[118] For Paul, it was a scandal that instead of unity, the ritual of the Lord's Supper had become a setting for divisions drawn along the lines of social status. By not "discerning the body" (1 Cor 11:29), such behavior was tantamount to an affront to Christ.

After exposing the hypocrisy of the elites, Paul provided the solution for an honoring way of celebrating the Lord's Supper. He drew the attention of the Corinthians to the fact that both the rich and poor were brothers and sisters in the family of God: "So then, my brothers and sisters, when you come together to eat, wait for one another. If you are hungry, eat at home, so that when you come together, it will not be for your condemnation" (1 Cor 11:33–34).

Why was there a need to exhort the elites to wait for the poor? First, this suggests that the celebration of the Lord's Supper together may not have been a religious meal but was also a means of practicing food distribution to the poor as part of a family, to ensure that everyone had enough to eat.[119] If

---

117. See Thiselton, *First Epistle to the Corinthians*, 878–82.

118. For example, see Isocrates *Or.* 4.43: "Now the founders of our great festivals are justly praised for handing down to us a custom by which, having proclaimed a truce and resolved our pending quarrels, we come together in one place where, as we make our prayers and sacrifices in common, we are reminded of the kinship which exists among us."

119. See also the discussion in Henderson, "'If Anyone Hungers,'" 295–308. See also Ehrensperger, "To Eat or Not to Eat," 131, who further argues that sharing in the Lord's

this is correct, then the celebration of the Lord's Supper was a clear demonstration of how a community cared and provided for the poor so that there could be equality in sharing the most basic means of survival—food. This is even more pronounced if Markus Öhler is correct. According to him, the distribution of food in a cultic meal in the Greco-Roman associations as mirrored by the Eucharistic meal of the Christ-followers, could have been a reenactment of the prevailing social hierarchy.[120] For Paul, this emphasis on the distinction between the rich and poor was to be corrected in light of the gospel of Christ if the poor were to be remembered. Exhorting the rich to wait and to eat at home if they were hungry would ensure a proper distribution of food. This could possibly be a strategy to offset poverty among the poor in Corinth. In this respect, caring for the poor became a ritual to be observed. To deny the poor brothers and sisters from sharing the same table or to humiliate them was a violation of their basic needs and tantamount to a threat against the community as a whole.

Secondly, unless the family of God embodied a concern for the poorer brothers and sisters rooted in the model of Jesus himself, it could not proclaim the Lord's death. In defending those who had nothing against those who had houses and plenty to eat, Paul was concerned not about the position or status of the person—but about economic relationships in the body of Christ. There was no room for the exploitation and humiliation of the have-nots. As such, the celebration of the Lord's Supper was one that was oriented towards the economy of God—an economy that welcomed and embraced the poor to share in the abundant banquet of the table of the Lord as a family. Failing to do so equaled social injustice.[121] It was when the needs of the poor were met that the celebration of the Lord's Supper became a proclamation of the death of Jesus—the very confession of the gospel.

Thirdly, by exhorting the wealthy to wait for the poor so that everyone had the same share, Paul was also going against the prevailing social convention of honoring the rich with the best food and the best seats.[122] In appealing to the richer members as siblings, Paul was reminding them that they were to play their roles as stronger brothers who honored the weaker

---

Supper not only establishes fellowship for the gentiles in a similar manner as the table fellowship they had to give up in conjunction with pagan temple cults, it also functions as providing actual nourishment for them through communal meals.

120. Öhler, "Cultic Meals," 496.

121. See Schottroff, "Holiness and Justice," 51–60.

122. For a discussion on social meals in the Greco-Roman world, see Coutsoumpos, *Paul and the Lord's Supper*, 39–55. See also Finney, "Social Identity," 273–87. Cf. Öhler, "Cultic Meals," 475–502. A lack of quality food for everyone present in a meal may have been a cause for social tensions (see 498).

brothers by waiting for them to have the meal together. This was a concrete expression of equality where class distinctions were immaterial. Paul was clear that abusing "the body" at the community meal eaten at the Lord's Table in honor of the Lord (1 Cor 11:20) was a mark of the church's failure to uphold family values and honor, and was ultimately an abuse of Christ himself. It is only when social class distinctions are removed that the significance of the meal and the celebration of the Lord's Supper is restored to its rightful place—"Do this in remembrance of me" (1 Cor 11:24–25). Feasting as a family not only proclaimed the Lord's death until he comes (1 Cor 11:26) but also discerned the body (1 Cor 11:29) by giving honor to those who lacked it.

Finally, Paul linked the failure of the Corinthians to remember the poor to an act deserving judgment.[123] He exhorted the Corinthians to examine themselves (δοκιμάζω) in 1 Cor 11:28 and made it clear that those who ate and drank without discerning the body (μὴ διακρίνων τὸ σῶμα) brought judgment on themselves resulting in some of them becoming weak, ill, and even dying (1 Cor 11:29–30). Paul's outburst here was not that the Christ-followers were "profaning a holy rite, but that they are fragmenting a holy society."[124] This violation of the body of Christ "hampers and restricts the redemptive and healing nature of the fellowship wherein the poor are fed, the lonely are befriended, the sick are visited, the grieving are comforted, and sinners are forgiven. . . . So serious is this situation in Corinth that Paul posits a connection between it and the death rate there."[125]

If we understand this background, we can appreciate Paul's use of sibling language in a deeper manner. By addressing the Corinthians as brothers and sisters, Paul was driving home the point that they belonged to one another, and also to Christ.[126] In this new family, all social and economic boundaries that divided the community were obliterated. All the ethnic boundaries that prevented it from growing were broken down. As brothers and sisters, they were to treat one another with respect and honor, protect one another, build up one another, and help the weaker and poorer broth-

---

123. See Jamir, *Exclusion and Judgment*, 166–217 for further discussion on judgment at the Lord's Supper.

124. Orr and Walther, *1 Corinthians*, 269.

125. Ibid., 274.

126. Theissen, *Social Setting of Pauline Christianity*, 147–74; and Meeks, *First Urban Christians*, 159–60, argue that the transfer of an individual through the initiation rites of baptism resulted in membership in a community comprising brothers and sisters. Meeks further contends that the use of sibling imagery is unique in Pauline communities and this signifies a "break with the past and integration into the new community" (88).

ers. The sibling image powerfully evoked the bonds of affection that bound the members of the community together. Any element that appeared to threaten this bond must be dealt with and removed.[127]

According to Paul's vision, this was a family with a distinct social identity rooted not in their cultural value systems but in his gospel. The unity and solidarity of this new humanity is to be demonstrated though the community meal—the Lord's Supper. At the same time, this meal also sets boundaries distinguishing the Christ-followers from outsiders. This demonstrates the extent Paul goes in creating the identity of the Christ-followers through rituals and the efforts put into negotiating the different social groups so that they could be united as the "body of Christ" and as a family. Any violation of the needs of the poorer brothers and sisters in this family is a threat to the entire family.[128]

Sharing of Recourses among Siblings: The Jerusalem Collection

More than half of the usage of ἀδελφοί in 2 Corinthians occurs within the context of Paul's appeal regarding the monetary collection for the Jerusalem Christ-followers. As siblings, the Corinthians were to share financial resources with one another, especially with those who were in need.[129] This demonstrates that Paul's choice and use of sibling imagery within these two chapters was deliberate. Paul was keenly aware of the need to provoke his readers to think and move them to act in ways that reflected the values of the Mediterranean family in the context of reciprocity and sharing of resources among siblings.[130]

---

127. Cf. Walters, "Paul and the Politics of Meals," 343–64, where he argues that Paul's rebuke of the Corinthians for their abuse in the Lord's Supper and corrective instructions are best seen as an attempt to limit the powers that his rivals could exert though meals. While Walters' suggestion may seem a bit far-fetched, his argument that Paul was siding with the "weak" and advocating for behavioral changes of the social elites remains valid.

128. For further discussion, see Ehrensperger, "To Eat or Not to Eat," 114–33.

129. Out of the twelve times where ἀδελφὸς or ἀδελφοί appears in 2 Corinthians, seven are directly related to the sharing of financial resources: six times are found in 2 Cor 8–9 (see 2 Cor 8:1, 18, 22 (twice); 9:3, 5), two major chapters dealing with the collection for Jerusalem, and once in 2 Cor 11:9.

130. For further treatment on Paul's understanding of generosity as the motivation behind the collection for Jerusalem, see Lim, "Generosity from Pauline Perspective," 20–33. The Mediterranean culture of sharing resources with others is not unique. Other cultures, for example, the Chinese kinship and clan system, also believe in sharing with those in need. See also Lim, "Paul the Economist?" and Briones, *Paul's Financial Policy*.

Organizing a major relief fund for the poor in Jerusalem from the Corinthian congregation was no easy task for Paul.[131] In 1 Cor 16:1–4, Paul lays down his instructions to the Corinthians. They were to set aside a sum of money on a weekly basis for the relief fund, so that on his next visit, the contribution would be ready for dispatch to Jerusalem. However, these instructions were ignored by the Corinthians, and were picked up again in 2 Cor 8–9.

In 2 Cor 8:1, Paul appealed to the sibling imagery in emphasizing the example of the Macedonians who had generously contributed to the fund despite their extreme poverty: "We want you to know, brothers and sisters, about the grace of God that has been granted to the churches of Macedonia."

According to Paul, the Macedonians literally begged Paul to accept the monetary gift despite the fact that they themselves had greater need for the money (2 Cor. 8:1–5). This act of generosity was a result of the Macedonians giving "themselves first of all to the Lord, and then by the will of God also to (Paul)" (2 Cor. 8:6).

Paul then appealed to the paradigmatic grace of the Lord Jesus Christ: "For you know the grace of our Lord Jesus Christ, that though he was rich, yet for your sake he became poor, so that you through his poverty might become rich" (2 Cor. 8:9). Paul's argument for generosity was rooted in the example of Christ. The standard reading of 2 Cor 8:9, as reflected in the NRSV, is to take the juxtaposition of opposites: the Christological movement from wealth to poverty ("though he was rich he became poor"), and the anthropological movement from poverty to wealth through Christ ("you through his poverty might become rich"). The notions of wealth and poverty have often been interpreted by a large majority of commentators in an allegorical or spiritual sense—the wealth of Jesus is generally read as the quality of his heavenly, pre-existent status as God, and his becoming poor referred to his incarnation or taking on the human form.[132] The paradoxical anthropological movement from poverty to richness is often interpreted as believers' benefits of salvation or spiritual enrichment.[133] This Christological and soteriological readings are by no means impossible.

131. For a detailed historical treatment on Paul's collection, see Georgi, *Remembering the Poor*. See also Downs, *Offering of the Gentiles*; and Verbrugge and Krell, *Paul and Money*, 107–201.

132. For example, see Harris, *Second Epistle to the Corinthians*, 579; Martin, *2 Corinthians*, 440–41; Plummer, *Second Epistle of St. Paul to the Corinthians*, 241, and Fee, *Pauline Christology*, 162–65. Contra Dunn, *Christology in the Making*, 121–23 and *Theology of Paul the Apostle*, 290–92, who offers an alternative reading in which Christ's wealth was the richness of his human relationship to God.

133. For examples, see Harris, *Second Epistle to the Corinthians*, 578–79 and Furnish, *II Corinthians*, 417. See also Hooker, "Interchange in Christ," 18.

However, we should note that 2 Cor 8:9 is directly related to the context where Paul is urgently appealing to the Corinthians to complete the contribution to the Jerusalem collection. As Barclay notes, since "wealth" is read as spiritual benefits, possessed, renounced and gained, the application to the appeal for financial contribution requires a shift from the metaphorical to the literal domain: What Christ has done in giving up his wealth for others, so the Corinthians must now do in giving up their material possessions for the Jerusalem saints.[134] However, this direct and parallel application has its problems, as highlighted by Furnish, where the call is to ensure that Jerusalem believers have sufficiency (2 Cor 8:15) and not riches, and that the Corinthians are not called to do what Christ did in giving up everything until they become poor. Furnish acknowledges the awkwardness in this reading:

> Paul is not presenting Christ's act of grace as an example for the Corinthians to emulate. If that were the case he ought to urge them to become "poor" for the sake of others as Christ did, but this he specifically does not ask them to do . . . The admonition implicit in this statement is not "Do what Christ did," or even "Do for others what Christ has done for you." It is, rather, "Do what is appropriate to your status as those who have been enriched by the grace of Christ."[135]

In light of this, Barclay questions if a closer parallel between a Christological statement in an economic metaphor which matches its financial context that governs the behavior of believers could be possible.[136] He proposes reading the participle πλούσιος ὤν in 2 Cor 8:9 as causal, rendering a nuanced reading as "because he was rich he became poor."[137] This reading carries the meaning that "it was precisely because of his wealth, and as an expression of it, that Christ made himself poor. Here, then, 'wealth' means not what Christ possessed, but, with a different and paradoxical sense, *the 'wealth' of his generosity.*"[138] Barclay justifies his reading by tracing Paul's flow of thought in 2 Cor 8 where the notion of generosity is clearly highlighted. Paul described the Macedonians' giving as the result of the wealth of their generosity in 2 Cor 8:2 (ἐπερίσσευσεν εἰς τὸ πλοῦτος τῆς ἁπλότητος). This same language of abundance is also seen in Paul's exhortation to the Corinthians to give generously in 2 Cor 8:7 (ἵνα καὶ ἐν ταύτῃ τῇ χάριτι

---

134. Barclay, "Because He was Rich," 337.
135. Furnish, *II Corinthians*, 418.
136. Barclay, "Because He was Rich," 338.
137. Ibid., 339.
138. Ibid., 340, emphasis his.

περισσεύητε), 2 Cor 9:8 (ἵνα ἐν παντὶ πάντοτε πᾶσαν αὐτάρκειαν ἔχοντες περισσεύητε εἰς πᾶν ἔργον ἀγαθόν) and 2 Cor 9:11 (ἐν παντὶ πλουτιζόμενοι εἰς πᾶσαν ἁπλότητα). Based on this observation, Barclay concludes that 2 Cor 8–9 is saturated with the language of abundance and wealth, and "people abound not in what they have but in what they give, and 'wealth' consists not in possession but in generosity."[139] As such, Barclay proposes the reading of 2 Cor 8:9 as follows:

> You know the χάρις of the Lord Jesus Christ, that in his wealth (that is, generosity) he became poor (a single term covering his incarnation, life and death), so that by his poverty (by all that is effected by "the son of God who loved me and gave himself for me," Gal 2.20) you might become rich, in the same momentum of generous love.[140]

This reading, according to Barclay, provides a tight fit between the Christological/soteriological statement of 2 Cor 8:9, and the exhortation to the Corinthians to give generously. Christ has made the Corinthians rich in generosity and thus, they are to give generously to the Jerusalem collection.[141]

If Barclay is right in his reading, we see Paul using the metaphor of generosity to effect a change of behavior in the Corinthians. Drawing on the narrative of Jesus, Paul challenged the Corinthians to finish the collection for the poor in Jerusalem by drawing on the principle of equality—the abundance that the Corinthians currently enjoyed would supply for the needs of the poor in Jerusalem (2 Cor 8:11–15). To challenge the Corinthians further, Paul reiterated that both he and the Corinthians would be shamed if the Macedonians found out that the collection was left unfinished by the Corinthians (2 Cor 9:1–5). Then Paul evoked an agrarian metaphor suggesting that all giving to the Jerusalem collection was like sowing seed that would reap a harvest. Finally, Paul underscored that true generosity was also a direct result of the confession of the gospel of Jesus Christ. This generosity would also bring about thanksgiving and praise to God from the recipients of the collection (2 Cor 9:6–15).

To emphasize that siblings share resources with one another, Paul recounts that it was the ἀδελφοί who came from Macedonia who supplied monetary assistance to alleviate his financial needs so that he need not depend on the Corinthians for support (2 Cor 11:9).[142] By using sibling

139. Ibid.
140. Ibid., 343.
141. Ibid.
142. See Table 3.2 above where οἱ ἀδελφοί is unfortunately translated as "friends"

imagery, Paul once again underscored the fact that as brothers and sisters, the Christ-followers were to share material resources with one another, especially those who were in need. By calling the Macedonians ἀδελφοί, Paul was challenging the Corinthians to reconsider their reluctance in completing the collection project for the brothers and sisters in Jerusalem. He was also attempting to set an example before the Corinthians that they could emulate the Macedonian ἀδελφοί in their giving and sharing of resources with those who were in need in the family.

Paul also used sibling imagery to emphasize the importance of the charge given to those who have been entrusted with the administration of the collection. The word ἀδελφὸς or ἀδελφοί appears a total of five times in 2 Cor 8:18, 22 (twice); 9:3, 5 in describing Titus, along with other men, who were entrusted with carrying the collection with Paul to Jerusalem. Paul also gave the credentials of these brothers. They were enthusiastic about the project, trustworthy, praised by others, proven in their service, and were representatives of the churches and an honor to Christ (2 Cor 8:16—9:5). Such superlative praise by Paul was to further reinforce the fact that these brothers were siblings full of integrity who could be trusted with the administration of finances. Any fear of fraud or doubt was completely removed with the use of sibling imagery.

Boundaries and Attitudes towards Outgroups

At numerous points in 1 Corinthians, Paul appealed to the Christ-followers to consider their status in Christ and their new identity against groups that were outside their boundaries.[143] One of the most forceful languages of separation is found in 1 Cor 5:11: "But now I am writing to you not to associate with anyone who bears the name of brother or sister who is sexually immoral or greedy, or is an idolater, reviler, drunkard, or robber. Do not even eat with such a one."

In his previous letter that is now lost, Paul exhorted the Corinthians not to associate with anyone who was sexually immoral (1 Cor 5:9). However, by the time of writing 1 Corinthians, it had been reported to Paul that a man was having a sexual affair with his "father's wife," who was most likely his stepmother (1 Cor 5:1). Paul was shocked that the Corinthians did nothing about this illicit relationship, and described it as a kind that even "pagans

---

in the NRSV.

143. Philip Esler has also argued that Paul uses family imagery in Galatians 5:13—6:10 to create an identity for his congregations that is very different from the dominant groups outside their boundaries. See Esler, "Family Imagery," 122.

do not tolerate" (1 Cor 5:1). Instead, they were proud and boastful about it. As a result, Paul was determined to have this "brother" removed from the family, and likened him to yeast that would affect the entire batch of dough (1 Cor 5:7–8). For Paul, such a person belonged to the outgroup and had no business with the family of believers, and should rightly be expelled. In this regard, Trebilco argues that ἀδελφοί language is "insider language for self-designation, used internally by members within the group" and not by outsiders.[144] He further notes that in the Pauline corpus, Paul reserved the language of ἀδελφοί strictly for Christ-followers, with only one exception in Rom 9:3.[145] This demonstrates that sibling language was a boundary-constructing term used by Paul in the formation of social identity where members of the community are considered as ἀδελφοί.

In 1 Cor 6:6, Paul contrasted ἀδελφὸς with ἄπιστος, clearly signifying that outsiders were not part of the family where ἄπιστος functions as the antonym of ἀδελφὸς. Similarly, in 1 Cor 7:12–15, ἀδελφὸς and ἄπιστος were being used to construct the insider-outsider boundary.

Paul also emphasized ingroup and outgroup relationship by calling into mind the former life of the Corinthian Christ-believers as ἔθνη (literally "gentiles" but translated as "pagans" in the NRSV) where they used to be "enticed and led astray to idols that could not speak" (1 Cor 12:2).

In 2 Cor 11:26, Paul compared true brothers and sisters with those who were false. In speaking of his own sufferings, Paul referred to the dangers he faced from various groups of people including his own people, gentiles, and "false brothers and sisters" (ψευδαδέλφοις), demonstrating that ψευδάδελφος was a reference to unacceptable members of the community.[146]

Given the strong linkage between kinship and identity in the Greco-Roman world, Paul's use of ἀδελφοί provided a strong sense of group identity for the Corinthians. In fact, ἀδελφοί was used as a central boundary marker in the formation of the Corinthians' social identity. In seeking to differentiate the community from outgroups, Paul grounded their identity in Christ and reminded them that they were a people of God.

SUMMARY

In this chapter, I highlighted that Paul used sibling imagery in addressing the various issues confronting the church, particularly in instances where there were divisions and conflicts such as disputes over the nature of leadership,

---

144. Trebilco, *Self-designations and Group Identity*, 37.
145. Ibid., 37.
146. Cf. Gal 2:4.

sexual immorality, church discipline, bringing each other before the pagan courts, disputes as to the consumption of food sacrificed to idols, chaos in the celebration of the Lord's Supper, and abuses in the operation of spiritual gifts. He also used the sibling imagery to exhort the Corinthians to participate in the sharing of financial resources and also in the administration of this financial collection for the Jerusalem church. Finally, Paul also used the sibling imagery to reinforce the boundaries between the Corinthian Christ-followers and the outgroups.

The fact that these problems existed demonstrated that the Corinthians failed to live up to expectations as a family of God. As such, Paul found the sibling metaphor the most appropriate in addressing these problems. Within the Greco-Roman setting, the image of siblings evoked physical and emotional security, care and belonging, and mutuality and respect that existed only within the familial and household kinship. Family members must not be in conflict with one another, and wealthy members may not invoke privileges that society granted them over others who were of lower status. In light of this, Paul's frequent use of sibling language clearly speaks of his vision that the Christ-followers should be a very close-knit group. This fictive kinship language promoted egalitarian structures compared to other groups that were organizationally a reflection of the structured hierarchical first-century society. It also eliminated all social, economic, and ethnic boundaries established by Greco-Roman society among different groups of people that divided the Christian community, stunned its growth, and hindered its witness as an alternative assembly. Paul wanted the Corinthians to pursue an attitude and course of action towards siblingship and thus create a social identity that was radically different from the community that surrounded them. By using sibling metaphor, a new expectation was now imposed on the Christ-followers in the way they thought and acted. They could no longer view their brothers and sisters through the lenses of socio-economic status and ethnicity. On the contrary, they were to honor, encourage, and build up one another as brothers and sisters. Therefore, "sibling" was a fitting metaphor to shape, guide, and rebuke the community towards peace and harmony, honor and respect, and in their relations with outsiders. It ultimately drove home the point that the Corinthians belonged together as one and within this family of Christ, blood was indeed thicker than water.

4

"In Christ Jesus I became Your Father"

Familial Metaphors

PAUL'S USE OF FAMILIAL METAPHORS

IN CHAPTER 3, I provided a brief survey of Paul's use of familial language in describing his relationship with the Corinthians and their relationship with one another, in particular his use of sibling imagery to reinforce their identity as members of a family. In this chapter, I will examine how Paul uses other familial imagery such as those involving father, mother, children, and slave to describe his relationship with the Corinthians.[1]

On at least six occasions, Paul explicitly takes on the role of a father in addressing the Corinthians. In 1 Cor 4:14–21 he speaks as a father,

---

1. When the word family is used, it is not simply a reference to the nuclear family that we are familiar with today, although the nuclear family did exist in antiquity. As for the metaphorical use, family will be used from the perspective of familial relationship: Paul's relationship with his converts (parent-child) and the relationship with each other (siblings). See Saller, "*Familia*," 336–55, and particularly the statement from 355: "Neither *familia* nor *domus* has a regular meaning the nuclear family, and yet much evidence suggests that this was the dominant family type . . . though the Romans had no word for it, they drew a conceptual circle around the mother-father-children triad and made it the centre of primary obligations." For further discussion on family and the metaphorical use of familial language in early Christianity, see Moxnes, "What Is Family?," 13–41.

addressing his beloved children and appealing to them to imitate him in his character and conduct. He also introduces Timothy as his faithful child and a role model for the Corinthians. He also warns them that he would not hesitate to wield his authority as a father when he visited them should they continue to cause divisions in the family. In 2 Cor 6:11–13, Paul pleads with the Corinthians to open their hearts as children would to their parents by using terms of endearment. He appeals to his emotional ties with the Corinthians in a parent-child relationship. The same language is also used in 2 Cor 11:2 where Paul sees himself as a jealous father, expressing his concern for the future of the Corinthians, his daughters. He bears the heavy burden of their future welfare and wants to present them as a perfect bride for their future husbands. Finally in 2 Cor 12:14, Paul brings the parent-child imagery to a climax declaring his deep love as a father who provides an inheritance for his children, to the extent that he is willing to sacrifice himself for them. Apart from these four explicit accounts, Paul also takes on the role of the *paterfamilias* in addressing the issues of marriage and divorce in 1 Cor 7:12–16. In 2 Cor 13:10, he describes his authority as a father who builds up his children rather than tearing them down.

This nurturing theme is also seen in Paul's assumption of the role of a nursing mother. In 1 Cor 3:1–2, he treats the Corinthians as infants and feeds them milk. He uses a striking and less flattering image of an infant who is abnormally born in describing himself in 1 Cor 15:8. Apart from the images taken from a nucleus family, Paul also applies the metaphor of a slave administrator on himself in 1 Cor 4:1–2 and 1 Cor 9:17.

Based on this brief survey, Paul's use of fictive familial language is replete with instruction, encouragement, and reinforcement of his roles within a family rather than being someone who is authoritative, abusive, and powerful. The Christ-followers are to relate to one another the way members of a family, with shared ethos, values, and structures, relate to each other. By creative use of fictive language, Paul highlights a distinctive and unique relationship within the household setting.

FAMILIAL METAPHORS IN THE STUDIES OF PAUL

In 1995, Jerome Neyrey, commenting on the Synoptic Gospels, highlighted the general lack of research into the connection between the social institution of the family in antiquity and the fictive kinship notion of the early Christ-movement: "More serious considerations need to be given to the basic social institution of antiquity, namely the family and the role of *paterfamilias* . . . Issues of family and (fictive) kinship remain underdeveloped in scholarship."[2]

This neglect is not only applicable to Gospel studies but also to the Pauline letters. Sibling imagery in Pauline studies has received some attention in recent years. However, Paul's use of familial imagery governing the relationship between parents and children, and vice versa, has received much less focus. Most of the treatment of familial language is dominated by two domineering perspectives. First of all, familial language has been discussed in Paul's use of household codes in Ephesians and Colossians.[3] These household codes have been generally seen as a development of post-Pauline era utilizing patriarchal or hierarchical household framework in identity formation or institutional developments.[4] These codes have also been regarded as Paul's attempt to govern relationships within the communities he founded based on the Greco-Roman concept of a household in which the *paterfamilias* yielded considerable power.

Secondly, closely related to the theme of power is the investigation of Paul's use of parental imagery, or *paterfamilias*, in reinforcing his power and authority in cases where his apostolic position has been contested.[5] This notion of power and authority has also been examined from a gender perspective such as the work of Elizabeth A. Castelli where she investigates Paul's idea of mimesis based on 1 Cor 4:16–21.[6] She argues that the notion of

---

2. Neyrey, "Loss of Wealth," 156–57.

3. For example, see Crouch, *Origin and Intention*; Hering, *Colossian and Ephesian Haustafeln*. Apart from Col 3:18—4:1 and Eph 5:22—6:9, the Household Codes are also found in 1 Peter 2:18—3:7, and to a certain extent, 1 Tim 2:8–15; 6:1–2; and Titus 2:1–10. See also Balch, *Let Wives be Submissive*; Verner, *Household of God*, 27–81. See also MacDonald, "Kinship and Family," 29–43 and Westfall, "This is A Great Metaphor!," 561–98.

4. For example, see MacDonald, *Pauline Churches*, 31–234. She sees development in the Pauline communities from Paul's undisputed letters to the Pastoral Epistles. From community-building institutionalization in the authentic letters of Paul, MacDonald argues that this subsequently develops into community-stabilizing institutions in Colossians and Ephesians that later leads to community-protecting institutionalization in the Pastoral Epistles. She also finds progressive development from a more egalitarian focus in the authentic letters to a more patriarchal development, a phenomenon she describes as "love patriarchalism." See also MacDonald, "Beyond Identification," 65–90; and Dunn, "Household Rules," 54–58.

5. For example, see White, "God's Paternity," 271–95; Hellerman, *Ancient Church as Family*; Chris Frilingos, "For My Child, Onesimus," 91–104; Joubert, "Managing the Household," 213–23. Contra Bartchy, "Who Should Be Called 'Father'?," 163–80, who questions Joubert's argument that Paul sees himself as *paterfamilias* of the communities he founded.

6. Castelli, *Imitating Paul*, 98–117. Castelli's view is further supported by Robbins, *Tapestry of Early Christian Discourse*, 195–99. See also Polaski, *Paul and the Discourse*

imitation forms part of Paul's discourse on power in which the apostle aims at having his apostolic authority in his privileged position uncontested as well as securing sameness instead of difference. Here, a picture emerges of Paul as someone who controls his communities and removing any degree of individuality or difference. In other words, those who saw things differently from Paul were called to practice self-discipline in order to re-orientate their perspectives in imitation of the apostle. Another example is the work of Lone Fatum, who sees Paul's use of parent-child metaphor as a tool to strengthen his authority. By employing a gender hermeneutical reading of 1 Thessalonians, Fatum argues that Paul communicated from within his symbolic universe. This translates into a view that "the lives of women are embedded in the lives of men, and women are defined and qualified by their dependence on men."[7] As a result, women were invisible and not integrated into the brotherhood of the community. They were only "attached to the faction of brothers through husbands or male heads of households with reference to their social roles as wife, daughter, mother or sister."[8]

There is no denying that Paul certainly wielded his power and authority as a father, or a *paterfamilias*. The importance of children cannot be denied either as the imagery appears again and again in Paul's letters.[9] Reidar Aasgaard highlights Paul's use of parent-child language and lists fifty one children and childhood related terms and expressions in the seven undisputed letters in alphabetically order and where they appear in the Pauline letters.[10] However, he does not tabulate them according to the frequency of their appearance in each of the letters. This I do in the table below.

---

of Power, 12–15.

7. Fatum, "Brotherhood in Christ," 193.

8. Ibid.

9. Not much attention has been given to children and parent-child relationship in the investigation of family in the Greco-Roman world. For example, see Sandnes, *A New Family*; Moxnes, *Constructing Early Christian Families*; Osiek and Balch, *Families in the New Testament World*; Hellerman, *Ancient Church as Family*; Burke, *Family Matters*; Balch and Osiek, *Early Christian Families in Context*; and Aasgaard, *My Beloved Brothers and Sisters!* See also Weima, "Infants, Nursing Mother, and Father," 209–29 and Osiek, "The Family in Early Christianity," 1–24.

10. Aasgaard, "Paul as a Child," 134. In a separate table, Aasgaard further sorts the terms and expressions in a thematic order, listing them under the heading of Kinship, Social Position, Formation and Belonging. See Aasgaard, "Paul as a Child," 135.

Table 4.1: Frequency of Children and Childhood-Related Terms and Expressions in Paul's Undisputed Letters Based on Aassgard's Tabulation

Letters	Number of Times Children and Childhood Related Terms and Expressions Appear	Percentage of Total
Romans	61	29%
1 Corinthians	42	20%
2 Corinthians	28	13%
Galatians	52	25%
Philippians	9	4%
1 Thessalonians	14	7%
Philemon	5	2%
Total	**211**	**100%**

The table shows that the words related to children appear most frequently in Romans (29 percent), Galatians (25 percent) and 1 and 2 Corinthians (20 percent and 13 percent) respectively. But the Corinthian letters when combined show the highest usage.

While the power of *paterfamilias* is acknowledged in the discussion of family, the strong bonds of affections, cooperation, and sharing of resources among family members within the collectivist culture of the Mediterranean world need to be reinforced. It is not until recently, the studies on children and how this influences the understanding of Paul's parent-child language and the place of children within the households or communities in the New Testament have been carried out.[11] In light of the recent scholarship, Margaret MacDonald notes that children and childhood in the New Testament era have been neglected in the investigation on early Christian families.[12] She firmly believes that children played significant roles in families, and suggests that much more attention should be paid to the role of children in the household, particularly in the area of education and custody of chil-

---

11. See, for examples, Strange, *Children in the Early Church*; Balla, *Child-Parent Relationship*; Gaventa, *Our Mother Saint Paul*; and McNeel, *Paul as Infant and Nursing Mother*. See also Burke, *Family Matters* (covering 1 Thessalonians); Aassgaard, *My Beloved Brothers and Sisters* (covering Pauline epistles); Yarbrough, "Parents and Children in the Letters of Paul," 126–41; Gundry-Volf, "The Least and the Greatest," 29–60; Gaventa, "Finding a Place for Children," 233–48; Aassgaard, "Like a Child," 249–77; Francis, "Children and Childhood," 65–85; and MacDonald, "A Place of Belonging," 278–304. For a study of other nuances of the father imagery, see Long, *Paul and Human Rights*, 119–30.

12. MacDonald, "Children in House Churches," 69–85.

dren, and living spaces that they shared with slaves.[13] MacDonald's study is significant as the role of the *paterfamilias* in the education of the children is also a metaphor Paul employed in 1 Corinthians. This I will further explore below. Beverly Gaventa, in her survey of a number of texts in Paul's letters related to parent-child relationship, also suggests that more attention should be given to the place of children in Pauline community.[14]

Balla's work is possibly the only major and extensive study on parent-child relationship.[15] He notes that many works on the theme on parent-child relationship are from the perspective of the parent. Balla fills the gap by examining this familial relationship from the perspective of a child. Specifically, Balla investigates the obligations of a child to the parents covering a range of duties including honoring, obeying, and caring for them, supporting them in old age, preparing a noble burial for them, and in some instances, venerating them as God.

Trevor Burke attempts to look into Paul's use of familial imagery in 1 Thessalonians by examining his relationship with them (as a father, mother, infant, and orphan) and their relationship with one another (as his children and as brothers and sisters). He explores standard assumptions or common expectations of ancient family by investigating a wide range of literary and non-literary resources such as epigraphic evidence and inscriptions covering both the Jewish and Greco-Roman sources. He concludes that there are defined roles and expectations for each party. Fathers are to exercise authority, instruction, and affection, and set themselves up as role models for imitation. Children are to reciprocate the love and care of the parents, submit to them in obedience, and care for the elderly. By applying paternal metaphors to himself, Paul exercises his apostolic authority to regulate his relations with the Thessalonians. At the same time, he also exhibits love and affection, and takes on the role of teaching, instructing, and exhorting the Thessalonians. As for Paul's use of maternal imagery of a nursing mother, Burke notes that this demonstrates the love, care, and anxiety Paul had for his converts. By using infant and orphan imagery, Paul places himself in a very vulnerable position and in non-authoritative familial roles. Burke suggests that by using a wide range of metaphors, Paul draws on different aspects of his relations with the Thessalonians in his struggle to communicate the depth of his feelings for them.[16]

---

13. Ibid.

14. Gaventa, "Finding a Place for Children," 233–48.

15. Balla, *Child-Parent Relationship*.

16. Burke, *Family Matters*, 252. See also Burke, "Pauline Paternity," 59–80; and Burke, "Paul's New Family," 269–87.

Another major monograph that addresses Paul's use of familial metaphors in 1 Thessalonians is the work by Jennifer Houston McNeel.[17] What is significant in this work is the examination of infant and nursing mother metaphors in relation to social identity formation. Using Conceptual Metaphor Theory or Cognitive Metaphor Theory in her analysis, McNeel argues that the infant and nurse metaphors served Paul's rhetorical strategy by emphasizing his trustworthiness, creating a kinship relationship among the Christ-followers and between Paul and the community. This would further encourage the Thessalonians to ground their identity in the Christian community rather than in their previous civic connections. Both metaphors also enhanced Paul's apostolic authority in the community and strengthened his emotional bond with them.

PARENT-CHILD AND ETHOS OF A FAMILY IN THE GRECO-ROMAN WORLD

While family relationship rooted in the Hebrew Scripture is deeply entrenched in Paul's worldview, recent studies have also pointed out that familial relationship is an important feature in the Greco-Roman world.[18] The recent growing scholarly interest in children and childhood in antiquity has contributed to our understanding of how a family functioned in the Greco-Roman world and Paul's use of parent-child imagery in his letters.[19] In this section, I will examine the notion of parent-child relationship in a family.

Paterfamilias

Aristotle dedicated an entire section on household management and discussed the responsibilities and obligations of parents towards children and vice versa. Since a household was considered the basic unit of the state,

---

17. McNeel, *Paul as Infant and Nursing Mother*.

18. See Dixon, "The Sentimental Ideal," 99–113; Eyben, "Fathers and Sons," 114–43; and Saller, "Corporal Punishment," 144–65.

19. For a survey of this, see Wiedemann, *Adults and Children*; Golden, *Children and Childhood*; Rawson, *Children and Childhood*; Neils and Oakley, *Coming of Age*; Lacey, *Family in Classical Greece*; Rawson, *Family in Ancient Rome*; Bradley, *Discovering the Roman Family*; Rawson, *Marriage, Divorce, and Children*; Kertzer and Saller, *Family in Italy*; Dixon, *Roman Family*; Saller, *Patriarchy*; Rawson and Weaver, *Roman Family in Italy*; Patterson, *Family in Greek History*; Cox, *Household Interests*; Nathan, *Family in Late Antiquity*; van Henten and Brenner, *Families and Family Relations*; and Dixon, *Childhood*.

household management (*oikonomia*), comprising master and slave, husband and wife, and father and children was essential.[20] Within a family, hierarchy was important. There were those who ruled, those who were being ruled, and those who served. If the basic structure of the household was disrupted, the rest of society would also be affected. In light of this, the role of the *paterfamilias*, who headed the Roman *familia* was crucial. Typically the oldest male, he exercised his power, *patria potestas*, over members of the family (*domus*) that included the wife, children, grandchildren, any other adopted children, plus slaves and their family.[21] This power included the right over life and death, inheritance, and control over the lives of the children including discipline, marriage, and divorce. His authority over members of his family was legally recognized and protected, and it did not cease even when the children had become adults and had married.

In addition, a *paterfamilias* could decide whether to recognize a newborn as his own, raise the child, or expose and kill the child. Although the frequency of exposition or casting the child out in a public place is debated, it was practiced at every level of society in the Roman world, as Peter Garnsey and Richard Saller have attested, until the late fourth century.[22] A letter from a husband to a pregnant wife, stating that, "If by chance you bear a child, if it is a boy, let it be, if it is a girl, cast it out," is often quoted to refer to the exposition of a newborn.[23] Infants that were exposed or cast out in a public place would die unless they were picked up by strangers, often raised only to be sold as slaves, prostitutes, or beggars later on.[24]

When it comes to the image of the *paterfamilias*, several questions need to be raised: In the Roman family, was the father seen as an authoritative and tyrannical figure who had at his disposal unlimited powers to wield as he wished in ruling his household? This question is crucial as it will determine the image of the father that was assigned to Paul—was Paul like

20. Aristotle, *Pol.* 1.1253b.

21. Ibid., 1.1259a–b. See also the Ulpian records in *Digest* 50.16.195.2. For further discussion, see Lacey, "Patria Potestas," 121–44; and Saller, "Pater Familias," 182–97.

22. Garnsey and Saller, *Roman Empire* 136. See also Wiedermann, *Adults and Children*, 36, who suggests that "belief in the exposition of unwanted babies was widespread."

23. POxy IV 744, as cited by White, *Light from Ancient Letters*, 111–12.

24. See the letter written by Pliny the Younger, *Ep.* 10.65–66. In this letter, Pliny the Younger, serving as a governor of Bithynia, wrote to Emperor Trajan in the early second century CE, asking for advice regarding the status of people exposed at birth but raised as slaves. In his letter, Pliny the Younger uses the word, *threptos*, to describe babies reared in strangers' home. The issue of children abandonment must have been serious enough to warrant Pliny the Younger seeking for advice.

the *paterfamilias* of the Roman family as he asserted his power and control over his community?[25]

The almost unlimited power and authoritarian figure of the *paterfamilias* gradually eroded from the days of the Empire onwards. During the era of the Late Republic and Empire, the more humane side of the family relationship emerged and flourished. The focus was on harmony, *concordia*, between husbands and wives. Affection, or *pietas*, was also more frequently demonstrated to the children and expressed as the basis of *patria potestas*. Personal fatherly love was often stressed as well.[26] At the same time, the absolute or lifelong paternal power over one's children was also limited by the increasing social independence of the children. Public opinion also developed "a distaste for undue strictness," as suggested by Emiel Eyben.[27] Increasingly, from the days of the Empire, "the legislators adapted themselves gradually to the altered mentality and took as their rule of thumb the maxim . . . of the third-century jurist Marcianus: 'paternal authority must be based on affection, not on cruelty (*patria potestas in pietate debet, non atrocitate consistere*).'"[28] While the exercise of the *patria potestas* gradually lessened by the time of the early Roman Empire, the control over property continued.[29]

The notion of *pietas* was an attitude of dutiful respect toward those in higher authority and power such as the gods, parents, and other kinsmen. Although the general understanding seemed to reflect a dutiful son being fully submissive to his father's authority, Richard Saller has demonstrated that this was not always the case.[30] There were instances where the virtue of *pietas* also encompassed expression of affection and compassion as well as duty. Furthermore, *pietas* may not necessary be a virtue exhibited only to higher powers and authority. The reverse could also be true. A person in higher authority, such as a father, could also display *pietas* to his children, as parents were obligated to look after the best interests of their

---

25. See Joubert, "Managing the Household," 213–23. Joubert argues that Paul served as the earthly *paterfamilias* of the Corinthians.

26. For further discussion, see Dixon, "Sentimental Ideal," 99–113. See also Balla, *Child-Parent Relationship*, 45–46; and Eyben, "Fathers and Sons," 114–43.

27. Eyben, "Fathers and Sons," 115.

28. Ibid. Cf. Saller, *Patriarchy*, 72, who states that "it is a gross oversimplification to represent Roman fathers as endowed with unlimited power, obeyed by children under unlimited obligation underwritten by the duty of *pietas*."

29. For further discussion, see Clarke, *Serve the Community of the Church*, 88. See also Lassen, "Use of the Father Image," 128. See also Joubert, "Managing the Household," 215.

30. For further discussion, see Saller, *Patriarchy*, 102–32.

children.[31] Plautus talks about a father's *pietas* in rescuing his daughters.[32] This reciprocal aspect of *pietas* is also seen in an early first-century BCE rhetorical treatise: "There is a natural law, observed *cognationis aut pietatis causa,* by which parents are esteemed by children and children by parents."[33]

A soldier's letter written by the turn of the century to his son, Horos, and wife, Tachinis, demonstrates a father caring for the welfare of the family and expressing anxiety for the needs of the family:

> Heraklas to Horos and Tachinis, greetings and good health. Don't worry about us. Since we've been on military duty we have been sailing in the boat for eight days. With the gods' will in three days we shall be on shipboard. As for the child keep an eye on him as you would an oil lamp, since I am worried about you ... Farewell ... and to Horos his son.[34]

The evolution of the image of an authoritarian father to one who exhibited affective and reciprocal qualities is well documented by the first century BCE.[35] In light of this, the image of a *paterfamilias* may not have been that of an authoritarian and tyrant who hungered for power by the time of the Common Era. This insight is significant to our understanding of Paul's use of the father metaphor.

Paterfamilias and the Education and Discipline of Children

One of the primary roles of a *paterfamilias* was the responsibility for the education of his children. Plutarch's *De liberis educandis* (*On Education of Children*) not only underscores the duty of a father but also reveals the conditions of education during the first century CE. According to Plutarch, "learning, of all things in this world, is alone immortal and divine."[36] He advised fathers "to make nothing of more immediate importance than the education of their children."[37] For him, the education of children begins almost immediately after birth in order "to regulate the characters of

---

31. See ibid., 106–14. Elsewhere, Saller also comments that "Roman culture drew a clear distinction between the father's relationship with his children, characterized by mutual obligation and concern, and the master's exploitative power over his slaves" (ibid., 73).
32. Plautus, *Poen.* 1137.
33. Rhet. Her. 2.19.
34. Horsley, *New Documents Illustrating Early Christianity,* 1:52.
35. See Saller, *Patriarchy,* 113.
36. Plutarch, *Lib. ed.* 5E.
37. Ibid., 6A.

children."³⁸ Recognizing that the environment in which the child grows up influences his moral and character formation, Plutarch suggested that only slaves with sound character be selected.³⁹ Similarly, when selecting teachers for the child, they must be "free from scandal in their lives, who are unimpeachable in their manners, and in experience the very best that may be found."⁴⁰

Apart from moral character, Plutarch also suggested that philosophy should be given primary attention, as it is "the head and front of all education,"⁴¹ in addition to rhetoric, general education, travel, physical training, and the control of tongue in speeches.⁴²

The ultimate aim of education for children can be summarized as follows:

> . . . how a man must bear himself in his relations with the gods, with his parents, with his elders, with the laws, with strangers, with those in authority, with friends, with women, with children, with servants; that one ought to reverence the gods, to honour one's parents, to respect one's elders, to be obedient to the laws, to yield to those in authority, to love one's friends, to be chaste with women, to be affectionate with children, and not to be overbearing with slaves; and, most important of all, not to be overjoyful at success or overmuch distressed at misfortune, nor to be dissolute in pleasures, nor impulsive and brutish in temper.⁴³

Interestingly, Plutarch did not stop at the education of children. He also provided advice on dealing with adolescents where the father should take a personal interest in the lives of the children by guiding them.⁴⁴ Plutarch emphasized learning from the examples of those who had gained success and suffered misfortune in life. At the same time, the role of the father is also to ensure that the children are kept away from bad examples and negative moral values that would drive animosity between the father and the children.⁴⁵

38. Ibid., 3E
39. Ibid., 4A–B.
40. Ibid., 4C.
41. Ibid., 7D.
42. Ibid., 6B–8B; 10A–F.
43. Ibid., 7E–F.
44. Ibid., 12C.
45. Ibid., 12D. See also 13A.

Plutarch's advice on education was not only reserved for the elites. For those from the lower strata of the society, he noted: "Even the poor must endeavour, as well as they can, to provide the best education for their children, but, if that be impossible, then they must avail themselves of that which is within their means."[46]

This suggests that Plutarch viewed education as something more than the mastery of knowledge; education also includes the development of the character and formation of a person. In this respect, the father plays a crucial role as *paterfamilias* in the upbringing of his children and in the ways they should go.[47]

Discipline and punishments carried out by the father also constituted education of a child. However, punishments should not simply be understood as inflicting pain on a person. Ultimately, the goal of punishment such as the use of the rod, more so if the whipping was done in public, was to shame the ones being punished where their dignity, or *dignitas*, was violated. Within an honor-shame culture, humiliation, more so if it was inflicted publicly, caused more pain than the rod. As such, punishment or public shame could potentially be a tool to shape a person to a particular behavioral norm.[48]

While the father may have the right to use the whip, there are also opinions that its use was inconsistent with the desire of a father to instill in their sons a sense of *dignitas*. It is in the context of the violation of one's dignity, particularly those from the elites, that led Quintilian, the *magister*, to criticize the practice of punishment:

> I disapprove of flogging, although it is the received practice and meets with the acquiescence of Chrysippus, because in the first place it is a disgraceful form of punishment and fit only for slaves and is in any case an insult, as you will realize if you imagine its infliction at a later age. Secondly, if a boy is so insensible to instruction that reproof is useless, he will, like the worst type of slave, merely become hardened to blows. Finally there will

---

46. Ibid., 8F.

47. The Roman poet, Horace, also talked about a father who teaches his son to live frugally and avoid squandering his patrimony, and to steer clear of vices and adultery. Horace also provides stories of fathers who lived badly as examples to avoid. See Horace, *Sat.* 1.4.105–106.

48. For further discussion see Saller, *Patriarchy*, 133–53 on discipline and punishment in Roman household. See also Aulus Gellius *Noct. att.* 10.3.17 where a comparison on the speeches of three great orators, Gaius Gracchus, Marcus Cicero, and Marcus Cato, was made. All of them condemned the public beatings being carried out by the Roman magistrates. In each account, the public humiliation of the Roman citizens or noble men caused more pain than the pain inflicted under the rod.

be absolutely no need of such punishment if the magister is a thorough disciplinarian.[49]

According to Seneca, the use of the whip on children was acceptable if a son was wayward[50] or if the children did not understand reason.[51] He also stated that in raising children, parents should take a middle ground to avoid encouraging the children's temper and anger and stifling their native spirits.[52] Horace preferred words over the whip in the household of the free-born, describing his father as being accustomed to shape him as a boy by words.[53]

Plutarch also suggested that beatings should not be inflicted on children as this form of punishment was reserved for slaves.[54] He also advised that children should not be constantly rebuked. At times, giving praise and encouragement might be in order according to the circumstances:

> Praise and reproof are more helpful for the free-born than any sort of ill-usage, since the praise incites them toward what is honourable, and reproof keeps them from what is disgraceful. But rebukes and praises should be used alternately and in a variety of ways; it is well to choose some time when the children are full of confidence to put them to shame by rebuke, and then in turn to cheer them up by praises . . . Moreover in praising them it is essential not to excite and puff them up, for they are made conceited and spoiled by excess of praise.[55]

How did the parent-child and household relationship play out in public? Saller highlights that in many Roman comedies, while conflicts between fathers and their youthful sons were common, fathers were portrayed as trying to guide the sons toward honorable behavior through reasoning.[56] Interestingly in the Roman plays, the fathers were never presented as beating

---

49. Quintilian, *Inst.* 1.3.13. See also Saller, *Patriarchy*, 148, where he mentions about the complaints of neighbours living next to a school room where the sounds of students being beaten awakened them early in the morning. Juvenal commented that even the great warrior, Achilles, was afraid of the *virga magistri* (*Sat.* 7.2.10).

50. Seneca, *Clem.* 1.14.1.

51. Seneca, *Constant.* 12.3.

52. Seneca, *Ira.* 2.21.

53. Horace, *Sat.* 1.4.120–121.

54. Plutarch, *Lib. ed.* 9A. Saller, *Patriarchy*, 137, noted: "One of the primary distinctions between the condition of a free man and a slave in the Roman mind was the vulnerability of the latter to corporal punishment, in particular lashings at another's private whim."

55. Plutarch, *Lib. ed.* 9A.

56. Saller, *Patriarchy*, 144.

or threatening to beat their sons. By contrast, the nature of punishment or discipline of slaves was often drawn clearly.[57]

Finally, Plutarch emphasized that the *paterfamilias* should set himself up as the best example for the children to emulate.[58] Plutarch also had some very strong words for fathers who failed in their duties of educating their children: "It is right to rebuke some fathers who, after entrusting their sons to attendants and masters, do not themselves take cognizance at all of their instruction by means of their own eyes or their own ears. Herein they most fail in their duty."[59]

In an epitaph for an infant who died just shy of her first birthday dated during the Imperial period, it was said: "When I had just tasted life fate snatched me, an infant, and I did not see my father's pattern (τύπος); but I died after enjoying the light of eleven months, then I returned it."[60] By suggesting that the child had yet to follow in the father's ways nor had she received her father's imprint, this inscription demonstrated the significant role he would have played in her life.[61]

In short, the responsibility of a *paterfamilias* was to ensure the proper education of his children and set himself as an example to be imitated. Discipline was necessary but children were not to be repressed to the point of being treated like slaves, thereby losing their dignity.

Mother and Children

While the responsibility for caring, nurturing, and providing moral guidance to children lay with the parents, ancient authors distinguished the relationships of the father and mother with their children. Aristotle highlighted

---

57. For example, Plautus' *Mostellaria* is a comedy that tells the story of the punishment to be meted out when the father, Theopropides, discovered his son, Philolaches, had sold the family house for money to buy the freedom of his *amica*, a slave girl he loved. The father decided that the slave, Tranio, who collaborated with Philolaches would be punished. The slave would receive the whip (*flagrum*) but the son was expected to receive a verbal rebuke (*increpare*). See Plautus, *Most.* 743–50. In Terrance's *Heauton timorumenos* written in second century BCE, the slave Syrus told his master's son, Clitipho, on the consequences of being caught by the angry father: "For you there will be words (*verba*); for this man (that is Syrus) there will be a beating (*verbera*) (Terrance, *Haut.* 356). Similarly, in another play, *Phormio*, a similar idea is expressed to the disobedient son, Phaedria, by the slave, Geta:"you will hear complaints; I will be hung up and beaten" (Terrance, *Phorm.* 220–221).

58. Plutarch, *Lib. ed.* 14A–B.

59. Ibid., 9D.

60. Horsley, *New Documents Illustrating Early Christianity*, 4:40.

61. Ibid., 4:41.

the fact that "parental affection is stronger in the mother"[62] because "parenthood costs the mother more trouble."[63] While the role of mother in a typical Roman family is less well documented compared to that ot the father, her role in nurturing and educating a child should not be downplayed. Eyben argues that a mother was often held in high regards, and "managed to impress her stamp on her children."[64] Plutarch suggested that mother should be the one feeding their infants, unless she was too weak to do so,[65] and in instances like this, a wet nurse was hired. However, care must be exercised in choosing an appropriate one.[66] Seneca also highlighted the differences between maternal and paternal love:

> Do you not see how fathers show their love in one way, and mothers in another? The father orders his children to be aroused from sleep in order that they may start early on their pursuits, even on holidays he does not permit them to idle, and he draws from them sweat and sometimes tears. But the mother fondles them in her lap, wishes to keep them out of the sun, wishes them never to be unhappy, never to cry, never to toil.[67]

Children's Responsibility to Parents

I have discussed the responsibilities of parents towards their children, focusing on the aspect of education. In this section, I will survey children's responsibility towards parents.

The utmost responsibility of children towards their parents is to honor and respect them. This is well documented in antiquity.[68] Aristotle regarded honor to parents as similar to the dues given to gods.[69] Cicero laid down the duty of a person in hierarchical order: ". . . in the social relations . . . our first

---

62. Aristotle *Eth. nic.* 8.12.3.
63. Ibid., 8.7.7.
64. Eyben, *Restless Youth*, 213.
65. Plutarch, *Lib. ed.* 3C.
66. Ibid., 3D–E.
67. Seneca, *Prov.* 2.5.
68. For a brief discussion on parents-children relationship in the Greco-Roman world, see Burke, *Family Matters*, 60–96. See also Balla, *Child-Parent Relationship*, 10–79, for sources ranging from Homer to third century CE. See particularly his tables on pp. 39–40 and 78–79 summarizing the duties of children to parents from Homer to the end of Greek classical period and from Hellenistic period to third century CE respectively.
69. Aristotle, *Eth. nic.* 8.12.5. See also 9.2.8.

duty is to the immortal gods; our second, to country; our third, to parents; and so on, in a descending scale, to the rest."[70]

Plato also explicitly stated that honoring parents was the duty of every person in conduct and also in one's speech towards one's parents.[71] He warned that if a son failed to observe reverence of speech towards his parents, Nemesis, the messenger of Justice who had been appointed to keep watch, would mete out a heavy penalty.[72] In addition, Plato said that the gods were more attuned to the prayers of parents when they were dishonored by the children.[73] Such sayings were meant to encourage children to honor their parents, and at the same time, warn them about the consequences should they fail to discharge their duties. At the same time, Plato also suggested that the gods would reward the children accordingly if they were obedient and honoring to their parents.[74]

Similarly, Plutarch also regarded parents as worthy of honor, and honor to them is seen as next to the gods: "... there is nothing which men do that is more acceptable to gods than with goodwill and zeal to repay to those who bore them and brought them up."[75]

Children's failure to please and honor their parents was considered unholy and unlawful: "... to our mother and father, if we do not always afford, both in deed and in word, matter for their pleasure, even if offence be not present, men consider it unholy and unlawful."[76]

This notion of reciprocity between a father and a son is also mentioned by Seneca. A son in return for the father's love was expected, based on *pietas*, to submit to the father's will.[77] Seneca further stated that "not to love one's parents is to be unfilial (*parentes suos non amare impietas est*)."[78] In this respect, love and *piestas* are inseparable.

---

70. Cicero, *Off*. 1.45.160. Further on in *Off*. 1.17.58, Cicero states: "Now, if a contrast and comparison were to be made to find out where most of our moral obligation is due, country would come first, and parents; for their services have laid us under the heaviest obligation; next come children and the whole family, who look to us alone for support and have no other protection."

71. See Plato, *Leg.* IV.717B–718A; IV.717B–718A.

72. Ibid., IV.717C–D.

73. Ibid., IV.913C; 931E–932A.

74. Ibid., IV.718A.

75. Plurarch, *Lib. ed.*, 479F.

76. Ibid., 480A.

77. See Seneca, *Prov.* 2.5.

78. Seneca, *Ben* 3.1.5. See also *Ben* 6.23.5 where Seneca says, "We owe filial duty to our parents."

Apart from honoring parents, Plato also explicitly stated that it was the duty of children to provide for parents while they were living to repay the debt they owed for what their parents had done for them, and ensure that parents be given a proper burial when they passed away. Furthermore, children were encouraged to venerate their parents and ensure that such memorial would be carried out continuously.[79] Children who failed to care for aged parents deserved to be punished by the gods.[80]

The Use of Familial Metaphors in the Public Sphere

The use of familial metaphors in the public sphere was not unusual in antiquity although siblings, mothers, brothers, and daughters featured less prominently than the father-son relationship.[81] For example, the bond between a *quaestor* and his superior, a *praetor*, or consul, was often described as that of father and son. Cicero referred to this in his speech against Caecilius. He described Caecilius as unable to go against his former *praetor* without violating the obligation of a son's *pietas*.[82] Elsewhere, he also described the relationship between a young man, who was a *quaestor* working for the governor of Cisalpine Gaul, as that of a son with his father.[83] Pliny the Younger also subscribed to the same tradition in explaining the relationship between a council elect with a *quaestor*: "I will only say, he is a young man, who deserves you should look upon him in the same relation, as our ancestors used to consider their *queastorts*, that is, as your son."[84]

The other familial metaphor used in the public sphere was *Pater Patriae* (Father of the Fatherland). Romulus, the founder of the Rome, was called the Father of Rome.[85] Military commanders were also addressed as "father" by their army.[86] The title *Pater Patriae* was also conferred on those who had made significant contribution to the ruling powers. For example,

---

79. See Plato, *Leg.* IV.717B–718A; 931E–932A. See also similar teaching in Aristotle, *Eth. nic.* 1165a. In Select Papyri, it documents a letter from a son, Philonides, who was living in Alexandria, to the father, Cleon, a chief engineer in the Fayum. In this letter, Philonides urged the father to resign from his job in order to spend a season with him so that he could honor the father. He assured his father of his duty to care for and to protect the father until he died. See Select Papyri, I/94, dated about 255 BCE.

80. Hesiod, *Op.* 331–332.

81. Lassen, "The Roman Family," 111.

82. Cicero, *Div. Caec.* 61–62.

83. Cicero, *Fam.* 13.10.1.

84. Pliny the Younger, *Ep.* IV.15.

85. See Cicero, *Rep.* I.64.

86. See Livy, *History of Rome* 1.16.3, 2.7.4, and 2.60.3.

Cicero was conferred the title by the *Princeps* Senatus for his efforts in rescuing the Republic from Catiline's treason.[87] Julius Caesar also used this title as well, and was called a father in Cicero's pleading with him.[88] Perhaps the best-known use of *Pater Patriae* was by Augustus who was conferred the title by the Roman Senate in 2 BCE.[89] It was during his reign that the image of *Pater Patriae* became increasingly important and was used extensively.[90] This demonstrates that the Empire functioned as a great *familia* in which the emperor was a *paterfamilias* for the entire Roman population who must accord him their *pietas*.[91]

FAMILIAL METAPHORS IN THE CORINTHIAN LETTERS

I turn now to examining Paul's use of familial metaphor in the Corinthian letters, specifically the imagery of father, mother, infant, and slave administrator that Paul applied to himself.

Paul the Paterfamilias

1 Cor 4:14–21: Will the Corinthians Listen to their Father?

That Paul took his role as the *paterfamilias* of the Corinthian assembly seriously and wielded his authority and power (*patria potestas*) over them is without question,[92] as he declares in 1 Cor 4:14–15:

> I am not writing this to make you ashamed, but to admonish (νουθετῶ) you as my beloved children (τέκνα μου ἀγαπητὰ). For though you might have ten thousand guardians in Christ, you do not have many fathers (πατέρας). Indeed, in Christ Jesus I became your father (ἐγὼ ὑμᾶς ἐγέννησα) through the gospel.

In 1 Cor 4:14–21, Paul wraps up his rebuke of the Corinthians over their fractions in the community by admonishing (νουθετῶ) them for their dismissive behavior. The word νουθετέω carries an ethical dimension where

---

87. See Cicero, *Pis.* 3.6.
88. Cicero, *Lig.* 30.
89. See *Res gestae divi Augusti*, 35, also cited in full in Suetonius, *Aug.* 58.
90. See Lassen, "Roman Family," 112–13; and D'Angelo, "Εὐσεβεία," 142. See also Strabo, *Geogr.* 6.4.2 on subsequent use of the title.
91. On the emperor as *paterfamilias*, see Lacey, "Patria Potestas," 139.
92. For further discussion of Paul as *paterfamilias* of the Corinthians, see Joubert, "Managing the Household," 213–23.

it includes "counsel about avoidance or cessation of an improper course of conduct."[93] This word appears eight times in the New Testament, all used by Paul or related to Paul, in admonishments or warnings related to their behavior or conduct.[94] In other words, Paul is deeply disturbed by what he sees in the Corinthian community, and he attempts to admonish the Corinthians on their misconduct based on his relationship with them as a father.

Paul addresses the Corinthians as τέκνα μου ἀγαπητὰ, "my beloved children" (1 Cor 4:14) whom he begot through his preaching of the gospel (1 Cor 4:15, cf. 2 Cor 10:14b). He also claims that he is the only legitimate father even though the Corinthians may have "ten thousand guardians (παιδαγωγός)." Formation of children is the responsibility of the guardian, παιδαγωγός, a person "who has responsibility for someone who needs guidance, guardian, leader, guide."[95] Often, this role was assigned to "a slave or paid attendant who accompanied the child for the purpose of protection, guidance, and general supervision of behavior, e.g., to and from school, or on occasions when a parent was absent"[96] and to offer some general basic education. When children grew older, a philosopher might play the role of guiding them. Garland highlights that a guardian in the Greco-Roman world was often described as a stern, ignorant, and uncaring person and suggests that Paul has in mind the other apostles or leaders of the various Corinthians factions.[97] Whether he did remains uncertain but what is clear is that by using this language, Paul set himself above the other παιδαγωγός in terms of hierarchy. This is because the fundamental responsibility of educating the children lay with the parents, especially in character formation. Parents were viewed as role models, especially the father.[98] As such, Paul's role as father takes precedence over that of the guardians. By taking his role and authority seriously, and by rebuking and chastising, he offers himself as

93. BDAG, s.v.

94. See Acts 20:31 (in the context of Paul's speech to the Ephesians elders); Rom 15:14; 1 Cor 4:14; Col 1:28; 3:16; 1 Thess 5:12, 14; and 2 Thess 3:15.

95. BDAG, s.v.

96. Thiselton, *First Epistle to the Corinthians*, 370. At the same time, Paul may also have in mind the Jewish tradition of instructing the children. Jewish literature contains numerous instructions on raising and disciplining the children. See Prov 13:24; 19:18; Sir 7:23–25; 22:3–6; 30:1–13, amongst others. Disobedient children who fail to follow the traditional piety will bring shame to the parents. See also 4 Macc 18:10–19.

97. Garland, *1 Corinthians*, 146.

98. See, e.g., Eyben, "Fathers and Sons," 112–43; Yarbrough, "Parents and Children in the Jewish Family of Antiquity," 41–49; Barclay, "Family," 66–72; Balla, *Child-Parent Relationship*, 62–73, 86–104. See also Dutch, *Educated Elite*, 184–91; Lietaert Peerbolte, "Paul and the Practice and Paidea," 261–80; and Lietaert Peerbolte and Groenendijk, "Family Discourse," 129–49.

someone whom the wayward and disobedient Corinthians could listen to, imitate, and obey. Paul also did not hesitate to threaten punishment should the conduct of the Corinthians remain unchanged. Since obedience was a central virtue and considered as *pietas* at all stages of life in antiquity, especially in children's relationship with parents, the use of the parental metaphor was to evoke an emotional response from the Corinthians and cause them to evaluate what should be the appropriate response concerning the divisions in their midst.

Paul the Example

In 1 Cor 4:16, Paul urges (παρακαλῶ) the Corinthians to imitate him, their father. Pointing to himself as a model, Paul had earlier talked about his own behavior and character; now he expects the Corinthians to grow and learn from him. Imitation, where children were expected to follow the example of the father, was part of the education of children in antiquity.

Paul also presents to them his another "beloved and faithful" son, Timothy, who was sent to remind them of what a father is like, and how Paul's way of life is consistent with his teaching to the churches (1 Cor 4:17).[99] By using terms of endearment to appeal to the emotions of the Corinthians, Paul presents himself as a loving father to both the Corinthians and Timothy. Timothy is portrayed as what a son should be—loyal, obedient, and bringing honor to the father, qualities that the Corinthians lacked. This challenged them to consider if they were good sons and daughters. At the same time, Paul cared deeply for his children. As in antiquity, children were looked upon as objects of care and affection,[100] and this is observed in the manner he addresses them—as "beloved" (ἀγαπητὰ, 1 Cor 4:12) and "my beloved and faithful child" (μου τέκνον ἀγαπητὸν καὶ πιστὸν in 1 Cor 4:17).

Paul's language of imitation and use of parent/child metaphor have attracted considerable attention, particularly from those interpreting it from a feminist perspective who picture him as an authoritarian figure exerting his control and authority over the Corinthians.[101] One needs to

---

99. See also Phil 2:22 where Timothy is described as a son to Paul. Similarly, Paul viewed Onesimus as his own son begotten in chains (Phlm 10, 12), and he sent his very heart back to Philemon. See also Mitchell, "New Testament Envoys," 641–62.

100. Dixon, *Roman Family*, 98–108.

101. For example, Fatum, "Brotherhood in Christ," 183–97, argues that Paul's use of familial metaphors served to advance male prominence to the effect that women only became associate members of the Thessalonian brotherhood through their men. See also Castelli, *Imitating Paul*, 98–117, where she argues that Paul's idea of imitation and the Corinthians imitating Paul as children do a father forms part of the discourse

bear in mind that Paul's language of imitation is being used in the context of the role of a father in educating and disciplining his children, and the tone of authority is expected.[102] Interestingly, Plutarch also provides some advice on dealing with adolescents in the family by using "instruction . . . threats . . . entreaties" and "by pointing out examples of men who through love of pleasure have become involved in misfortunes, and of those who, through their steadfastness, have gained for themselves approval and good repute."[103] Furthermore, Plutarch also states that a father's role is also to ensure that the children are kept away "from any association with base men; for they carry away something of their badness."[104] If not, these bad influences would threaten the relationship of father and son, bringing sorrow for both parties.[105] Therefore, it is not surprising that Plutarch strongly urges that the father should be the best example for the children to emulate:

> Fathers ought above all, by not misbehaving and by doing as they ought to do, to make themselves a manifest example to their children, so that the latter, by looking at their fathers' lives as at a mirror, may be deterred from disgraceful deeds and words. For those who are themselves involved in the same errors as those for which they rebuke their erring sons, unwittingly accuse themselves in their sons' name. If the life they lead is wholly bad, they are not free to admonish even their slaves, let alone their sons. Besides, they are likely to become counsellors and instructors to their sons in their wrongdoing. For, wherever old men are lacking in decency, young men too are sure to be most shameless.[106]

The language of imitation in 1 Cor 4:16 should be understood in the light of this. Paul is operating within the boundaries of what is expected of a father in the education of his children. He sets himself as an example of

---

of power that aims to have his authority uncontested and exerting his control over the communities. For similar argument, see also Polaski, *Paul and the Discourse of Power*, 12–15. See Thiselton, *First Epistle to the Corinthians*, 371–73, for a critique of Castelli. Contra Ehrensperger, "Be Imitators of Me," 241–61, who argues that imitation language, rather than being an instrument of domination and control, serves to guide the Corinthians into life in Christ and to deconstruct the social convention of the Greco-Roman society. Cf. Clarke, "Be Imitators of Me," 329–60; Fiore, "Paul," 228–57.

102. See Belleville, "Imitate Me," 120–43, especially 121 on the language of imitation where Paul is appealing to the Corinthians as a father, not an apostle.

103. Plutarch, *Lib. ed.* 12C.

104. Ibid., 12D. See also 13C, where schoolmates that were of bad influence were to be removed as friends of the children.

105. Ibid., 13A.

106. Ibid., 14A–B.

someone who lives by what he preaches. Paul underscores that his way of life is rooted in Christ by embracing the weakness and suffering of Christ and in the embodiment of this suffering for the sake of others (1 Cor 4:17, cf. 11:1).[107]

Notably, Paul's language of imitation is found within the context of his catalogue of sufferings in 1 Cor 4:9–13 where he views himself as a fool, one who is weak, held in disrepute, hungry and thirsty, poorly clothed, beaten and homeless, persecuted, slandered, and ultimately treated as scum of the world (περικαθάρματα τοῦ κόσμου) and refuse (περίψημα). Paul's language here is targeted at the elites of the community, a group with the most to lose and least to gain from any inversion of cultural norm. This group would have had the most difficulty in accepting Paul's status of reversal or taking on a less privileged status, as stated by Horrell: "Paul's Christianity . . . is often critical of and offensive to the socially prominent members of the community. It makes strenuous demands upon them, demands which will have an impact upon their worldly position and social interaction."[108] By encouraging others in giving up their rights for the sake of the weaker brothers, Paul's language of imitation is, therefore, a language of transformation, of change, and yet of authority demanding that the Corinthians imitate him as their father. As such, Paul uses his power and authority constructively, not to suppress his church but to empower them towards maturity. Paul's power, far from being domineering (although recognizing the patriarchal context of the Greco-Roman world), has a transformative objective, as argued by Kathy Ehrensperger: "Paul emphasizes again and again that the aim of his teaching is to *empower* those within his communities to *support each other*. He acts as a parent-teacher using power-over them to empower them and thus render himself, and the power-over exercised in this role, obsolete."[109]

Paul the Disciplinarian

Finally, in 1 Cor 4:18–21,[110] Paul takes on the role of a disciplinarian, asserting his authority over the community as a father disciplining his rebellious

---

107. See Kim, "'Imitators,'" 147–70. See also Ehrensperger, "Be Imitators of Me," 241–61; and Young, "Paidagogos," 150–76. On Paul's embracing the sufferings of Christ, see Lim, *Sufferings of Christ*. For further discussion on the embodiment of suffering for the sake of others, see chapter 6 below on Paul's use of body metaphor.

108. Horrell, *Social Ethos*, 233.

109. Ehrensperger, *Paul and Dynamics of Power*, 136, emphasis hers. For further discussion, see Talbott, *Jesus, Paul, and Power*, 93–161.

110. There are disputes whether this pericope belongs to the preceding argument on divisions in the church or marks a new beginning of a section linking it to the

"*In Christ Jesus I became Your Father*" 115

children.[111] One of the most dominant functions of a paternal metaphor is to "evoke images of authority: authority of God over humans, senior officials over junior officials, state leaders over subjects."[112] Since the Romans viewed themselves as a society of fathers and sons, so the metaphor of father holds a very important position in the context of the family. Hence it is only fitting that Paul used it in addressing issues related to disciplining the Corinthians, but not when he dealt with their relationship with one another within the community of ἐκκλησία. As a father, Paul poses a rhetorical question of whether the Corinthians preferred him to come with a rod (ῥάβδος), or in love and with a spirit of gentleness. He would not hesitate to exercise punishment if the Corinthians failed to submit themselves to his discipline and correction. Moreover, some among the Corinthians had accused Paul of being an absentee father, believing he would not come to them, and thereby becoming arrogant.[113] Paul brushes this charge aside by stating that the manner of his arrival would depend on the attitude and response of the Corinthians.

The notion of a father punishing with rod has often been understood as having its roots in the Old Testament. The word ῥάβδος in the LXX is used in the context of paternal discipline of children.[114] Within the Greco-Roman context, ῥάβδος was the traditional instrument for punishing small

---

following argument on the issues surrounding sexual immorality and lawsuits of 1 Cor 5–6. See Ciampa and Rosner, *First Letter to the Corinthians*, 189–92, who argue that it is a beginning of a new section linking together 1 Cor 4:18—7:40, and Garland, *1 Corinthians*, 151, who insists that 1 Cor 4:18–21 forms part of chapters 1–4. In light of the continuity of the use of the father-child metaphor, it is best to take 1 Cor 4:18–21 as part of the overall argument of chapters 1–4.

111. Lockwood, *1 Corinthians*, 153 and Fee, *First Epistle to the Corinthians*, 209, view the rod as a fatherly discipline, and not one wielded by a pedagogue, as suggested by Schneider, in "ῥάβδος, ῥαβδίζω, ῥαβδοῦχος," TDNT 6:969–70. See Daube, "Paul a Hellenistic Schoolmaster?," 67–71. Cf. the NIV1978 translation of ῥάβδος as "whip" in 1 Cor 4:21, giving the impression that this is a task carried out by a schoolmaster. However, the NIV2011 rightly corrected it to "rod of discipline," reflecting the use of the metaphor of father-child. For further discussion, see Dutch, *Educated Elite*, 261–68, who argues that Paul's use of "rod" here could also be read within the social contexts of family and school where the pedagogues could be those who are household slaves, or freedmen hired to supervise the children. If Dutch is correct, it does not minimize the role the father plays in the discipline of the children. The pedagogues would have exercised their roles under the authority of the *paterfamilias*. See also White, *Where is the Wise Man?*, 187–90.

112. Lassen, "The Roman Family," 114.

113. On Paul as an absentee father, see Wanamaker, "Power of the Absent Father," 339–64.

114. See 2 Sam 7:14; Prov 22:15; 23:13–14; 26:3.

children at home and in school. By speaking of the rod, Paul shows that he views the Corinthians as children requiring discipline.

In view of the universal nature of paternal discipline, it is not surprising that the rod was a common instrument of discipline.[115] What is significant here is the purpose of the rod. Bartchy suggests that Paul needed to use a domineering tone in addressing those who considered themselves to be wise, powerful, and of noble birth.[116] Stricter measures of punishment might be taken in order to bring them under control.[117] It is in this spirit that Paul appeals to them to surrender their status-linked privileges in favor of caring for one another as siblings in a family. If Bartchy is correct, Paul was presenting the Corinthians with a choice: a rod for punishment of disobedience, or love for obedience. He uses the image of a disciplinary father to prompt the Corinthians into considering their relationship with him and with the other members in the community. The Corinthians are now required to consider their divisive conduct and close ranks as a family.

2 Cor 6:11–13: Will the Corinthians Reciprocate with Affection?

In 2 Cor 6:11–13, Paul uses terms of endearment to plead with the Corinthians and expresses his affection for them publicly so that they can be reconciled with him. Earlier on in 2 Cor 5:11–21, Paul reminds the Corinthians about the ministry of reconciliation in Christ, and in 2 Cor 6:1–10, he presents himself as a true apostle who suffered for the sake of the gospel and the Corinthians in order to bring this message of reconciliation to them. In 2 Cor 6:11–13, Paul turns to focus on the Corinthians with the hope that they too would be reconciled to him. He does so by appealing to the metaphor of *paterfamilias* in declaring his affection for them. However, the Corinthians are withholding their affection from him (2 Cor 6:12). Like a father pleading with a wayward son (τέκνον), Paul entreats the Corinthians that in return (ἀντιμισθία), they should open wide their hearts to him.

---

115. See Lassen, "Use of the Father Image," 127–36, for an argument that Paul's father image is drawn from the Greco-Roman world, particularly from the Imperial propaganda where Augustus is protrayed as a father of all. See also Swift, "A Group of Roman Imperial Portraits," 142–59, for further discussion on the statue of Augustus.

116. Bartchy, "Who should be called Father," 173–75. Bartchy argues that Paul adopted different tones in addressing different groups of people in the Corinthian community. To the insecure, he was gentle, but tough to the arrogant.

117. Saller, *Patriarchy*, 133–53. See also Saller, "Corporal Punishment," 144–65; Eyben, "Fathers and Sons," 121–24; and Rawson, *Children and Childhood*, 175–77.

The word ἀντιμισθία suggests that children are obligated to repay parents the debt of raising them.[118] In this respect, Paul's choice of words is careful and deliberate. In asking the Corinthians to reciprocate what is rightly due him as their father, he places them in a position of being indebted to him. In that position, the Corinthians have a moral obligation as children to give back to their father honor, respect, and love as there is no way they could ever repay their debt to Paul for sacrificing and raising them up in Christ. The highest honor children can give to their father includes paying heed to his advice. By opening wide their hearts to Paul, the Corinthians would not only be acknowledging Paul as their father but would also be treating his advice as worthy of being followed. Using familial metaphor, Paul entreats the Corinthians to carefully evaluate their actions and allegiance, a theme that is repeated in 2 Cor 7:2–4. By using the metaphor of *paterfamilias*, Paul reinforces the Corinthians' identity as members of a family that should be characterized by love, acceptance, and reconciliation. If God has reconciled them to Christ and to one another, how could they, by withholding their affection, be estranged from their apostle who is their father in Christ?

2 Cor 11:2: A Father with Divine Jealousy

When confronted with the "super apostles" (2 Cor 11:5) who attempt to drive a wedge between Paul and the Corinthians by leveling accusations against him (2 Cor 10:1—11:6), Paul responds by taking on the role of a father in 2 Cor 11:2, one with divine jealousy (ζηλῶ γὰρ ὑμᾶς θεοῦ ζήλῳ),[119] guarding and protecting the dignity of the daughters before they are given in marriage.[120] Paul speaks as a concerned father, expressing his love and care for his daughters and their future. As such, the Corinthians owe their obedience and allegiance to Paul, and not to the super apostles who are

118. Yarbrough, "Parents and Children in the Letters of Paul," 133–34. See also Yarbrough, "Parents and Children in the Jewish Family of Antiquity," 49–55. According to BDAG, s.v., ἀντιμισθία "expresses the reciprocal (ἀντι) nature of a transaction as requital based upon what one deserves, *recompense, exchange*, either in the positive sense of *reward* or the negative sense *penalty*, depending on the context."

119. Paul plays with two words in 2 Cor 11:2, ζηλῶ and ζήλῳ, in the same phrase, declaring that he is "jealous with the jealousy of God," possibly drawing from the attributes of the God of Israel as a jealous God as in Exod 20:5; 34:14. Cf. Num 25:11–13.

120. Paul's role as bethrothing the Corinthians as the bride of Christ has been subjected to numerous interpretations. Harris, *Second Epistle to the Corinthians*, 736–38, lists four possibilities: 1) friend of the groom or the groomsman; 2) friend of the bride; 3) the father's agent, and 4) the father of the bride. In light of the immediate context, it is best to see Paul's role as a father. So Guthrie, *2 Corinthians*, 505.

luring them away. For Paul, there is no common ground between the Corinthians and the super apostles. Here, he once again evokes his emotional ties with the Corinthians, picturing himself as a jealous father who only wants the best for them. By painting himself as a jealous father, Paul is not only guarding them from outsiders but also exposing his opponents as not having the welfare of the Corinthians at heart, the way a father would.

2 Cor 12:14-15: A Father who Provides for the Children

Confrontation is one of the most difficult aspects of any relationship. Paul has confronted the Corinthians earlier and now needs to prepare them for his upcoming third visit (2 Cor 12:14). He frames his relationship with them as one of family by declaring his deep love for them just as parents love their children to the extent of sacrificing for them (2 Cor 12:14-15). He states that he is not a burden to the Corinthians, although he could rightly expect that as his children, they would provide for him (see also 2 Cor 11:7-15).[121] Instead, he discharges his responsibility as a father by providing an inheritance for his children,[122] instead of taking from them (2 Cor 12:14b-15a). Aasgaard has noted that by doing so, Paul views the relationship from the perspective of the weaker party in which the older generation must act for the benefit of their descendants.[123] This idea of parents providing for children is also well documented in antiquity.[124]

However, the manner in which Paul emphasizes this idea is nevertheless striking. He goes further than merely providing for the Corinthians, he is willing to be sacrificed for their sake. This is repeated twice with the word δαπανήσω and the compound word ἐκδαπανηθήσομαι in 2 Cor 12:15a: ἐγὼ δὲ ἥδιστα δαπανήσω καὶ ἐκδαπανηθήσομαι ὑπὲρ τῶν ψυχῶν ὑμῶν.[125]

In 2 Cor 12:15b, Paul moves from providing an inheritance to taking care of children by using the language of mutual love (ἀγαπάω). He has

---

121. Plutarch's *Cupid. divit.* 526a and Philo's *Moses* 2.245 have often been cited as parallels to what Paul is saying here. For discussion on ancient sources on parental beneficience, see Harrison, "Paul the 'Paradoxical' Parent," 405-18.

122. On Paul talking on inheritance here, see Yarbrough, "Parents and Children in the Letters of Paul," 134-36. See also Harrison, "Paul the 'Paradoxical' Parent," 399-425.

123. Aasgaard, "Paul as a Child," 139.

124. See Yarbrough, "Parents and Children in the Letters of Paul," 131, 134-36, with references.

125. This word, δαπανάω, also occurs in Mark 5:26 in describing the woman with the issue of the blood who spent all she had on doctors, and also in Luke 15:14 in the story of the prodigal son who spent all he had. The word δαπανάω carries the idea that one is "to use up or pay out material or physical resources" (BDAG, s.v.).

brought the gospel to them, nurtured them, sacrificed himself for them, and suffered hardships. The least the Corinthians could do is to reciprocate by expressing their love and affection for him as rightly noted by Yarbrough.[126] The obligation of the children to parents is clearly illustrated by Hierocles:

> We should, therefore, procure for our parents liberal food . . . a bed, sleep, unction, a bath, garments; and in short, all the necessaries which the body requires, that they may never at any time experience the want of any of these; in thus acting, imitating their care about our nurture, when we were infants.[127]

In this respect, Paul is moving the Corinthians to decisive action with the use of the image of *paterfamilias*. Yet he is clear that he is not an abusive father. He is using his paternal authority for building up and not tearing down (see 2 Cor 13:10), in wrapping up his argument in 2 Cor 10–13. In his reference to himself as a generous father, Paul's readers would be able to discern the point he was trying to make with regards to his love and care for them and his having gone beyond the normal bounds of generosity. The real issue now is whether the Corinthians, as his pious children, would repay the beneficence of their father-in-Christ.

Summary: Paul the Father

Although the image of the father creates anticipation of a hierarchical space between father and children where those in the subordinate roles are expected to recognize and submit to the father as one with positions of power and authority, it also evokes a strong sense of affection and bond that father has for the children. Seen from the perspective of Paul in his letters to the Corinthians, Adrian Long rightly argues that "it would seem safer to find in Paul's claim to be the community's father a statement of power which is gospel-defined; which aims not as self-aggrandizement but at the edification of the community through service and love."[128] What emerges from the nuanced way in which Paul portrays himself as a *paterfamilias* is not a harsh and authoritarian father who abuses his authority. Rather, it is of one who is deeply concerned with his children and attentive to their needs: he communicates with them according to their level (2 Cor 6:13), acts lovingly toward them (1 Cor 4:14–17), strives to provides for them and stores up

---

126. Yarbrough, "Parents and Children in the Letters of Paul," 137.

127. Cited in Yarbrough, "Parents and Children in the Letters of Paul," 137.

128. Long, *Paul and Human Rights*, 130. See his wider discussion on Paul and power in 56–147.

their inheritance (2 Cor 12:14), and exhorts them in a benevolent manner, as a firm but yet loving father (1 Cor 4:14). As I have argued, the father's role in antiquity was more flexible than has often been suggested, and Paul appears to utilize the whole spectrum of the nuances for this role in how he relates to his children.

1 Cor 3:1–3: Paul as a Nursing mother

Paul's use of the paternal image in which he sees himself as the *paterfamilias* of the Corinthian assembly may not have surprised the Corinthians as much as his use of a maternal image. In 1 Cor 3:1–3 Paul declares:

> And so, brothers and sisters, I could not speak to you as spiritual people, but rather as people of the flesh, as infants in Christ. I fed you with milk, not solid food, for you were not ready for solid food. Even now you are still not ready, for you are still of the flesh.

The metaphorical use of mother or wet nurse is rather common. It is found elsewhere in the New Testament (Heb 5:12–14; 1 Peter 2:2) and in the writings of the orators of the day. Epictetus uses similar imagery about milk and solid food: "Are you not willing at this late date, like children, to be weaned and to partake of more solid food, and not to cry for mothers and nurses—old wives' lamentations?"[129]

Based on these seeming parallels, it is not surprising that many commentators have adopted a two-tier diet reading in 1 Cor 3:1–2. According to this interpretation, milk is equated to Paul's initial preaching or instruction while solid food is analogous to further instruction for the matured, and the Corinthians should have already been weaned off milk and moved on to solid food.[130] However, this line of argument does not do justice to Paul's

---

129. Epictetus, *Diatr.* 2.16.39. See also ibid., 3.24.9. Furthermore, similar usage of milk and solid food has also been found in Philo where he compared milk and solid food to different level of instructions. See Philo, *Good Person* 160. See also his *Prelim. Studies* 19; *Agriculture* 9; *Migration* 29; and *Dreams* 2.10. For further discussion on nursing and wet nurse in the Greco-Roman world, see McNeel, *Paul as Infant and Nursing Mother*, 71–80.

130. Robertson and Plummer, *First Epistle of St. Paul to the Corinthians*, 52–53. For interest in correlating milk and solid food with different levels of instructions, see Lovacs, "Echoes of Valentinian Exegesis," 317–29. So Hays, *First Corinthians*, 48: "The metaphors used here (adults vs. infants and solid food vs. milk) are stock language in relation to philosophical and religious instruction throughout the ancient world. The assumption is that spiritual progress can be graded and that a different sort of curriculum is appropriate to each level of maturity."

argument here. First of all, it fails to take into consideration Paul's extended stay in Corinth for eighteen months if the testimony from Acts 18:1–2 is to be considered as accurate. To suggest that Paul could have only offered the initial proclamation of the gospel to the Corinthians ignores the fact that his extended stay could have included substantial instruction on matters related to faith.

Secondly, it does not fully account for the force of the maternal metaphor that Paul uses and applies to himself, "I feed you milk." This language evokes the imagery of a nursing mother or a wet nurse nurturing a baby. If food is all that matters, Paul could have said, "You are still drinking milk and you should move on to solid food," as seen in Epictetus and Philo, and refrained from applying the image to himself. It is noteworthy that neither Epictetus nor Philo takes on the role of nursing or providing milk and applying the maternal image to themselves. Furthermore, Epictetus' references to wet nurses or those feeding milk to infants are largely negative, conveying a picture that the nurses care for those who lack maturity.[131] In this regard the use of a feminine imagery by Paul should not be ignored.

Finally, it seems that the comparisons between milk and solid food representing different levels of maturity may have been read into the Corinthian letter from other New Testament passages, particularly Heb 5:12–14 and 1 Pet 2:2, further reinforcing the two-tiered diet system.

In light of this, a number of scholars have rightly challenged the difficulties in adopting this two-tiered diet interpretation.[132] However, what most commentators miss is the fact that Paul is applying a maternal role to himself in nurturing the Corinthians.[133] This use of a feminine metaphor[134]

---

131. See Epictetus, *Diatr.* 2.16.28; 2.16.39; and 2.16.44.

132. Hooker, "Hard Sayings," 19–22. See also similar argument by Francis, "As Babes in Christ," 41–60, where the problem of the Corinthians was not a failure of progression from babes to adults but a failure of comprehension. In his respect, Francis argues that the Corintians were behaving in a childish manner (57). See also Gaventa, *Our Mother Saint Paul*, 42–43.

133. Gaventa, *Our Mother Saint Paul*, 45. See also Gaventa, "Mother's Milk," 101–13. McNeel, *Paul as Infant and Nursing Mother*, 7, rightly notes that Paul's use of nursing metaphor has been neglected.

134. Yarbrough has argued that the person feeding milk in 1 Cor 3:1–3 refers to a male nurse. See his "Parents and Children in the Letters of Paul," 126–41; here, 132–33. See also Bradley's chapter on "Child Care at Rome" in his *Discovering the Roman Family*, 37–75. He also advances similar argument. While there is no denying that there could have been a male nurse in view, he often fed children not of his own. In the Corinthian context, Paul has clearly argued that the Corinthians were his children through the gospel, so the male nurse imagery would not have been applicable in this context. For a further critique of Yarbrough's and Bradley's view, see Gaventa, *Our Mother Saint Paul*, 45–46. For the suggestion that the nursing mother is compared to the philosophers, see

is striking for several reasons. First, the use of maternal imagery is often neglected in Pauline studies as rightly lamented by Gaventa[135] despite its frequent use in Paul's letters.[136] In her studies, Gaventa notes that maternal imagery conveys something distinctively different from the imagery of *paterfamilias*, and this is even more pronounced in an ancient community where gender construction and identity are often emphasized. Gaventa suggests that Paul's use of maternal imagery appears in context referring to the ongoing nature of the relationship between Paul and the communities he founded, while paternal imagery often refers to the initial stage of preaching the gospel or conversion, or a single event that occurred at one moment in the past.[137] While it may be true that maternal imagery often depicts the continuing process of nurturing children to health and growth, Paul's use of paternal imagery (especially in the formation of the children), also appears within the context of the ongoing nature of relationship, as we saw earlier in this chapter.

Secondly, the use of maternal imagery reinforces the notion of a family. As a father, Paul leads, provides, and sets himself as an example for the Corinthians. As a mother, he cares for the children, nurtures them, and loves them. Margaret Aymer argues that the role, authority, and power of a mother within a Roman family should not be discounted.[138] While the mother may not wield the absolute powers of a *paterfamilias*, she remains a powerful figure in the family who demands respect and obedience from the children. At the same time, she is the one exercising her influence in ensuring the physical nurture and moral formation of the children. This suggests that the roles Paul played are not only complementary, but emphasized his apostolic role in building and nursing the community towards maturity.

Thirdly, underlying the maternal imagery is the intimacy Paul feels towards the Corinthians. Paul cares for his children whom he begot. And he knows precisely what to feed the Corinthians for their nourishment, rather than the alternative food of philosophical knowledge, rhetorical eloquence,

---

Malherbe, "Gentle as a Nurse," 203–217. Cf. also Num 11:12 where Moses applied the role of a nurse to himself and the 1QH 15.20–22 where the teacher of righteousness described himself as a father to the children who open their mouth wide like a nursing child. See also Bradley, "Wet-nursing at Rome," 201–29.

135. Gaventa, *Our Mother Saint Paul*, 5–6. See Ciampa and Rosner, *First Letter to the Corinthians*, 139–42, where the maternal imagery is not even mentioned at all in the commentary of 1 Cor 3:1–4.

136. See Rom 8:22; Gal 1:15; 4:19; 1 Thess 2:7; 5:3 amongst others.

137. Gaventa, *Our Mother Saint Paul*, 6–7. For example, Gaventa sees the paternal imagery as the act of begetting the believers metaphorically as in Phlm 10 and 1 Cor 4:15.

138. Aymer, "Mother Knows Best," 188–97.

and speculative wisdom provided by the worldly system (1 Cor 3:3). The maternal imagery of feeding milk to the children leads Aymer to suggest the dependency of the community on Paul for its existence and sustenance.[139] This underscores Paul's ongoing maternal authority among them, which would give him the right and responsibility to care, correct, and instruct them in matters related to virtue and morality. Aymer further argues that with this authority Paul is able "to hold them accountable for their moral lapse—their 'jealousy and envy,' which he characterizes as 'merely human'... Paul, thus, stands firmly in her role as a moral agent to curb the immoral and childish behaviour evidenced in the factionalism at Corinth."[140] As a mother, Paul also expects the Corinthians to listen to him and to obey him, since *pietas* is also expected from children to their mother.

Finally, the maternal imagery is even more striking if we take into consideration the series of metaphors Paul uses in his subsequent flow of thought. Following 1 Cor 3:1–3, Paul describes himself and his co-workers by drawing from agriculture and construction. Farmers and builders are masculine images: they plant, water, and build for God, the owner of the field and building. The comparison becomes obvious where the feminine nursing imagery stands out significantly.

This is where my earlier attempt to read metaphors not simply as devices to decorate or illustrate the writings, but to provoke reflection and change of worldviews comes into play. The cognitive function forces readers to re-look things differently and alters their perspective. As a nursing mother, Paul demonstrates his deep love and pastoral care for the Corinthians by providing them affection, comfort, and suitable nourishment to ensure their well-being. This nursing imagery also evokes the bonds shared intimately by the mother and the infant. At the same time, the nursing mother also has authority over the children. By using maternal imagery—a very unusual and unlikely metaphor—and applying it to himself, Paul is not only inviting the Corinthians to reconsider their relationship with him in the hope of evoking a response from them, but also risking attacks on his masculinity.

Paul's Masculinity under Attack?

How would the Corinthians view Paul's application of maternal imagery to himself? Was he taking a calculated risk in doing so, in that his masculinity may be compromised? I now turn to examining gender roles in the

---

139. Ibid., 192.
140. Ibid.

Greco-Roman world which illuminate the impact of Paul's use of a feminine metaphor.[141]

In *Physiognomonics* attributed to Aristotle, the description of a male is clearly distinguished from that of a female. For example, "The male is larger and stronger than the female, and the extremities of his body are stronger, sleeker, better conditioned and more fit for every function."[142] A long list of physical characteristics and traits that describe a real man deemed as brave and a coward or less manly are further described in a rather amazing and elaborate fashion.[143] Similarly, Seneca also claimed that men who dress like women behave contrary to nature.[144] Apart from appearance and behavior, masculinity in the Greco-Roman world also featured prominently in competitive arenas such as the battlefield and gymnasium.

However, there is another category in physiognomy that is often emphasized in demonstrating one's masculinity as suggested by Maud Gleason: rhetorical education and public performance.[145] Physiognomy forms part of rhetorical theory, and the manner of delivery of an orator is often used to judge a person's character and masculinity. Cicero pursued this subject at some length where he believed that nature "has so formed his (human) features as to portray therein the character that lies hidden deep within him, for not only do the eyes declare with exceeding clarity the innermost feelings of our hearts, but also the countenance, as we Romans call it, which can be found in no other living being, save man, reveals the character."[146]

Physiognomy is also used in rhetorical invective, a speech of condemnation or blame. The oratory of Cicero in employing physiognomic distinctions in invective against L. Calpurnus Piso Caesonius, one of the consuls in office during his exile in 58 BCE, is commonly highlighted. Here, Cicero focused his invective on Piso's deceptive facial features:

> We were not deceived by your slavish complexion, your hairy cheeks, and your discolored teeth; it was your eyes, eyebrows, forehead, in a word, your whole countenance, which is a kind of silent speech of the mind, that pushed your fellow-men into

---

141. See Gleason, *Making Men*; and Parsons, *Body and Character* on the importance of gender construction. See also Martin, *Corinthian Body* for a discussion on his approach in reading Paul's letter related to issues of gender construction, and Conway, *Behold the Man*, 15–34 on constructing masculinity in the Greco-Roman world.

142. Aristotle, *Physiogn.* 806b.

143. Ibid., 807a–b.

144. Seneca, *Ep.* 122.7. See also Quintilian, *Inst.* 11.1.3.

145. Gleason, *Making Men*.

146. Cicero, *Leg.* 1.9.26. For further discussion, see Parsons, *Body and Character*, 17–37.

delusion. This is how you tricked, betrayed, inveighed those who were unacquainted with you. There were but few of us who knew of your filthy vices, the crassness of your intelligence, and the sluggish ineptitude of your talk . . . You crept into office by mistake, by the recommendation of your dingy family busts, with which you have no resemblance save color.[147]

Maud Gleason further examines the writings of two Sophists—Favorinus, a eunuch, and Polemo, a man who met the conventional gender expectations during the second century CE.[148] The careers of these popular orators offer interesting insights into how the notion of masculinity was constructed or presented. The mastery of rhetoric marked the transition of a boy to an adult and this remained crucial in a man's social standing in society. Rhetoricians were trained to develop traits that would be considered masculine. These included gesture, facial expression, voice and gait; these traits were often subject to close and intense scrutiny by others, and served to divide men into legitimate and illegitimate members based on their masculinity.[149]

If a man's public speech was part of the criteria for masculinity, Paul would have failed miserably as far as the Corinthians were concerned. In 1 Cor 2:1–5, Paul testified to his lack of rhetorical eloquence (bearing in mind Cicero's invective attack against Piso's "sluggish ineptitude" of speech as one of the characteristics that lacked masculinity). Harrill further argues that "to accuse a person of a weak bodily presence and deficient speech is to call that person a slavish man unfit for public office or otherwise to dominate others."[150] If this is true, we see Paul deliberately introducing his lack of masculinity in 1 Cor 2:1–5 when he spoke about his lack of rhetorical eloquence in addressing the Corinthians during his initial visit. Furthermore, Paul claimed weakness and trembling, traits that depicted a shameful, cowardly, and incompetent person in his speech. In addition, the content of his message, Christ crucified, was also considered foolish. As such, Paul would already have shocked his audience. In 2 Cor 10:10, his opponents judged him severely for lacking in appearance.[151]

Taking into account all the above, it would not have been surprising if the Corinthians judged Paul as not a real man. This would have been made

---

147. Cicero, *Pis.* 1.
148. Gleason, *Making Men*, 3–54, 131–58.
149. See Parsons, *Body and Character*, 27–34 for examples of physiognomy in practice in antiquity.
150. Harrill, *Slaves in the New Testament*, 48.
151. Harrill, "Invective against Paul," 189–213; and Lim, *Sufferings of Christ*, 160–96.

worse by his taking on a maternal imager in 1 Cor 3:1–3. As a "biological father" to this community of faith, surely Paul would not have been a nursing mother, what more feeding the infant with milk. A man's masculinity was called into question when he took on a feminine role, and in this respect, the listeners would have reacted negatively to Paul abandoning his manly role. This would have also brought him shame when he presented himself as a "female-identified male," as testified by Gaventa.[152]

But Paul turned things around with the use of a feminine metaphor. Regardless of how the Corinthians may have judged or thought of him, he remained their caring mother. As a nursing mother, he would not abandon them. On the contrary, he insisted that as the one feeding the Corinthians, he knew the right food to give them, which was milk, and yet urging them to move on to solid food when the time was right. He was unlike others who may have fed them the wrong type of food. Paul's role was not different from that of a wet-nurse—described by Dio Chrysostum—who sweetens an unpleasant drink for the baby with honey to make it easier to consume.[153] Plutarch talked about a nurse who speaks gently in time of misfortune[154] and how a nurse also offers nourishment after causing the baby to cry.[155] These examples express the bond of affection, care, and love that characterized the parental relationship between Paul and the Corinthians.

Paul used the language of belonging and a metaphor of care and concern in addressing children who still required constant care and feeding, something that the imagery of *paterfamilias* could not achieve. This image suggests that Paul saw the Corinthians as a close-knit, fictive family that should re-evaluate the divisions that threatened to divide them along the lines of the nature of leadership. Paul used maternal imagery to represent a nursing mother caring for an infant who was helpless and in danger. Likewise, he was also protecting the community from the danger arising from divisions in the community. Some among the Corinthians may have been dislocated from their family of origin,[156] and the Corinthian family served as a surrogate family. If the Corinthians saw themselves as brothers and sisters, and Paul as their begetting father and nursing mother, and God as the father of all, then it was foolish for the Corinthians to maintain their divisiveness over the nature of leadership within the Christ-believing community.

---

152. Gaventa, *Our Mother Saint Paul*, 14.
153. Dio Chrysostum, *Or.* 33.10.
154. Plutarch, *Adul. amic.* 69C.
155. Plutarch, *Lib. ed.* 3C–F.
156. For example, see 1 Cor 7 where there could be some cases of husbands divorcing their wives.

To Paul, the Corinthians were like children with their strife and divisions. As a result, Paul could only communicate and treat them as such and feed them with suitable food. In this respect, they needed more care and concern. The metaphor of a mother breasting a child signaled not primarily authority and correction, but care and provision.[157] The Corinthians were now left to evaluate for themselves whether they had failed to discern the implications of their divisions.

1 Cor 15:8: Paul as a Child

Closely related to Paul's use of maternal imagery is the metaphor of a child. In antiquity, children were often viewed as immature. Physically, they were considered weak and emotionally unstable. In terms of their mental faculty, they were thought to be intellectually deficient. As for their social status, they were not treated as adults and as members of society. This is the common pattern noted when Paul addressed the Corinthians as children or infants. They were described as unspiritual, people of the flesh, and not having the mind of Christ in 1 Cor 3:1–13. In other words, the Corinthians fell short of the ideal spiritual or perfect human.

Paul also applies the metaphor of a child to himself. Like maternal imagery, this metaphor has also been neglected in Pauline scholarship.[158] In 1 Cor 15:1–8, in describing himself as one of those who witnessed the post-resurrection appearance of Christ, Paul uses a very surprising and unusual imagery: one "abnormally born" (ἔκτρωμα), referring to "a birth that violates the normal period of gestation (whether induced as abortion, or natural premature birth or miscarriage... or birth beyond term)."[159] The exact meaning of this word in 1 Cor 15:8 is open to debate.

Louw and Nida recognize the problem of translating the word ἔκτρωμα. They suggest that since the context of 1 Cor 15:8 refers to the listing of people witnessing the post-resurrection appearance of Christ in which Paul comes last, the word is best understood as describing a birth beyond term,

---

157. So Aasgaard, "Paul as a Child," 144; Gaventa, *Our Mother Saint Paul*, 32–33; Collins, *First Corinthians*, 140–41,143; and Balla, *Child-Parent Relationship*, 183–84. Contra White, *Where is the Wise Man?*, 138–40, who sees Paul drawing the meaning and usage of the nursing metaphor from ancient education, and downplaying the role of a mother.

158. See Aasgaard, "Like a Child," 249–77; Aasgaard, "Paul as a Child," 129–59; MacDonald, "A Place of Belonging," 278–304; Gaventa, "Finding a Place for Children," 233–48; and Moo, "Of Parents and Children," 57–73. See also McNeel, *Paul as Infant and Nursing Mother*, 7–8.

159. BDAG, s.v.

and translated as "untimely birth" or "born at the wrong time."[160] Instead of rendering the more usual meaning "born too soon," this reading suggests that Paul is rather late in the process of conversion, compared to the rest of the Twelve. Likewise, Ciampa and Rosner also adopt this line of argument, proposing a reading of "birth beyond term" which conjures up "the image of Paul as a grotesque infant whose birth experience was far from what might normally be expected."[161] But this reading is inadequate and misses the forcefulness of the image of a baby that is abnormally born, which carries with it a rather negative connotation.

A brief study of how ἔκτρωμα is used elsewhere yields rather interesting results. Although it occurs very rarely (a hapax legomenon in the New Testament and only appearing three times in the LXX), each of its occurrences in the LXX refers to unfortunate birth or birth in unwanted circumstances. In Num 12:12, Aaron, in pleading with Moses for Miriam's leprosy, describing her situation "like one stillborn (ἔκτρωμα), whose flesh is half consumed as it comes out of its mother's womb." In Ecc 6:3, Qoheleth bewails that the person who "does not enjoy life's good things, or has no burial" is worse off than a ἔκτρωμα. Similarly, in Job 3:16, Job curses the day he was born by asking why was he not "buried like a stillborn (ἔκτρωμα), like an infant that never sees the light."

As further noted by Aasgaard, the usage of ἔκτρωμα is also rare in classical literature, and was only used in the context of abortion, miscarriage, or stillborn.[162] Miscarriage or premature birth was common in antiquity and the survival rate was low.[163] In the event of an infant that was abnormally born, the father could lift the baby up from the ground as a sign of acceptance into society, or he could expose or abandon the child.[164] Infant abandonment was not unusual in the days of Paul, as testified by Cicero and Seneca.[165]

---

160. Louw and Nida, s.v.

161. Ciampa and Rosner, *First Letter to the Corinthians*, 751.

162. See Aasgaard, "Paul as a Child," 141 note 42 where he highlights that ἔκτρωμα occurs only once in Aristotle, *Gen. an.* 4.5.18, in the sense of "abortion," and twice in Philo, *Alleg. Interp.* 1.76, in the sense of "miscarriage" or "stillborn." See also Aasgaard, "Like a Child," 249–77 and Nickelsburg, "An *Ektroma*," 198–205.

163. Rawson, *Children and Childhood*, 116–17.

164. For further discussion, see Lassen, "Roman Family," 104–5; Corbier, "Child Exposure," 58–60, and McNeel, *Paul as Infant and Nursing Mother*, 65–66.

165. See Cicero, *Leg.* 3.8.19; and Seneca, *Ira.* 1.15. Both advocated severely deformed infants be exposed.

By using ἔκτρωμα to describe himself, Paul once again prompts the Corinthians to think of someone vulnerable, weak, and socially marginal.[166] He compounds this by describing himself using two other derogatory terms in 1 Cor 15:9—as "the least of the apostles" (ὁ ἐλάχιστος τῶν ἀποστόλων) and "unfit to be called an apostle" (ἱκανὸς καλεῖσθαι ἀπόστολος).

Why would Paul adopt a derogatory description of himself by using an image of a stillborn child, ἔκτρωμα? To describe oneself in a derogatory way not once but thrice in quick succession in an honor-shame culture was nothing short of daring. But far more important is how the Corinthians heard and thought of Paul. In describing himself as ἔκτρωμα, Paul led the Corinthians to judge him as being exposed as a child that was untimely born by an earthly father, yet accepted by God, the heavenly father. In 1 Cor 15:10, Paul declares that "by the grace of God I am what I am, and his grace toward me has not been in vain." In other words, Paul was relating the grace of God to his seemingly inferior position. He turned the tables on his opponents by comparing himself to them. They came with lofty words and eloquence, and in positions of superiority, but Paul could only come in most humble status with deficiency of speech. Yet this resulted in the Corinthians accepting and believing in the message of the cross. As an infant, Paul underscores the fact that he was not capable of any hidden motives and deceit, not used to flattery to get his way, unlike his opponents. Infants were innocent, and were not in any position to manipulate others for their advantage. As such, the image of an infant is an appropriate metaphor for Paul to use in defending himself against his opponents.

By turning what was shameful to honor, and what was degradable and socially marginal to one who was accepted by God, Paul was evoking an emotional evaluation from the Corinthians as to who their real apostle was. He placed himself in a very vulnerable position, and the metaphor of an unwanted child longing for acceptance and yearning for his parents must have been striking.

By associating himself with one who was untimely born and presenting an image of an abandoned child accepted by God, Paul presses the metaphor far indeed. He chooses this metaphor not to enhance his authority but to make himself "vulnerable and subject to the mercy of his addressees."[167]

---

166. Collins, *1 Corinthians*, 537, suggests that ἔκτρωμα could also be used to describe someone whose situation is deplorable, and carries with it the meaning "monster" or "horrible thing."

167. Aasgaard, "Paul as a Child," 159. Contra Mitchell, "Reexamining the 'Aborted Apostle,'" 469–85, where he argues that Paul's use of ἔκτρωμα carries with it a sense of "abortion" from the rest of the apostles. Mitchell's reading sees Paul as one that had been cast aside and rejected in the same manner as an aborted fetus by the rest of the

In addition, Paul also risked forfeiting the respect the Corinthians had for him. He expresses himself in a paradoxical fashion, like what Aasgaard suggests, "not only on a rhetorical level but also on a social and ideological level."[168]

The Corinthians is now forced to give a careful evaluation of their apostle in comparing to his opponents. By using this metaphor, Paul creatively constructs a new reality for his role as an apostle. As an apostle, he was not held in high esteem and honor (1 Cor 4), and worked hard and paid for his labors (1 Cor 9). He was humble, weak, beaten, and became the scum of the world. The apostle shared the lowly status, the weakness, and the rejection of the stillborn infant. The question that Paul placed in front of the Corinthians is this: How would they respond? This was deliberately done in order to evoke an emotional and evaluative response from the Corinthians to consider accepting or rejecting Paul as their apostle.

1 Cor 4:1–2: Paul as a Slave Administrator

Another image that is often neglected in Paul's use of familial imagery is the role of a slave. While the use of slavery imagery has been widely discussed in Pauline scholarship,[169] its social impact within the discussion of familial language has yet to be fully explored[170] despite slaves being considered as part of the family in the Greco-Roman world.

Paul's use of οἰκονόμος appears in two significant passages in 1 Corinthians. In 1 Cor 4:1–2, Paul describes himself as οἰκονόμος, an administrator of a household.[171] The same language is also used in 1 Cor 9:17 where Paul is entrusted with οἰκονομία by God. In these passages, the οἰκονόμος/οἰκονομία metaphor is used in instances where his apostleship is being questioned and in clarifying his role, rights, and responsibilities as an apostle.

Dale Martin's treatment of οἰκονόμος metaphor is influential. He argues that the metaphor is drawn from the backdrop of managerial slavery,

---

apostles, and thus Paul needed to defend his apostolic commission. While this reading may be possible, there is no way of being certain about it.

168. Aasgaard, "Paul as a Child," 159.

169. Byron, *Slavery Metaphors*; Martin, *Slavery as Salvation*; Harrill, *Slaves in the New Testament*; Harris, *Slave of Christ*; and Tsang, *From Slaves to Sons*. See also Reumann, "Stewards of God," 339–49; and Reumann, "Oikonomia-Terms," 147–67.

170. Goodrich, *Paul as an Administrator*, 13.

171. In 1 Cor 4:1, Paul describes himself and the apostles as "ὑπηρέτας Χριστοῦ καὶ οἰκονόμους μυστηρίων θεοῦ." See Goodrich, *Paul as an Administrator*, 133–39, for an extended discussion on the use of ὑπηρέτης, and how this word ὑπηρέτης is to read in light of οἰκονόμος, occupying a servile position.

"In Christ Jesus I became Your Father" 131

where a slave was in charge of or managed a household and other household slaves.[172] In this context, Martin sees Paul's use of οἰκονόμος drawing a positive impression from those of a lower social status but frowned upon by freed persons. Although Martin's study focuses on Paul's use of οἰκονόμος in 1 Cor 9:16–23, his argument remains relevant:

> It is important to see . . . Paul has made no move toward humility or self-lowering, even though he has defined himself as a slave of Christ. He has however, redefined the categories for leadership and authority. Instead of thinking about leaders in the normal ways—as patrons, wealthy, kings those who are free and do as they will—Paul moves the debate into the common discourses of early Christianity, which talks of its leaders as slaves of Christ. Again, this is not to make Christian leaders less powerful or authoritative but to insist that the discussion be carried on in the context of Christian discourse rather than in that of the upper class or of moral philosophers. Far from giving up his authority, Paul seeks in 9:1–18 to establish it beyond question.[173]

In a recent and perhaps most extensive investigation of metaphor of οἰκονόμος, John Goodrich investigates Paul's use of this imagery by examining what it indicates about his apostolic authority and how it is employed to bring about ecclesial and ethical change.[174] Goodrich begins by examining how οἰκονόμος is used from the Hellenistic period to the early Roman period. He carefully surveys how the administrators who bore the title οἰκονόμος executed their roles in regal, civic, and private contexts.[175] He argues that Paul would most likely had in view a private administrator when he metaphorically used οἰκονόμος since he was familiar with the urban setting of the ancient world, and particularly Corinth.[176] Corinth's vibrant commercial activity and prosperity provided Paul with a familiar field from which he could have drawn his metaphor to illustrate his apostolic position.

Goodrich argues that Paul was defending himself in 1 Cor 1–4 as he perceived his authority to be under threat. As such, in describing his role as an apostle, Paul employed the imagery of an administrator subject to a higher authority (in the case of Paul, God), but possessing power and

---

172. Martin, *Slavery as Salvation*. Curiously, Martin does not consider 1 Cor 4:1–2 in his investigation. For a critique of Martin's view, see Harris, *Slaves of Christ*, 129–30; and Byron, *Slavery Metaphors*, 241–53.
173. Martin, *Slavery as Salvation*, 84.
174. Goodrich, *Paul as an Administrator*, 117–18.
175. Ibid., 27–102.
176. Ibid., 108–15.

authority over those under him (in this case, the Corinthians). Although Goodrich's conclusion on the metaphor is similar to Martin's, he takes on a slightly different interpretation of its social connotations. Goodrich remains doubtful that the role of an administrator was highly admired and honored in antiquity. By examining οἰκονόμος from a hierarchical position (including the notion of subordination, legal, and social status and authority), the responsibilities assigned, and accountability of the role, Goodrich argues that Paul used this metaphor in portraying himself and other apostles as God's οἰκονόμος. In this role, Paul occupied a position of insignificance in comparison with the principal, yet attributed to them a subordinate role allowing them to negotiate the difficult terrain of defending his apostleship. At the same time, οἰκονόμος also portrays the apostles as slaves of Christ, serving the purpose of Paul's argument. Goodrich argues:

> By casting apostles as enslaved, status-depleted subordinates, as well as divinely authorised, critically immune administrators, Paul sought to censure the Corinthians for their inappropriate, power-implicit evaluations—and thus to reaffirm his own apostolic ethos—without also providing them with additional grounds for adulating their leaders.[177]

Applied to the context in 1 Cor 9:16–23, we see a similar picture emerging but for a different purpose. Paul declares in 1 Cor 9:16–17: "If I proclaim the gospel, this gives me no ground for boasting, for an obligation is laid on me, and woe to me if I do not proclaim the gospel! For if I do this of my own will, I have a reward; but if not of my own will, I am entrusted with a commission (οἰκονομίαν)." Here, Paul explained why he had the right to receive financial support but gave it up in order to preach the gospel without pay but at great personal cost. Paul's reward in lieu of pay was to deliver (τίθημι) the gospel free of charge (1 Cor 9:18) in order to gain (κερδαίνω) converts (1 Cor 9:19). It is interesting to note that both delivering the gospel and gaining converts are described in commercial language.[178] The emphasis here is that this metaphor of a slave administrator is used to emphasize the servility and humility of the apostle to counter the divisions in the church. Paul was unlike those who peddle God's word for selfish gain (2 Cor 2:17). Instead, he enslaved himself to the Corinthians by giving up his rights, power and authority for the sake of others, and for the sake of winning others for Christ. This attitude was no different from that of his master, Christ, as seen in 2 Cor 8:9 (cf. Phil 2:6–11).

---

177. Ibid., 163–64.
178. Ibid., 188–95.

FAMILIAL METAPHORS AND SOCIAL IDENTITY FORMATION

Paul's use of familial metaphors is more nuanced and varied than has been previously recognized, as demonstrated in this chapter. He takes on many roles—*paterfamilias*, nursing mother, stillborn child, and slave, all within the context of a typical Roman family—in negotiating his discourse with the Corinthians. Although a predominant function of Roman familial metaphors was to evoke images of authority—authority of gods over humans, state officials over subjects, and master over slaves,[179] Paul's use of these metaphors goes beyond that. While Paul follows the Greco-Roman convention of his day of using metaphors to communicate, he maneuvers them creatively and imaginatively to introduce new dimensions in social identity formation of the Christ-followers where the focus on the cognitive dimension is strengthened, the emotive dimension is emphasized, and the evaluative dimension is reinforced, to compel the Corinthians to evaluate their identity in Christ and move them to act accordingly.

Cognitive Dimension

Roger Keesing argues that in social groups, kin terms are used rarely and only in situations when the norms of kinship are violated.[180] Keesing's insight provides interesting lenses through which to read Paul's use of familial metaphors, more so as the Corinthian letters contain the most frequent usage within the Pauline corpus. This frequent use corresponds to the deep concern Paul had for the Corinthians because of the various conflicts and divisions in the family. Paul uses the image of *paterfamilias* in exercising his *patria protestas* to ensure that the household members submit themselves to the family norms in order to maintain concord and harmony. Paul conforms to patriarchal patterns in depicting the Corinthians as children who are in a position inferior to himself. He imposes on them the need to obey and imitate him. Using his authority as *paterfamilias*, he also rebukes them when family norms have been violated. What emerges is an image or a father whose role is one of instruction, encouragement, and reinforcement rather than one who is authoritative, powerful, or punitive as one might assume from true patriarchy. He is a father who cares for and is attentive to the needs of his children. In light of this, the family is built less around

---

179. Lassen, "Roman Family," 114.
180. Keesing, *Kin Groups*, 126.

the father's authority than around the father's teaching and nurturing.[181] He underscores cohesiveness in the family of Christ, a family with a nurturing environment that promotes growth towards maturity. At the same time, family honor that is central to kinship must also be defended. In light of this, Paul uses familial metaphor in exhorting how members of the Corinthian family should behave towards one another where divisions and strife bring dishonor and shame to the family.[182] Furthermore, refusing to listen to the instructions of the father is an act of shame. Paul defines norms and values that lead to what are acceptable and unacceptable actions, behaviors and attitudes for group members. Norms help members to enhance and maintain cohesiveness within the group, and at the same time define the boundaries that set them apart from outsiders.

Emotive Dimension

It is surprising that in the use of familial imagery, Paul does not, considering the situation he was addressing, place greater emphasis on his apostolic power. In a context where power is clearly seen as contesting, and where stronger apostolic statements might be helpful for strengthening his grip on power, we see Paul speaking of himself in a rather derogatory manner. He describes himself as a stillborn, an image that would have invited shock, shame, and even scorn from his hearers. Here, Paul places himself in a vulnerable position. In using familial language to reaffirm commonly held group assumptions, especially when the communities were falling short of the Mediterranean family ideal of social solidarity, Paul showed himself as willing to relinquish his power to reflect his master, Christ, who gave up everything for the sake of others.

Seen in this way, Paul's call to imitation is not merely a discourse of power, but a discourse of weakness as well. He is not to be identified with the strong, noble, and wealthy, but with the refuse and the scum of the earth. Paul identifies with the margins of the Corinthians, who probably suffered the most in this family as they potentially may have been ostracized. Here, Paul redefines the social identity of the church which is to be characterized by caring for the weak, thus going against the prevailing social convention of his day where the strong and powerful were honored and glorified. Ultimately, Paul's use of metaphors was to move the Corinthians to behavioral changes so they could live out the reality of the family relationship in the

---

181. See Bossman, "Paul's Fictive Kinship Movement," 163–71, especially 165.

182. Esler, "Family Imagery," 121–49.

ἐκκλησία as a true family of Christ under God with Paul as their founder and apostle.

Evaluative Dimension

Within the ancient Mediterranean world, kinship is the dominant institution and the basic social distinction is that between kin and non-kin.[183] Distrust of non-kin is also a prominent characteristic within group-oriented culture. The defection of members from ingroup to outgroup remains a possibility especially when members of the ingroup feel disadvantaged in relation to other groups. In addition, obstacles in providing its members with positive social identity may also result in members abandoning one group and moving to another. This threat of social mobility was real in Corinth with Paul's opponents luring the Christ-followers away from their allegiance to Paul. Finally, the lack of a family environment may also have contributed to the possibility of defection, as demonstrated by Karl O. Sandnes, especially if the fictive family was full of strife that not only threatened the ideal familial environment, but also weakened the social relations and sense of belonging.[184] Worse, the accusation of Paul as an absentee father further painted a picture of a missing *paterfamilias* who failed to care for the welfare of the family.

Paul used familial metaphors examined in this chapter to address these issues. One common feature of social comparison is to stereotype outgroups in a negative manner and provide positive stereotype to members of the ingroup. Paul's language of separation is evident throughout the letter—the pagans, the world, those outside, the unrighteous, the immoral, unbelievers, idolaters—such language was used to reinforce the Corinthians' solidarity and sense of belonging to a new community. These were people not within the circles of a family and as such, the Corinthians had no common ground and no business with these outgroups. The Corinthians were exhorted to think about themselves and see themselves differently. Hence, the familial imagery worked strategically for Paul to affect a positive re-evaluation of the ingroup in comparison with the outgroups.

These metaphors were used without diminishing the hierarchical dimension of Paul's apostleship. He remained the founder, the apostle of the community. Even in moments of his weakness, suffering, and failure, he was also endowed with power and authority—and that power is intimately bounded with the shared values of the gospel, and not the prevailing social

---

183. For further discussion, see Esler, "Keeping It in the Family," 145–84.

184. See Sandnes, *A New Family*.

convention that the Corinthians remained so deeply rooted in. Paul was not working according to how power was defined, but consistently sought to redefine power according to the framework of the gospel. This was the very identity formation that Paul wanted the Corinthians to embrace. His desire was for a maturing community, a community whose social identity was firmly rooted in Christ.

SUMMARY

Paul uses the whole range of familial metaphors in addressing the Corinthians. As a father, he is associated with instruction and discipline. As a nursing mother, he loves, cares, and nurtures his children. As an infant, he is innocent and without any motive to harm them. As a slave, he is humble in carrying out the task assigned for him. Here, Paul uses the familial imagery that is authoritative, yet filled with intimacy, nurture and love, implying he would do anything for the Corinthians to shape and build them. It also demonstrates that Paul speaks as an insider, as their father, mother, child, and slave. He is not an outsider or stranger to them. Taken together, we see a range of emotions Paul displays towards the Corinthians.

Therefore, the familial image is a very powerful metaphor evoking the bonds of affection that not only Paul has for the Corinthians but also the ties that bind the members of the community together as a family where togetherness, goodwill, interdependence, friendship, protection, provision, honor, respect, love, kinship, and glory are among the values that come to mind when one think of family relationship, and these values must be upheld within the family. For Paul, this family is the body of Christ who is the head, another image I will examine in chapter 6, and this family ultimately belongs to God. Any attempts to destroy this family would only bring dishonor to God.

5

"You are God's Temple"
Temple Metaphor[1]

LIVING UNDER THE SHADOW OF THE TEMPLES

THE CITY OF ROMAN Corinth in the days of Paul was a center for cultic worship graphically attested to by its many magnificent and imposing temples, statues, and shrines dedicated to both Greek and Roman gods such as Apollo, Athena, Tyche, Aphrodite, Pantheon, Demerter, Kore, Dionysus, Asklepios, Venus, Octavia, and Poseidon. Pausanias referred to at least twenty four sanctuaries and temples found in Corinth.[2] In addition, there were also temples dedicated to the Roman imperial cult and the Egyptian cults of Isis and Sarapis. Such juxtaposition not only clearly defined the varieties of deities that were well represented but also the extent to which religion penetrated the fabric of life in Corinth. The strong religious attitudes of Corinth were reflected in coins, terracotta and marbles statues,

---

1. Some of the materials in this chapter have been previously published in an essay titled, "Paul's Use of Temple Imagery in the Corinthian Correspondence," 189–205.

2. See Pausanias, *Descr.* Book II on Corinth. For further discussion, see Engels, *Roman Corinth*, 92–120; Lanci, *A New Temple for Corinth*, 25–43, 89–113; Bookidis, "The Sanctuaries of Corinth," 247–59; Schowalter and Friesen, *Urban Religion in Roman Corinth*, in particular the article by Bookidis, "Religion in Corinth," 141–64; Coutsoumpos, *Paul and the Lord`s Supper*, 171–80; Coutsoumpos, "Paul, the Cults in Corinth," 171–80; and Liu, *Temple Purity in 1–2 Corinthians*, 70–105. On textual and archaeological evidence on social, political, and religious activities in Corinth, consult Murphy-O'Connor, *St. Paul's Corinth*.

mosaic flooring, and other daily household wares.³ When travelers arrived in Corinth from the port of Cenchreae or left the city to head west to Sicyon, they would be greeted by the temples of Aphrodite and Isis and the temple of Apollo respectively. As such, the Corinthians literally lived continually in the shadow of the temples with the smell of fragrant offerings wafting out of these places of worship. Paul was keenly aware of this, having stayed there for more than a year (cf. Acts 18:11).

Much of life in Corinth centered on the temples and their associated activities. Apart from being places of worship, temples were also centers for social activities, providing platform for expanding one's social network. Therefore, encounters or participation in activities within the temples and shrines in Corinth were almost unavoidable for the Christ-followers. As noted by Garland: "If Christians took part in civic life, they would have been expected to participate in festivals which included sacrificial meals in some form or another."⁴ This is evident from Paul's extensive discussion related to pagan cultic practice in the canonical letters to the Corinthians.⁵ In 1 Cor 8–10, Paul deals with the issue of consuming food sacrificed to idols both in the temple precincts (1 Cor 8:7–11; 10:14–17) and in private homes (1 Cor 10:27–30). Since meat sold in the meat market or *macellum* had already been sacrificed to idols, consuming such meat is almost unavoidable (1 Cor 10:25).⁶ Paul may have also dealt with some of the Christ-followers participating in temple prostitution in 1 Cor 6:12–20.⁷ In addition, Paul's reference to the body imagery in 1 Cor 12:12–26 is most likely drawn from the prevailing practices of offering terra cotta replicas of the parts of the body healed by Asklepios in the temple.⁸

From his correspondence with the Corinthians, it is evident that many of the issues that Paul dealt with the Christ-community arose not because

---

3. For images of some of these statues now housed in the Corinth Museum at ancient Corinth, see Papahatzis, *Ancient Corinth*, 88–97.

4. Garland, *1 Corinthians*, 347.

5. Apart from addressing and appealing to the Greco-Roman cultic practices, Paul also alluded to Jewish cultic imagery as reflected in 1 Cor 5:6–8; 9:1–14; 10:14–22, amongst others. See Lim, *Sufferings of Christ*, 64–96 for further treatment on the use of cultic imagery in 2 Cor 2:14–16.

6. See Murphy O'Connor, *St. Paul's Corinth*, 186–91; Willis, *Idol Meat in Corinth*, 13–15; and Coutsoumpos, *Paul and the Lord's Supper*, 9–37. For further treatment on the issue of food sacrificed to idols, see Newton, *Deity and Diet*; Cheung, *Idol Food in Corinth*; Winter, *After Paul Left Corinth*, 269–301; Fotopoulos, *Food Offered to Idols*; and Shen, *Canaan to Corinth*.

7. See Rosner, "Temple Prostitution," 336–51.

8. See Hill, "The Temple of Asclepius," 437–39; and Murphy O'Connor, *St. Paul's Corinth*, 186–91. For further discussion, see chapter 6 on Paul's use of body metaphor.

this community existed in the pagan world but that too much of the pagan values and practices from the members' former religious beliefs were carried over and practiced in this new found community in Christ.[9] As rightly argued by Winter, these problems arose partly because the Christ-followers, as citizens of Roman Corinth, "had grown up in, and imbibed that culture" and they reacted to some of these issues "on the basis of the learnt conventions and cultural mores of Corinthian *Romanitas.*"[10] If the Corinthians were so rooted in the Greco-Roman convention and cultural norms, how would Paul shape the social identity and values of the Christ-followers so that they were aligned to the message of the gospel of Christ that was proclaimed to them (cf. 1 Cor 1:17—2:5), and being transformed in their symbolic universe as a result of their new status in Christ? If Paul were concerned about establishing an alternative assembly in Corinth,[11] how would he address his audience?

In this chapter, I will be examining temple imagery used by Paul in the Corinthian correspondence. If one were to live in such an environment where temple worship and rituals were closely associated with one's symbolic universe, culture, and existence, and where its activities were clear demonstration of one's social network and participation in the communal life, how would one, who used to be a part of this social and cultural background but was now a member of the Christ-community, have reacted and responded when the following words were heard:

> Do you not know that you are God's temple and that God's Spirit dwells in you? If anyone destroys God's temple, God will destroy that person. For God's temple is holy, and you are that temple (1 Cor 3:16–17).

> Or do you not know that your body is a temple of the Holy Spirit within you, which you have from God, and that you are not your own? (1 Cor 6:19).

> What agreement has the temple of God with idols? For we are the temple of the living God (2 Cor 6:16).

---

9. See Winter, *After Paul Left Corinth*, 27–28.

10. Ibid., 27. See also Tucker, *You belong to Christ*, 152–80, who argues that the Corinthians were continuing to identify primarily with key aspects of their Roman social identity rather than their salient "in Christ" social identity. As a result, this confusion over identity positions contributed to the problems within the community.

11. For the argument that Paul seeks to realign the identity hierarchy of the Corinthians that was grounded in the Greco-Roman convention to one that is rooted in Christ, see Tucker, *You Belong to Christ*. Cf. Horsley, "Paul's Assembly in Corinth," 369–95.

Would temple imagery recall the Christ-followers' understanding of their previous cultic activities and participation in one of the many temple festivals? Would the use of temple imagery cause them to pause and reflect on their current status in Christ? What function did the temple imagery that once represented the powerful expression of one's former symbolic universe and existence played in the social identity formation of this fledging community of Christ-followers? How would the use of temple imagery create the maximum impact desired by Paul in communicating the truth of the gospel? These are the questions I will attempt to answer in this chapter.

PAUL'S USE OF TEMPLE METAPHOR IN THE CORINTHIAN LETTERS

In both the Corinthian letters, Paul uses the word, ναός, usually translated as "temple," a total of six times: 1 Cor 3:16, 17 (twice); 6:19 and 2 Cor 6:16 (twice). Commentators frequently emphasize that Paul chooses ναός over ἱερόν and highlight the semantic differences between these two words, with the former denoting the dwelling place of deities and the latter a reference to the entire temple precinct.[12] Support for this argument is often drawn from the usage of these words in the Gospels where ναός is used to refer to the Holy of Holies while ἱερόν the entire temple precinct. Further argument is made that this distinction is also maintained in the LXX. The problem with such a view is that it presumes a very neatly and tightly defined meaning for both ναός and ἱερόν.[13] This may not always be the case. An example can be seen in Matt 27:5 where Judas threw the 30 pieces of silver into the ναός, which certainly refers to the temple precinct and not the Holy of Holies to which he had no access.[14] Hence, whether Paul narrowly had in mind the Holy of Holies of the Jerusalem Temple when he used the word ναός in the Corinthians is difficult to sustain.[15] On the other hand, one cannot discount

---

12. For example, see Robertson and Plummer, *First Epistle of St. Paul to the Corinthians*, 66; Fee, *First Epistle to the Corinthians*, 158; Thiselton, *First Epistle to the Corinthians*, 315; and Konsmo, *Pauline Metaphors*, 118.

13. This has been pointed out by Lanci, *A New Temple for Corinth*, 91–93. Cf. Levison, "Spirit and the Temple," 191n5.

14. Cf. O. Michael, *TDNT* 4:884. Note also that in Josephus, *Ag. Ap.* 2.119 and *J. W.* 5.207, ναός and ἱερόν are used interchangeably. See also the use of ναός in John 2:20 that most likely refers to the entire temple precinct rather that the Holy of Holies.

15. As noted in Fee, *First Epistle to the Corinthians*, 158n423, where he admits that the distinctions between the two words, ναός and ἱερόν, "do not necessarily hold in all the Greek and NT period." However, Fee maintains the distinction in semantic differences in his argument. For further discussion, see Gupta, *Worship that Makes Sense*,

completely that ναός could also refer to one of the numerous Greco-Roman temples or shrines found scattering in the city of Corinth. As such, it is best not to assume that when Paul speaks of the community as ναός, the only sole referent is the Jerusalem Temple.

The first temple metaphor appears in 1 Cor 3:16–17 where Paul declares: "Do you not know that you are God's temple and that God's Spirit dwells in you? If anyone destroys God's temple, God will destroy that person. For God's temple is holy, and you are that temple."

The stern warning against destroying God's temple comes in the midst of a larger rhetorical unit of 1 Cor 1–4 where Paul deals with the issue of dissentions within the community over the nature of leadership as reported to him by Chloe's household (1 Cor 1:10–12), as I suggested in chapter 3. In this context, the Christ-followers are metaphorically referred to as God's temple indwelt by the Holy Spirit. Significantly, this temple imagery is used not to address individual or sub-groups, but the entire community as underscored by the frequent use of second person plural pronouns and verbal forms in 1 Cor 3:16–17. It is also interesting to note that earlier on in 1 Cor 3:5–23, Paul uses a series of metaphors in his address to the Corinthians. In 1 Cor 3:5–9a, Paul describes the Corinthians as God's field where he and his co-workers were laborers in this field. Then in 1 Cor 3:9b–15, Paul shifts the imagery to describe the Corinthians as God's building. As a master builder, Paul laid the foundation, Jesus Christ, upon which the entire building was built. Paul also warns that one must take great care in how one builds. If one is a negligent worker where inappropriate materials are used in the construction, the building will be destroyed, and thus endangering the work of God in the Christ-community in Corinth.[16] Taken together, these two agricultural and building metaphors emphasize the notion of Paul as the apostle responsible for building up the Corinthians. The building metaphor progresses further in 1 Cor 3:16–17 where Paul brings his argument to a climax by declaring that this building that he had laboriously worked for is the very temple of God, a dwelling place of God.[17]

Moving on to 1 Cor 6:19, Paul once again employs temple metaphor: "Or do you not know that your body is a temple of the Holy Spirit within you, which you have from God, and that you are not your own?" In this context, Paul deals with the issue of sexual immorality (πορνεία). By declaring that the Christ-community is the temple of the Holy Spirit, Paul once

---

65–66.

16. On temple construction in Greco-Roman world and in Roman Corinth, see Bitner, *Paul's Political Strategy*, 212–42.

17. Gupta, *Worhsip that Makes Sense*, 67.

again emphasizes that their behavior should reflect that of their new status in Christ and be consistent with the presence of God indwelling within them.[18]

The temple metaphor appears for the third time in 2 Cor 6:16: "What agreement has the temple of God with idols? For we are the temple of the living God." This metaphor appears in one of the most debated controversial pericopes in the Corinthian correspondence where its authenticity and integrity have been questioned.[19] In addition, this pericope is surrounded by a host of interpretive issues.[20] As a result, the use of temple imagery has been somewhat marginalized in the interpretation of this passage. Whether 2 Cor 6:14—7:1 is a later interpolation or not does not minimize the forceful impact of the use of temple imagery within this self-contained pericope. In this passage, Paul exhorts the Corinthians to live up to their status as the temple of God by drawing clear social boundaries that demarcated their relationship with those outside the community, as reflected in the initial statement in 2 Cor 6:14: "Do not be mismatched with unbelievers" (Μὴ γίνεσθε ἑτεροζυγοῦντες ἀπίστοις).

CHRIST-COMMUNITY AS TEMPLE REPLACEMENT?

It seems that one of the primary motivations for claiming the semantic distinction in the usage of ναός and ἱερόν as highlighted earlier is to advance the understanding of temple-replacement theology. This is seen in Bertil Gärtner's work where he argues that the reason ναός is chosen over ἱερόν is because Paul had in mind that the *Shekinah* presence of God no longer

---

18. Fee, *First Epistle to the Corinthians*, 277, argues that Paul applies the temple imagery to individual believers and not the entire community, as reflected in the pairing of a singular noun and a plural genitive pronoun (τὸ σῶμα ὑμῶν) in 1 Cor 6:19. So Fitzmyer, *First Corinthians*, 269–70. However, this argument may not be that strong if the entire context is taken into consideration. While Paul may have some of the individuals in mind in 1 Cor 6:12–20, his ultimate concern was the entire community, as the actions of each member affected the larger community. See also Kempthorne, "Incest and the Body of Christ," 568–74; Newton, *Concept of Purity*, 56–57; de Lacey, "οἵτινές ἐστε ὑμεῖς," 401–09; Mitchell, *Paul and the Rhetoric of Reconciliation*, 119. See also Gupta, "Whose Body Was a Temple?," 518–36; and Wardle, *Jerusalem Temple*, 218–20.

19. For a survey of scholarship on the integrity and authenticity of 2 Cor 6:14—7:1, see Thrall, *Second Epistle to the Corinthians*, 1:3–49; and Adewuya, *Holiness and Community*, 13–43. See also Nathan, "Fragmented Theology," 211–28. For bibliography, see Lim, *Sufferings of Christ*, 28–29.

20. See Thrall, *Second Epistle to the Corinthians*, 1:25–36. For further discussion, see Harris, *Second Epistle to the Corinthians*, 14–25; Furnish, *II Corinthians*, 375–83.

rested on the Jerusalem Temple but "has been removed to the Church"[21] in Corinth that now constitutes "the true Temple."[22] Similarly, Michael Newton, by comparing the notion of purity in the Qumran and Pauline community, argues that Paul's use of the idea of purity centers upon the view that "the believers constitutes the Temple of God and as such enjoy the presence of God in their midst."[23] In light of this, those who enter this community must observe the standards of purity, distinguishing between the sacred and the profane, the pure and the impure, in order to retain the presence of God. Newton further argues that the priestly office and the accompanying purity regulations of Jerusalem Temple have also been replaced "by those who are ministers of Christ Jesus in proclaiming the Gospel . . . (and) the offering of the faith of converted believers"[24] respectively. Like Gärtner, Newton also insists that Paul's choice of ναός instead of ἱερόν is significant in support for the temple-replacement theology.[25]

In his work, *The New Temple: The Church in the New Testament*, R. J. McKelvey adopts a biblical theology approach and begins his study by examining the significance of the temple in the Old Testament and Jewish and Greek literature.[26] For McKelvey, the eschatological non-literal, spiritual temple "made without hands has displaced the temple made with hands"[27] where "the temple of Jerusalem surrendered its redemptive significance to Christ and his church and thereby dropped out of the plan of God."[28] According to McKelvey, this temple-replacement theology takes on its full development in texts like 1 Cor 3:16–17; 6:19; 2 Cor 6:16—7:1; Eph 2:20–22; 2 Cor 5:1–5; 1 Pet 4:17; 1 Tim 3:15; and numerous texts in Revelation, amongst others.[29] In light of this development, McKelvey argues that the new temple comprising the church is the final fulfillment of God's

---

21. Gärtner, *Temple*, 58.

22. Ibid., 57. Gärtner also further argues that the evidence that supports the Church as the true Temple is the presence of the Spirit dwelling among Christians now, unlike the past where the Spirit dwelt among the Israelites in the tabernacle and temple (58). See his wider argument in 49–60.

23. Newton, *Concept of Purity*, 52. See also his discussion in 10–51.

24. Ibid., 62. See his wider discussion in 60–70.

25. Ibid., 53–59.

26. McKelvey, *New Temple*.

27. Ibid., 74.

28. Ibid., 75. See also his discussion in 75–91.

29. See ibid., 92–178.

promises made by the prophets.[30] As such, sacrifices in this new temple take on an ethical form reflected in Christian service.[31]

In his work on the biblical theology of the temple, Greg Beale traces the development of the notion of temple from both the Old and New Testaments.[32] Beale demonstrates that the Old Testament never called for a new temple to be built. In fact, Beale argues that the "the Old Testament tabernacle and temples were symbolically designed to point to the cosmic eschatological reality that God's tabernacling presence, formerly limited to the holy of holies, was to be extended throughout the whole earth."[33] For Beale, the physical temple is to disappear only to be replaced by a literal nonphysical temple, the Church, which is "fulfillment of the end-time temple prophesied in the Old Testament."[34] In his examination of the cultic imagery in the Corinthian letters, Beale argues that "Paul thinks the faithful Corinthians are part of the final end-time temple that will withstand the fiery storm winds of the last judgment."[35] In 2 Cor 6:14—7:2, Beale argues that Paul's allusions to the Old Testament texts are drawn from texts that predict a future temple, and that Paul sees Christians "*are* the beginning fulfillment of the actual prophecy of the end-time temple."[36] In light of this, Beale sees Christ and the church as having done what Israel failed to do in extending the temple of God's presence throughout the world.

Tim Wardle is more nuanced than those who argue for the Christian community as temple replacement. For Wardle, the issue is not so much the legitimacy of the Jerusalem Temple but the worthiness of the priesthood charged with the administration of the Temple. He argues that the use of temple imagery should be read against the backdrop of conflict, dispute, and critique against the priestly overseers of the Jerusalem Temple, resulting in the construction of alternative temples as seen in examples of the Samaritans and the temple on Mount Gerizim, the Oniad Temple at Leontopolis, and the idea of a communal temple identity at Qumran. He further argues that the Christian community should be seen as the fourth community who also established a new, eschatological temple as a way to register their dissent against the Jerusalem Temple.[37] The impulse to construct an alternative

30. Ibid., 180.
31. Ibid., 183–87.
32. Beale, *Temple*.
33. Ibid., 25.
34. Ibid., 253. See also his exposition in 253–59.
35. Ibid., 251.
36. Ibid., 254, emphasis his. See also his wider exposition in 253–59.
37. Wardle, *Jerusalem Temple*.

temple and the way Pauline community uses this metaphor contributed to the formation of the social identity of the early Christians.[38] According to Wardle, a significant part of this new temple is "the startling claim that Gentiles could now enter this new community and become integral components of the true temple of the God of Israel."[39] This creation of alternative temples brought with them the expectation that the God of Israel who was present in the Temple in Jerusalem is now present in the community in the same way. It is only after the destruction of the Jerusalem Temple in 70 CE that the idea of the Christian community as a new temple lived on.

From this brief survey, there appears to be an overwhelming support for the understanding that Paul's use of temple imagery is rooted in the notion that the church has now replaced the Jerusalem Temple.[40] The primary assumption is that the sole reference point for Paul's use of temple imagery is rooted in his Jewish eschatological understanding and association with the Jerusalem Temple cult. As McKelvey clearly puts it, Paul, as an "orthodox Jew by upbringing . . . did not and could not think of many temples, but of one."[41]

Lanci has rightly taken issue with this problematic reading by suggesting that the Jewish temple cult also bears several resemblances to gentile cultic practices, and often, it is difficult to determine whether Paul is specifically referring to Jewish or gentile religious traditions.[42] This is further supported by Malina: "The Corinthians need not be concerned about the Jerusalem Temple or pilgrimage or whatever is bound up with Israelite Temple worship, since what that temple offers can be experienced in their gathering."[43] Furthermore, while comparative studies between Paul's use of temple imagery and wider temple theology in the Old Testament, contemporary Judaism, and Qumran scrolls may have yielded significant results, they unfortunately reduce the temple imagery into a survey of parallels or

38. Ibid., 225.

39. Ibid., 223.

40. This reading also finds wide support in a number of commentaries. For example, Snyder, *First Corinthians*, 41–42, argues that "the faith community has now replaced the Jewish temple . . . the movement from Jewish temple to Christian faith community became an absolute necessity for the first Christians." See also Konsmo, *Pauline Metaphors*, 120, who contends that "the believing community as the Temple of God has now replaced the Temple in Jerusalem." Similarly, Plummer, *Second Epistle of St. Paul to the Corinthians*, 208; and Martin, *2 Corinthians*, 366.

41. McKelvey, *New Temple*, 106.

42. For a brief survey of scholarship that challenges the notion of temple replacement theology, see Lanci, *A New Temple for Corinth*, 7–23, especially 11–13. See also Hogeterp, *Paul and God's Temple*, 271–378.

43. Malina and Pilch, *Social Science Commentary*, 75.

connection of ideas through usage of certain catch words.[44] In addition, attempts to explain the use of temple imagery from a biblical theology approach often fail to take into account the context of the passage and what the use of temple imagery would have meant to Paul's audience who were predominantly gentiles, leaving the significance of such temple imagery grossly undervalued in the minds of the recipients. Furthermore, one must not forget that the Temple of Jerusalem was still standing at the time of writing the Corinthian letters and any notion of temple replacement would probably have been quite alien to Paul.[45] For useful means of communication and for the full force of the metaphor to be felt, it is crucial that both the author using the imagery and recipients reading or hearing it should be able to give such imagery the same content. But if discrepancy in understanding the metaphor occurs, then both parties might be speaking in two different languages. As such, it is essential that in using temple metaphor, Paul would have to ensure that it conveys the message that is not only clear to the predominant gentile Christ-community but also one that they are able to readily identify with.

The power of metaphor lies not only in the mind of the author but also how the audience understands and interprets the imagery within their symbolic universe. A large majority of the Christ-community in Corinth not only originated from a pagan background, but continued to live in an environment where temple architecture and buildings still greeted its members daily. Furthermore, participation in temple worship and related activities continued to be part of their lifestyle, as highlighted earlier (see 1 Cor 8:1—11:1). This clearly establishes that the symbolic universe of the Christ-community remained aligned and associated to the pagan temples. While Paul did allude to the Jewish cultic practices elsewhere in the Corinthian letters,[46] it is not unlikely Paul would have used an imagery that resonated well with the gentile believers. Hence, it is reasonable to assume that any mention of "God's temple" would naturally conjure up the reality that was closest and most familiar to the gentile Christ-followers. This reality was almost certainly the pagan temples, such as those found along the Lechaion Road or one of the many shrines in the agora in Corinth, and not the Jerusalem Temple that was far removed from their reality. As such, an understanding of temple-replacement theology operative in the mind of the gentile believers living under the shadow of the pagan temples would not only appear to be odd but also remote.

44. This is seen prominently in Beale, *Temple*.
45. Nathan, "Fragmented Theology," 225.
46. For example, see 1 Cor 5:7–8; 9:13; 10:18.

However, the following questions remain. What did Paul hope to achieve by using the temple imagery in addressing the problems within the Corinthian community? If temples in the Greco-Roman world were seen as powerful symbols and expression of the identity of the adherents, what role did the temple imagery play in the formation of Christian identity and the transformation of the Christ-followers in light of the truth of the gospel of Christ?

PAUL'S USE OF TEMPLE METAPHOR IN THE FORMATION OF SOCIAL IDENTITY

I will examine the social identity process primarily involving three dimensions in establishing the ethos, values, status, and boundaries for a particular group as against other groups in a society—the cognitive, emotional and evaluative dimensions. As I reviewed earlier in chapter 2, the cognitive dimension provides the group members with a strong sense of belonging and distinctiveness as compared to other groups. The emotional dimension brings various rituals and practices to enhance the emotional ties ingroup dynamics to establish a strong sense of solidarity, identity, and belonging to the group. The evaluative dimension deals with how the members within the group rate themselves in relation to other groups.

Cognitive Dimension: Temple as Unifying Symbol

In the first use of the temple imagery in 1 Cor 3:16–17, Paul begins with a rhetorical question: Οὐκ οἴδατε ὅτι ναὸς θεοῦ ἐστε καὶ τὸ πνεῦμα τοῦ θεοῦ οἰκεῖ ἐν ὑμῖν.[47] Interestingly, similar construction is also found in 1 Cor 6:16 where temple imagery appears for the second time: οὐκ οἴδατε ὅτι ὁ κολλώμενος τῇ πόρνῃ ἓν σῶμά ἐστιν. William Wuellner suggests that rhetorical questions beginning with οὐκ οἴδατε function to increase adherence to what is already accepted in the community.[48] If Wuellner is right, then it strongly suggests that Paul's use of temple imagery here is of utmost significance and importance. By using the οὐκ οἴδατε construction, Paul was not advocating a new teaching nor reiterating anything that the Corinthians

---

47. This is the first in a series of ten rhetorical questions in 1 Corinthians that begins with οὐκ οἴδατε. See 1 Cor 5:6; 6:2, 3, 9, 15, 16, 19; 9:13, 24. Apart from 1 Corinthians, οὐκ οἴδατε only appears once elsewhere in the Pauline corpus in Romans 6:16.

48. Wuellner, "Paul as Pastor," 60. Cf. Collins, "Constructing A Metaphor," 205, who suggests that the using of οὐκ οἴδατε implies that the Corinthians may have consciously or sub-consciously forgotten or neglected that they were God's temple.

were not aware of. On the contrary, he was reinforcing what they already knew—that they were God's temple. At the same time, the οὐκ οἴδατε construction may also imply a rebuke for their failure to comprehend this truth.[49] As such, temple imagery is not simply a convenient rhetorical device that Paul employs; instead, it is a deliberate and calculated attempt to reinforce the truth of the gospel by appealing to the religious reality that the Corinthians believers were familiar with and the importance of which in their existence cannot be denied.

Considered to be center of the universe or icons of the world, temples in the Greco-Roman world were central to the life and experience of the city dwellers. Pausanias referred to the sanctuary of Apollos at Dephi as the *Omphalos* or navel of the world.[50] Livy described the Capitol in Rome as the stronghold of the Roman Empire and the head of the world.[51] Tacitus further described the Capitol as a temple that was founded as the symbol of imperial greatness and its origin, building and dedication were considered as part of the Roman heritage.[52] The Parthenon in Athens, the temple of Zeus in Olympia, the temple of Apollos in Delphi, and the temple of Artemis in Ephesus testified to the centrality of the temple in the civic life of the Greco-Roman world.

Temples typically occupied prominent and often elevated ground in the most strategic location of the city. The structures were very elaborate and imposing, and were buildings that first greeted the eyes of visitors making their travel or pilgrimage to the cities.[53] Apart from being places of dwelling for the deities[54] and for cultic activities, temples also played significant roles in the communal development of the society where they functioned as meeting and dining places for social gatherings. They also offered a resting place for weary travelers. Temples also made major contribution to the economic growth and prosperity of cities.[55] Apart from the cultic, social and economic functions, the Roman Empire also added another dimension

---

49. Robertson and Plummer, *First Epistle of St. Paul to the Corinthians*, 66.

50. Pausanias, *Descr.* 10.16.3. Interestingly, Jerusalem was also considered as the navel of the country for the Jews. See Josephus, *J. W.* 3.52.

51. Livy, *History of Rome* 1.55.5–6.

52. Tacitus, *Hist.* 3.72.

53. For discussion on architecture for temples in ancient Greek, see Pedley, *Sanctuaries and the Sacred*, 57–77. See also Orlin, *Temples*.

54. For Greek understanding that temple functioned as the house of God, see Burkert, "Meaning and Function," 29–31.

55. Acts 19:8–41 portrays the temple of Artemis as representing the wealth, power, status, and influence within the community and the wider world. It was also the economic engine that supported the city's wealth and employment (Acts 19:23–25).

to the function of the temples, those that were officially sanctioned serving to advance the political propaganda of the Empire.[56]

Participation in temple rites not only cemented the relationship between the deities and the adherents, but also served to bind all classes of the city together.[57] In Corinth, the temple of Aphrodite played a very significant role in the civic life and identity of the city (throughout the classical period, the city of Corinth, for example, was known as Aphrodite's city).[58] Her temple became one of the motifs found on the Roman Corinthians coins.[59] As such, temples not only defined the existence of the community but also symbolized that community's unity. Each of these temples functioned as a "vehicle for promoting central systems of values which served to hold ancient societies together."[60] Therefore, temples—and not palaces, town halls, commercial buildings—were the most important structures, defined the identity of the city and were a major source of pride in civic society.

Paul's use of temple imagery is not merely a serious reminder to the Corinthians about the importance of temples in their symbolic universe, it also constitutes nothing less than a frontal critique of their failure to appreciate and comprehend what a temple should be and all that it represents. Rather than appropriating the unifying presence of Christ to bind them together as a powerful and attractive icon to the immediate society and beyond, where the values aligned to the gospel of Christ could be promoted, the Corinthians had allowed their dissentions to create divisive provincialism and dire damage to the temple of God. Instead of building up the temple of God that would have defined their identity in Christ, they were heading in the opposite direction by destroying the temple. In Paul's eyes, these acts of causing dissentions were not merely casual, but criminal.[61] In failing to remember the symbolism of temples, the severe penalty that corresponded with the seriousness of the crime awaited them: God would destroy those who destroyed his temple (1 Cor 3:17).

---

56. For further discussion on functions of Greek and Roman temples, see Lanci, *A New Temple for Corinth*, 95–104. See also Burkert "Meaning and Function," 39–44; Pedley, *Sanctuaries and the Sacred;* and Fay, "Greco-Roman Concepts of Deity," 51–79.

57. Pedley, *Sanctuaries and the Sacred*, 11.

58. Strabo, *Geogr.* 8.6.20c, 21b, described Corinth as the sacred city of Aphrodite. While this description may have referred to the pre-146 BCE city and not the Roman Corinth Paul visited, it nevertheless underscored the importance of the temple as a unifying symbol of the city. See Burkert, "Meaning and Function" 27–47.

59. Walbank, "Image and Cult," 190–94.

60. Lanci, *A New Temple for Corinth*, 104. See also Burkert, "Meaning and Function," 39–44.

61. Levison, "Spirit and the Temple," 192.

Emotive Dimension: Temple Destruction and Desecration

Since temples define the existence of the community, any destruction of an iconic symbol that fosters self-definition, pride, and identity of the community is viewed as a shameful and despicable act of desecration. Tacitus described the destruction of the Capitol in Rome, which brought the entire city into chaos, as "the saddest and most shameful crime that the Roman state had ever suffered since its foundation."[62] As the stronghold of the Roman Empire and the head of the world acknowledged by Livy,[63] its destruction was tantamount to the destruction of the metaphorical head of the government. Tacitus attributed the cause of the destruction to the "mad fury of the emperors,"[64] and not the invasion of or war with any foreign enemies which Rome had none. Tacitus' outrage on the destruction of the Capitol suggests that in the Roman world, a temple was not simply a place of worship or a dwelling place for the deity. It was an icon of civic identity. Its destruction only brought upon the people shame and horror, and this was more so due to internal fights.

Paul picks up this notion in his warning to the Corinthians in 1 Cor 3:17, where he declares: "If anyone destroys (φθείρει) God's temple, God will destroy (φθερεῖ) that person." What did Paul mean when he used the word φθείρω? Lanci argues that φθείρω refers to ruin or damage of a building[65] while Shanor contends that it refers to partial damage done to a building under construction.[66] Garland rightly points out that this interpretation fails to appreciate Paul's use of metaphor.[67] In this context, Paul was issuing a stern warning to the Corinthians. Two interesting facts are to be noted in Paul's language of temple destruction in 1 Cor 3:16–17. First, Paul was not talking about the temple being destroyed by the enemies or outsiders, but by the devotees themselves. Secondly, the language of destruction in 1 Cor 3:17 stands in sharp contrast with the flow of Paul's argument in 1 Cor 3:10–15, where the imagery of construction was employed to describe the building of the temple of God that constituted the people of God.[68] This contrast is

62. Tacitus, *Hist.* 3.72.
63. Livy, *History of Rome* 1.55.5–6.
64. Tacitus, *Hist.* 3.72.
65. Lanci, *A New Temple for Corinth*, 67–68
66. Shanor, "Paul as Master Builder," 470–71.
67. Garland, *1 Corinthians*, 120.
68. For the argument that the building imagery in 1 Cor 3:10–15 constitutes the construction of God's temple that climaxes at 1 Cor 3:16–17, see Levison, "Spirit and the Temple," 193; Mitchell, *Paul and the Rhetoric of Reconciliation*, 99–105; Hogeterp, *Paul and God's Temple*, 311–31.

further amplified in 1 Cor 6:19 where Paul appealed to temple imagery in rebuking the Corinthians for desecrating it by participation in sexual immorality. By drawing on the construction imagery, Paul was evoking before the minds of his audience the picture of a building being constructed by many groups of people. The idea of bringing many people with diverse background and talents in a construction project served to underscore the common and united purpose of the project—to see the building of the temple, which is the pride of every builder, completed. Hence, Paul's greatest fear was to see his labor in building the temple wasted should it be destroyed by the Corinthians. Therefore, the impact of Paul's rhetoric and the force of temple imagery could be strongly felt. Paul could not have made it clearer that any destruction of God's temple is tantamount to a serious offence and a sacrilegious act of desecration, and this warrants a corresponding severe penalty of divine judgment.

It is interesting to note that the announcement of severe punishment appears in a series of failures of the Christ-followers—adultery involving a person's father's wife (1 Cor 5:1–13); lawsuits among believers (1 Cor 6:1–8); visiting prostitutes (1 Cor 6:9–20); marriage and divorce (1 Cor 7); consuming idol food (1 Cor 8–10); chaos in worship (1 Cor 11:2—14:40); and possible doctrinal error (1 Cor 15)—but none mentioned evokes such severe penalty as on those who caused divisions in the church. This penalty of divine judgment is extraordinary. Even an act that outstrips the most outrageous pagan sexual practice only receives the penalty of temporary ostracism from the community (1 Cor 5:1–8). But those who divided the church were subject to a more severe divine judgment, a fact that not only underscores the seriousness of the offence but creates a deep sense of shock to the hearers and serves as a stern warning for those who deliberately attempted to cause dissentions in the community.

By publicly declaring their failures, Paul was shaming the Corinthians. The divisions of the Corinthian community into numerous parties contradicted the unity of the one Temple in which God chooses to dwell through his Spirit. Instead of building up the temple that could be a source of pride and identity for the Christ-followers, their practices of competitive partisanship (1 Cor 1:10–13), boastful arrogance (1 Cor 1:29; 3:21; 4:7), and jealousy and strife (1 Cor 3:3) had, on the contrary, contributed to its destruction. Paul allowed his readers to imagine that their own actions were not only incompatible with the ethos of their existence as a temple of God but also undermined the survival of this fledging community.

As such, Paul's use of the temple metaphor speaks of shame, horror, and shock that are beyond words. This imagery conjures up a very powerful visual appeal to the emotions of the Corinthians, causing them to pause and reflect on how far they had fallen short through their error in causing dissentions in the community. It is a harsh imagery that evoked their memory the despicable act of temple destruction. By calling the community to function in a way that was similar to the way temples in the Greco-Roman world would have functioned, Paul was able to underscore the fact that the temple of the deities served as a powerful symbol of the unity existed between the deity and the worshippers. It also powerfully conveyed the message of how serious their error was that, in their own internal strife, they had forgotten the common good they should uphold. Just as a particular deity was understood to dwell in a Greek temple dedicated to it, so Paul envisioned the Corinthian community as a temple indwelt by the Holy Spirit.[69] By using this metaphor, Paul was realigning the Corinthians into the new symbolic world of the gospel he proclaimed. Paul was certainly very concerned that the temple he had been building (cf. 1 Cor 3:10–15) was now being destroyed by the Corinthians. To bring home the seriousness resulting from the actions of the Corinthians in dividing themselves into fractions, Paul declared that God's judgment would inevitably and inescapably fall on them.

Evaluative Dimension: Temple Purity and Holiness

In 1 Cor 6:12–20, Paul expresses his concern that the Christ-followers were still behaving like the society surrounding them, some justifying their sexual immorality practices as "all things are lawful for me" (1 Cor 6:12). In order to emphasize the seriousness of such immorality, Paul appeals to temple imagery in 6:19: "Or do you not know that your body is a temple of the Holy Spirit within you, whom you have from God?" As I have argued earlier, Paul's use of οὐκ οἴδατε is to underscore that the Corinthians were already aware that they were the temple of God.

It is also interesting to note elsewhere in this letter, Paul advocated that believing spouses were to remain with unbelieving spouses in order to make the unbelieving partners holy (1 Cor 7:12–16). In other words, Paul believed the Christ-community was intended to make those who are outsiders holy. But the direct opposite was taking place where the Christ-followers were polluting themselves by uniting with prostitutes by means of illicit sexual activity, and thereby further polluting the Christ-community. Paul

---

69. Cf. Thiselton, *First Epistle to the Corinthians*, 474–75: "The universal presence of images of the deities in Graeco-Roman temples would have made the principle more vivid to first-century readers . . . and Paul declares that the very person of the Holy Spirit of God, by parity of reasoning, stands to the totality of the bodily, everyday life of the believer . . . in the same relation of influence and molding of identity as the images of deities in pagan temples."

thus appealed to the temple imagery by imposing the holiness boundary as one of the critical pillars of the community's self-understanding and self-definition for the Christ-followers.

Moving on to 2 Cor 6:11—7:1, the theme of holiness emerges with greater intensity with Paul's charging the believers of being "unequally yoked" with those outside the Christ-community. Interestingly in 2 Cor 6:11, Paul addressed his readers as Κορίνθιοι, instead of the usual ἀδελφοί that is scattered throughout the letter. Throughout the Pauline corpus, there are only two other incidents where members of the Pauline communities were being addressed by the collective designation, as seen in Gal 3:1 and Phil 4:15. Guthrie notes that all these three vocatives addresses in 2 Cor 6:11; Gal 3:1; and Phil 4:15 are charged with emotion.[70] In the Galatian context, it was frustration while in case of Philippians, it was one of warmth and appreciation.[71] In the Corinthian context, Paul spoke clearly with "deep emotion and tender affection."[72] This further magnified the seriousness of the issue of holiness and purity that Paul attempted to address in this passage, particularly the Corinthians' "unequally yoke" relationship with the outsiders.

To provoke the Corinthians to evaluate their relationship with outsiders, Paul once again appeals to temple imagery by declaring in 2 Cor 6:16: "For we are the temple of the living God." Here, Paul's use of temple metaphor comes immediately after a series of five rhetorical questions formulated in an antithetical fashion that demonstrates the incompatibility of relationships between Christ-followers and pagans. Each pair speaks of the mutually exclusive relationships standing in direct and stark opposition between the "insider" and "outsider" respectively, as seen in the following diagram:

righteousness	against	lawlessness
light	against	darkness
Christ	against	Beliar
believers	against	unbelievers
temple of God	against	temple of idols

The declaration that the Christ-followers are the temple of God in 2 Cor 6:16 further justifies the separation of incompatible relationships. This

---

70. Guthrie, *2 Corinthians*, 343.
71. Ibid.
72. Harris, *Second Epistle to the Corinthians*, 487.

is further elaborated by a direct command (2 Cor 6:17–18) and an exhortation to purity and holiness (2 Cor 7:1). It is significant to note that in 2 Cor 6:17, Paul's command to the Corinthians requires them to "come out (ἐξέλθατε) from them, and be separate (ἀφορίσθητε) from them . . . and touch (ἅπτεσθε) nothing unclean" before they could be welcome by God. The idea of "come out" and "be separate" depicts "spatial movement"[73] from one sphere to another, and this denotes that there must be a clear distinction and separation between the people of God and the outsiders.

Paul's language here also clearly highlights the fact that the more positively outsiders are esteemed, the more positive conformity with them is valued. As noted by Barnett: "it is precisely at the point where that 'temple' meets the culture of 'idols' in the Gentile metropolis of Corinth that the challenge to compromise and syncretism becomes most painful, and to which the Corinthians are in danger of succumbing."[74] As can be seen from Paul's call to preserve purity of the community by expelling the sinful brother (1 Cor 5:1–13) and shunning sexual immorality (1 Cor 6:18), it is evident that purity and holiness were the social boundaries that defined the Corinthians believers from the rest of the society.[75] Paul's urgent tone suggests there is a pressing need to correct the behavior of the Christ-followers. Already there were disunity and dissention and numerous other problems and issues of non-conformity affecting the unrepentant and recalcitrant community, summed up in 2 Cor 12:20–21. Paul could not afford to allow the non-conformity of those Christ-followers to continue persistently. Thus he made a desperate cry by appealing to the temple metaphor to urge the Christ-followers to align themselves to the value of the gospel of Christ, without which the very existence of the Christ-community as an alternative assembly would be at stake and its life and witness severely compromised.

There is no doubt that Paul could have drawn from the Hebrew Scripture on the notion of temple purity as evidenced by a string of citations and allusions to it in 2 Cor 6:16–18, and this would appeal to the Jewish believers in Corinth.[76] However, for the majority of Gentile Christ-followers,

---

73. Guthrie, *2 Corinthians*, 356.

74. Barnett, *Second Epistle to the Corinthians*, 351.

75. For discussion on Paul laying down conditions for the maintenance to preserve purity of the community as a temple of God, see Newton, *Concept of Purity*, 79–114. See also Liu, *Temple Purity*, 198–233.

76. The strings of references to the Hebrew Scripture include Exod 25:8; Lev 26:11–12; Ezek 20:41, 37:27; 2 Sam 7:14; Isa 43:6, 52:11. Collectively, these references express two dominant themes: First, the presence of God in the midst of his people, and secondly, the presence of God demands separation from uncleanness. For further discussion, see Gupta, *Worship that Makes Sense*, 160–67.

temple purity was also a notion widely documented in the Greco-Roman world, and this source domain would have resonated with them when the temple metaphor was used. An inscription dated first-century BCE found in Smyrna concerning a temple of an unknown goddess states that any one who dared to behave inappropriately by stealing or vandalizing the temple "be destroyed wretchedly by a terrible destruction being eaten by fish."[77] A third-century BCE test from the island of Astypalais reads: "Let not anyone enter the sanctuary who is not pure."[78] Another first-century CE Rhodian inscription states that anyone "who enters within the temple fragrant with incense, must be holy; pure not through washing, but in mind."[79] Similarly, a second/third century CE inscription concerning the temple of Asklepios and Hygieia asserts that the precinct is sacred, and all those who sacrifice to these two deities must do so "in the way which is right."[80] Likewise, a late first-century/early second-century CE inscription discovered in Sardis dedicated to Zeus warns the temple wardens who "enter the innermost sanctum and who serve and crown the god, not to participate" in mystery cults and with those who bring offerings to these cults.[81] There were also rules governing how one is to behave, dress, and observe all ritual of purifications.[82] From these sources, the language of temple purity is clearly exhibited.

For Paul, the issue of holiness for the Christ-community is not simply a matter of ritual purity but a reflection of the moral nature of the God who dwells in the community.[83] In this respect, the community was to separate themselves from anything that would bring defilement to the temple and detach themselves from any continuing involvement with idol worship that was incongruous with their new identity as the people of God and members of the new temple. If the behavior of the members of this community brought dishonor to God, it was expected that God would repay by destroying those dishonoring him in order to protect his honor. It is within this framework that Paul's use of temple metaphor drives home the transformative effect on how the Corinthians think and behave.

77. Horsley, *New Documents Illustrating Early Christianity*, 4:105.

78. Ibid., 4:111.

79. Ibid.

80. Ibid., 4:108.

81. Ibid., 1:21–23.

82. See ibid., 4:109–11. See also Elliot and Reasoner, *Documents and Images*, 247–48, for further examples of inscriptions highlighting the requirement of holiness in approaching the temples. For further discussion on temple purity in the Greco-Roman world, see Liu, *Temple Purity*, 70–105.

83. Lanci, *A New Temple for Corinth*, 132 and Wanamaker, "Metaphor and Morality," 424.

In using temple imagery, Paul was differentiating his audience from the surrounding society by promoting positive group identity and moral standards that were compatible with their new status in Christ.[84] According to Pickett, Paul's use of cultic language emphasizes that only certain patterns of behavior are congruous with the identity conferred by this language.[85] As such, a temple must remain pure if God is to be present, and this means that the members must preserve strict standards of behavior that reflects the attributes of the dwelling deity. This is to encourage behavior that does not negatively impact the well-being of the holy community in which the Spirit of God dwells. In this respect, Paul was challenging the Corinthians to evaluate their relationships with the outsiders. It is worthwhile observing that Paul casts his opinion of the outsiders in 2 Cor 6:14—7:1 in an extreme negative and condescending manner, calling them "unbelievers" (ἄπιστοι) twice in 2 Cor 6:14 and 15.[86] This only magnifies Paul's rhetorical force in highlighting the fact that he now had reasons to believe the Corinthians had given up their quest for holiness with a passion for the unholy. For Paul, simultaneous worship of the living God and the practices associated with the worship of idols constituted "an impossibility."[87] By doing so, Hogeterp rightly argues that Paul wants to "protect the Christian community against the threat of corrupting influences from outside."[88] It is these faults that the temple metaphor so acutely addresses. Paul emphasizes the point that the temple of God evokes an image of a community of holiness that is aligned to a holy God, a community comprising Christ-followers who devote themselves to God and to one another, and a community that is distinct and unlike the other communities existing in Corinth—and these are the standards that the Christ-community has failed to live up to. And the key for Paul that the Corinthians could begin to change their thinking and behavior is to separate themselves from the "unbelievers" (2 Cor 6:14: Μὴ γίνεσθε ἑτεροζυγοῦντες ἀπίστοις).

Finally, Paul appeals to the Corinthians to be open once again to him, assuring them his deep affection for them: "We have spoken frankly to you

---

84. Cf. Neyrey, *Paul, in Other Words*, 96–97. See also Rabens, "Paul's Rhetoric," 229–53.

85. Pickett, *Cross in Corinth*, 92.

86. Although "unbelievers" (ἄπιστοι) in this context clearly refer to those outside the Christ-community, Rabens suggests that they could also refer to "unbelievers" inside the community, namely Paul's opponents and false prophets. See Rabens, "Paul's Rhetoric," 229–53. See also Keener, *1–2 Corinthians*, 193; and Guthrie, *2 Corinthians*, 350.

87. Harris, *Second Epistle to the Corinthians*, 504.

88. Hogeterp, "Community as a Temple," 287.

Corinthians; our heart is wide open to you. There is no restriction in our affections, but only in yours. In return—I speak as to children—open wide your hearts also" (2 Cor 6:11–12; cf. 2 Cor 7:2). Paul ends this section with a call to cleanse oneself from defilement and to make holiness perfect (2 Cor 7:1). The focus in identity formation ends with a positive tone, with a stronger focus on their identity in Christ by applying temple imagery to the Corinthians. This provides a decisive identity marker for them as they consider and evaluate the relationship of the community to competitive forces outside the community.

To sum up our discussion, we see Paul's creativity at work in the use of temple imagery, appealing to both his Jewish and gentile audience by drawing from their shared understanding of the temple located within their respective social and religious background in order to negotiate for a new identity in Christ. By evoking references to the Hebrew Scripture, Paul was able to draw the Jewish Corinthians into the story of Israel, reminding them that the temple was a symbol of the presence of God, the very dwelling place of God and that holiness preceded the worship of God that invoked God's presence. At the same time, the gentile Christ-followers were also able to identify with the imagery drawn from their Greco-Roman conventions. As a temple where not only the God of Israel dwelt but one that comprised both the Jewish and gentile Christ-followers that were united in Jesus the Messiah, it was both sacred and distinct. By employing this imagery, Paul addressed the community of Christ-followers to be distinctive not only in the ethical and moral dimensions compared to other communities but also drew both Jews and gentile into relationship with one another. A positive group identity and moral standards that were compatible with their new status in Christ was now being promoted. Certainly, the use of temple imagery is much more than "an *artistic* way of saying something else"[89] as suggested by Konsmo.

SUMMARY

By employing temple metaphor in the Corinthian correspondence, Paul creatively draws on the previous symbolic universe of the Christ-community and uses it powerfully in his appeal to realign the community to the ethos of the gospel of Christ in the formation of a distinct Christian identity. What emerges from Paul's use of temple imagery is a vivid and extraordinary image that holds together a number of different notions such as community identity, the building up of community, and the appearance of the

---

89. Konsmo, *Pauline Metaphors*, 117, emphasis his.

community to the outsiders. For Paul, what identifies the Christ-community and what will identify it to the outside world is the fact that this community is a unified community, a holy community, a distinct community being set apart from the surrounding society—one that is transformed by the gospel of Christ. Paul's vision in creating an authentic Christian identity rooted in this gospel is for the ultimate purpose that this Christ-community will serve both as an attraction and invitation to those outside of it, thus preventing it from being conformed to the value systems of this world.

6

"You are the Body of Christ"
Body Metaphor

PAUL DEALS WITH THE abuse of spiritual gifts, particularly the gift of tongues, during community worship in 1 Cor 12–14.[1] The word γλῶσσα dominates these chapters, occurring twenty one times throughout.[2] Much has been written concerning the nature, source, and function of speaking in tongues. Extensive studies and reviews on these issues exist elsewhere, and any further review will necessarily duplicate these efforts.[3] In this chapter, I will first examine the reason why speaking in tongues became an obsession with the Corinthians and how this eventually contributed to conflicts and disunity in the assembly. This will be followed by paying attention to how Paul uses the metaphor of body in addressing the abuse of spiritual gifts.

---

1. On the literary structure of 1 Cor 12–14, see Chiu, *1 Cor 12–14*. Note that in 1 Cor 12:1, Paul states: "Now concerning spiritual gifts, brothers and sisters, I do not want you to be uninformed." The phrase, "I do not want you to be uninformed" (οὐ θέλω ὑμᾶς ἀγνοεῖν) suggests that prior instructions concerning the gifts of the Spirit have been given to the Corinthians.

2. The word γλῶσσα appears four times in 1 Cor 12 (1 Cor 12:10 [twice], 28, 30); twice in 1 Cor 13 (1 Cor 13:1, 8); and fifteen times in 1 Cor 14 (1 Cor 14:2, 4 [three times], 6, 9, 13 [twice], 18 [twice], 22 [twice], 26 [twice] and 39).

3. For selected major monographs dealing with ecstatic speech, see Cartledge, *Charismatic Glossolalia*; Crone, *Early Christian Prophecy*; Forbes, *Prophecy and Inspired Speech*; Hovenden, *Speaking in Tongues*; Hiu, *Regulations Concerning Tongues and Prophecy*; Poirier, *Tongues of Angels*; Tibbs, *Religious Experience*; and Turner, *Holy Spirit*. There is also long list of journal articles written on the subject that are too numerous to list here. See the bibliography in Poirier, *Tongues of Angels*, 165–202, and Hiu, *Regulations Concerning Tongues and Prophecy*, 205–18.

THE CONTEXT: ECSTATIC SPEECH AS SOCIAL STATUS MARKER?

The Corinthians prized speaking in tongues more than any other spiritual gifts. There was excessive use of tongues (1 Cor 14:2–19) to the extent that Paul needed to downplay its value and to limit its use in an orderly fashion (1 Cor 13:1; 14:5–6, 12, 16–19, 23), but short of forbidding it (1 Cor 14:27, 39). According to Dale Martin, this phenomenon arose because the Greco-Roman society viewed esoteric speech as an activity that was related to one's social status.[4] Martin quotes a number of sources drawn from the *Testament of Job*, Montanists, Lucian, and Celsus and argues that esoteric speech was portrayed as "unequivocally high-status behavior, often connected with leadership roles."[5] Martin also appeals to Dio Chrysostom where superior, heavenly beings were believed to speak languages different from humans. In his work, Dio Chrysostom asked rhetorically, "Tell me, do you think Apollo speaks Attic or Doric? Or that men and gods have the same language?"[6] Dio Chrysostom also suggested that Homer seemed to know the divine language as he "talks to us almost as though he were acquainted with their language, tells us that it was not the same as ours, and that they do not apply the same names to the various things we do."[7]

In addition, Martin also alludes to Irenaeus who wrote in the second century CE and gave a rather glowing testimony to the high status of glossolalia:

> For this reason does the apostle declare, "We speak wisdom among them that are perfect," terming those persons "perfect" who have received the Spirit of God, and who through the Spirit of God do speak in all languages, as he used Himself to speak. In like manner we do also hear many brethren in the Church, who possess prophetic gifts, and who through the Spirit speak all kinds of languages, and bring to light for the general benefit the hidden things of men, and declare the mysteries of God, whom also the apostle terms "spiritual," they being spiritual because they partake of the Spirit, not because their flesh has been stripped off and taken away, and because they have become purely spiritual.[8]

---

4. Martin, *Corinthian Body*, 87–92. See also his "Tongues of Angels," 547–89, especially 556–58.
5. Martin, *Corinthian Body*, 90.
6. Dio Chrysostom, *Or.* 10.23.
7. Ibid., 11.22.
8. Irenaeus, *Haer.* 5.6.1.

Based on the above evidence, Martin concludes that speaking in tongues represented spiritual perfection in those who partook in the higher realms of reality. However, he cautions that while esoteric speech indicated an activity of those who belonged to high social status, it cannot be proven that those in the Corinthian assembly who spoke in tongues belonged to this category.[9] On the contrary, those from humble beginnings could be the ones desiring or emphasizing the gift of tongues with the perception that possession of this gift might elevate them to be on par with the elites of the community.[10] Some might even attach higher value and honor to speaking in tongues, as suggested by Collins: "Some considered glossolalia to be the spiritual reality par excellence, almost to the point of being the sole gift that was recognized by the Corinthians."[11]

From 1 Cor 12–14, we see evidence of Paul speaking against a hierarchical understanding of spiritual gifts. Paul hinted that not everyone possessed the gift of tongues in 1 Cor 12:30 when he asked, "Do all speak in tongues?" (μὴ πάντες γλώσσαις λαλοῦσιν). This rhetorical question anticipates a negative answer. Paul also spoke against the universality of the practice of tongues in 1 Cor 14:5, where he wished that everyone would speak in tongues, suggesting that there were some who did not.[12] The Corinthians might have thought that the tongues were some angelic languages (1 Cor 13:1) but Paul clearly downplayed it by indicating its temporal nature (1 Cor 13:8). By declaring that tongues would cease, Paul pointed out the misguided beliefs the Corinthians had in placing higher value on something that was only temporal instead of focusing on the virtue of love that was permanent (1 Cor 13:1, 13).

1 Cor 14 contains a concentrated discussion on regulating the use of tongues. Paul insisted that unless tongues were interpreted, speaking in tongues was useless, meaningless, and non-edifying (1 Cor 14:1–21,

---

9. Martin, *Corinthian Body*, 91. For a critique of Martin's use of sources that postdate first century CE, see Hiu, *Regulations Concerning Tongues and Prophecy*, 48. However, Hiu does not dispute the fact that the use of tongues may reflect a high social status. See the summary of his discussion in *Regulations Concerning Tongues and Prophecy*, 74. See also Tibbs, *Religious Experience,* who argues from a religious experience that Paul was actually writing about communicating with the spirit world in 1 Cor 12–14. See also Forbes, *Prophecy and Inspired Speech* and his "Early Christian Inspired Speech," 257–70.

10. See Theissen, *Psychological Aspects*, 300–301; and Ciampa and Rosner, *First Letter to the Corinthians*, 603 n. 184.

11. Collins, *1 Corinthians*, 461.

12. For further discussion, see Hiu, *Regulations Concerning Tongues and Prophecy*, 48–50; Fee, *First Epistle to the Corinthians*, 689; and Turner, "A Response," 297–308, reference here 297.

27–28). He also limited the number of people speaking in tongues (1 Cor 14:27). By regulating the use of tongues, Paul suggested that the utterance of tongues was the responsibility of the tongue-speakers. They should keep quiet if there were no interpreters (1 Cor 14:28). This strongly suggests that there were some Christ-followers in Corinth who constantly spoke in tongues simultaneously until the situation became chaotic in the gathering (1 Cor 14:23).

Paul also consistently compared prophecy and tongues, and placed higher value on prophecy that edified and built up the church (1 Cor 14:1, 3–5, 12, 24–25, 39). He made it clear that although he possessed the gift of tongues and spoke in tongues more than the Corinthians, he would rather speak five intelligible words to instruct others than ten thousand words in tongues (1 Cor 14:18–19).

From the above, abuse and excessive use of tongues as some form of self-promotion, affecting those who did not speak in tongues, is evident.[13] This caused disorder and confusion in the assembly. The tongue speakers might feel they were more superior while those who were not tongue speakers might feel they were treated as outsiders (see 1 Cor 12:14–26).[14]

How did Paul address conflict in a community that seemed to reinforce the elevation of the status of the elites and powerful and, at the same time, reminded the poor and less honorable of their position which not only existed in society but was being practiced in the church? How did Paul expose the false notion that certain gifts of the Spirit, particularly the gift of tongues, were more desirable, valuable, and could possibly enhance one's status within the church? How did Paul remind the community that they were interdependent and needed one another in order to be powerful witnesses to the community surrounding them? To address these concerns, Paul employs the imagery of body, which I will now examine in greater depth.

COMMUNITY AS THE BODY OF CHRIST

The image of the church as the body of Christ is used frequently in Paul's letters.[15] In Rom 12:4–5, Paul declares, "For as in one body we have many

---

13. See Hiu, *Regulations Concerning Tongues and Prophecy*, 53.

14. So Garland, *1 Corinthians*, 596. So Ciampa and Rosner, *First Letter to the Corinthians*, 603. For a detailed reconstruction of the situation in Corinth, see Chiu, *1 Cor 12–14*, 240–41.

15. For a survey of this issue, see the discussion in Son, *Corporate Elements*, 102–8; Lee, *Paul*, 1–5. See also Gundry, *Sōma in Biblical Theology*, 223–44; and Daines, "Paul's

members, and the members do not all have the same function, so we, though many, are one body in Christ, and individually members one of another." This statement follows a plea for humility appropriate to believers in Rom 12:3. Then moving on in Rom 12:6–8, Paul dwells on the need to complement each other in this body whereby the gifts that had been deposited in each member ought to be used to build up the body of Christ. By emphasizing mutual dependence on each other, Paul exhorts the Roman Christ-followers that each person in the body of Christ plays different roles in building up this body.

The notion of Christ-followers as the body of Christ also received prominent treatment in Ephesians and Colossians.[16] In Eph 1:22–23, Paul refers to the church as the body of Christ in his prayer for the Ephesian believers (Eph 1:15–23; cf. Eph 4:13; 5:23, 29–30). Within the context of Ephesians, Paul specifically uses the word ἐκκλησία to designate the community of Christ-believers and subsequently identifies it as the body of Christ of which Christ is the head (see also Eph 4:14–15 and Col 2:19). In Eph 2, Paul emphasizes that both Jews and gentiles are now reconciled to God in one body through the cross of Christ (Eph 2:16, see also Eph 3:6). This body is to be built up through different gifts and functions until it reaches the fullness of Christ (Eph 4:4–16). In Eph 4:4–16, Paul's focus is not merely the unity of believers with one another, but also their ultimate unity with Christ. Likewise, in Col 1:18, Christ is described as the head of the church (cf. Col 1:24), and the Christ-followers are called in the one body (Col 3:15).

However, the most extensive treatment of the church as the body of Christ is found in 1 Cor 12. In this chapter, Paul compares the Corinthian Christ-followers with a human body by emphasizing the diversity of the body, the unity of the body, and also the mutual dependence of the body (1 Cor 12:12–27).

PAUL'S USE OF BODY METAPHOR IN 1 COR 12

The repeated use of the word "body," σῶμα, in 1 Cor 12:12–27 is striking. In these few verses, this word appears eighteen times (or 39 percent) out of a total of forty six times in 1 Corinthians. It also occurs the most in 1

Use of the Analogy," 71–78.

16. The Pauline authorship of Ephesians and Colossians has been vigorously disputed. For a survey of scholarship, see Hoehner, *Ephesians*, 2–61; and Barth and Blanke, *Colossians*, 114–26. For treatment on the notion of body in Ephesians, see Dawes, *Body in Question*.

Corinthians compared to the rest of the Pauline corpus,[17] suggesting how significant it is in Paul's argument when he was addressing issues related to the operation of spiritual gifts.

First of all, Paul states in 1 Cor 12:12: "Καθάπερ γὰρ τὸ σῶμα ἕν ἐστιν καὶ μέλη πολλὰ ἔχει, πάντα δὲ τὰ μέλη τοῦ σώματος πολλὰ ὄντα ἕν ἐστιν σῶμα, οὕτως καὶ ὁ Χριστός" (1 Cor 12:12). Here, Paul likens the Corinthian Christ-followers to a body with many members. Interestingly, the analogy that Paul draws here is that of the body to Christ rather than to the church. It would have been logical for Paul to say that a body has many parts and yet one, "so it is with the church," or "so also is the body of Christ." Instead, Paul makes a direct reference to Christ when σῶμα is being compared—"so also is Christ" (οὕτως καὶ ὁ Χριστός). This is significant as it indicates that there exists a special relationship between the church and Christ.[18] The description of the church as a body of Christ carries with it the idea that the church belongs to Christ. It is Christ who establishes the body, and it is Christ who is the head of this body. By referring to Christ, Paul impressed upon the Corinthians that their behavior ultimately affected not only each other but, more importantly, Christ who is the head of the body. Earlier on in 1 Cor 1:13 where Paul addressed the issue of division in the church, he appealed to Christ in a rhetorical question: "Has Christ been divided?" Similarly, in 1 Cor 6:12–20, Paul warned against sexual immorality on the grounds that the Corinthians' bodies were members of Christ: "Do you not know that your bodies are members of Christ? Should I therefore take the members of Christ and make them members of a prostitute? Never!" (1 Cor 6:15). The reference to the members of the church as the body of Christ also appears in 1 Cor 8:12 within the context of consuming food sacrificed to idols where a weaker brother was being stumbled: "But when you thus sin against members of your family, and wound their conscience when it is weak, you sin against Christ." From these references, it is clear that the Corinthians'

---

17. The word σῶμα appears a total of ninety one times in the Pauline corpus as follows: thirteen in Romans; forty-six in 1 Corinthians; ten in 2 Corinthians; once in Galatians; nine in Ephesians; three in Philippians; eight in Colossians; and once in 1 Thessalonians.

18. As noted by Barrett, *First Epistle to the Corinthians*, 287; and Lee, *Paul*, 126–27. Fee, *First Epistle to the Corinthians*, 668, dubiously believes that the phrase "so it is with Christ" is a metonymy where "Christ" is a shortened way of referring to the church as the "body of Christ." Robinson argues that the body of Christ refers to the physical body of Christ (see Robinson, *Body*, 49–55). See also Cerfaux, *Church in the Theology of St Paul*, 262–86; Conzelmann, *An Outline of the Theology*, 260–63; and Schweitzer, *Mysticisicm of Paul the Apostle*, 109–40. This interpretation has been rightly challenged by Gundry, *Sōma in Biblical Theology*, 228, who argues for a metaphorical reading of the body of Christ. So Best, *One Body in Christ*, 95–114; Lee, *Stoics*, 105–52; Carter, "Looking at the Metaphor," 94; and Tuckett, "The Church as the Body of Christ," 161–91.

relationship with Christ became the foundation for their moral injunction and ethical behavior. This awakened the need to consider others in one's actions, particularly the weaker members of the body, failing which it would jeopardize the cohesiveness and sense of belonging in the body.[19]

Secondly, the metaphor also conveys the idea that while the body is one, it comprises many parts.[20] Members within the body of Christ are not merely individuals but are mutually interdependent and every part deserves appropriate respect from each other (see 1 Cor 12:14–16). This is why not every part of the body is given the same function (1 Cor 12:17), and as such, the eye or the head cannot disparage the hand or the foot.

Next, Paul emphasizes that honor must be given to the weaker, less honorable, and inferior members of the body (1 Cor 12:22–24). This would have been shocking to the Corinthians. As noted in chapters 3 and 4, in the honor-shame culture of the Greco-Roman world, honor was always due to the strong, mighty, rich, and powerful. Hardly would anyone accord honor to those who were weak, less honorable, and inferior. Instead, shame was often associated with this group of people.[21] Furthermore, it is significant that the lesser or weaker members of the body is described as ἀναγχαῖα (indispensable/necessary) (1 Cor 12:22) for the body.

Finally, Paul attributes the arrangement of different parts of the body, both the strong and weak parts, to divine activity. Since God has placed all these parts together, there should be unity where honor is given to the parts of the body that lacked it and every members care for one another (1 Cor 12:24–26).[22] To question the existence of the other parts of the body is tantamount to questioning the action of God in putting them together.

---

19. See Käsemann, *Perspectives on Paul*, 102–21, where he argues that the body of Christ is used as a metaphor related to ethical exhortation.

20. See Son, *Corporate Elements*. Cf. Gundry, *Sōma in Biblical Theology*, 224.

21. For a discussion on honor-shame culture in the Greco-Roman world, see deSilva, *Honor*, 23–93. See also Finney, *Honour and Conflict*, 5–48, 178–96.

22. See Mitchell, *Paul and the Rhetoric of Reconciliation*, 20–64. See also Lee, *Paul*, 105–52; Bultmann, *Theology of the New Testament*, 1:310.

POSSIBLE BACKGROUNDS FOR BODY METAPHOR

There are many possible provenances of the body metaphor, ranging from Jewish apocalyptic and Rabbinic writings,[23] the institution of the Eucharist,[24] and the Hellenistic literature.[25] Probably the most compelling argument with the greatest support is that Paul draws inspiration from the contemporary Hellenistic world where the body metaphor was used to reinforce the unity and harmony of the city, state, and cosmos.[26] Evidence that is often cited to support this view include the following:

1) Seneca's depiction of the Roman Empire as the body in which Nero the Emperor is described as the head.

2) The Stoic description of the cosmos as a single unified body that comprises units that are held together.

3) Josephus' description of the various dissenting parties in Jerusalem as one body.

4) The fable of the belly and the members attributed to Menenius Agrippa that is similar to the body analogy in 1 Cor 12:14–16, as recounted by Livy, *History of Rome* 2.32.7–33.1.

The above Hellenistic sources for the imagery of body can be further investigated based on the following broad categories:

1) The political image of the body; and

---

23. For example, Albert Schweitzer is a major proponent for the Jewish concept of corporate personality where he roots Paul's notion of the body of Christ in the concept of the solidarity of the Elect with the Messiah and with one another found in Jewish apocalyptic writings. See Schweitzer, *Mysticism of Paul the Apostle*, 116. See also Davies, *Paul and Rabbinic Judaism*, 55–57, where he argues that Paul adapted the rabbinic idea of Adam representing the oneness of humanity to the newly created humanity that is in Christ where there is neither Jew nor Greek, male nor female, slave nor free in the eschatological body of Adam. See also Kim, *Origin of Paul's Gospel*, 252–56, where Paul's personal experience at the Damascus Road in which the concept of solidarity of the people with Christ is another possibility for the use of the body metaphor.

24. Rawlinson, "Corpus Christi," 225–54. This view is supported by Conzelmann, *An Outline of the Theology*, 261–62.

25. For a detailed analysis of the possible source of Paul's notion of the body, see Jewett, *Paul's Anthropological Terms*, 201–304. For a discussion on the possible background of Paul's ideas of the body imagery, see Son, *Corporate Elements*, 111–20; and Lee, *Paul*, 8–11.

26. See Barrett, *First Epistle to the Corinthians*, 287; Fee, *First Epistle to the Corinthians*, 600–603; Witherington, *Conflict and Community*, 258–59; and Dunn, "'The Body of Christ'," 162, amongst others.

2) The philosophical image of the body.

Political Image of the Body

The image of body is used as a model of social unity and harmony in ancient rhetoric as reflected in the works of Plato, Cicero, Seneca, Epictetus, Dio Chrysostom, Dionysius of Halicarnassus, Josephus, and Philo, amongst others.[27] It is also a very common metaphor used in political discourses.[28] Some well-known examples are the speeches of Antiphon's *On Concord* and Isocrates' *Panegyricus* where body or household are used as metaphors to champion political unity for the common good of the city or *politeia*.

Probably the best-known political discourse that is commonly held as the source of Paul's body imagery is the speech by Menenius Agrippa in the fifth century BCE persuading the plebeians to cease their rebellion against the senate. In his speech, Menenius Agrippa drew on the human body as an analogy for the relationship between the plebeians and the senate. This fable is passed on by Dionysius of Halicarnassus and is worth quoting in full:

> A commonwealth resembles in some measure a human body. For each of them is composite and consists of many parts; and no one of their parts either has the same function or performs the same service as the others. If, now, these parts of the human body should be endowed, each for itself, with perception and a voice of its own and a sedition should then arise among them, all of them uniting against the belly alone, and the feet should say that the whole body rests on them; the hands, that they ply the crafts, secure provisions, fight with enemies, and contribute many other advantages toward the common good; the shoulders, that they bear all the burdens; the mouth, that it speaks; the head, that it sees and bears and, comprehending the other senses, possesses all those by which the thing is preserved; and then all these should say to the belly, 'And you, good creature, which of these things do you do? What return do you make and of what use are you to us? Indeed, you are so far from doing

---

27. See, for example, Plato, *Resp.* 370A–B; Cicero, *Off.* 3.5.22–23; 3.6.26–27; *Top.* 6.30; Seneca, *Ira* 2.13.7; Epictetus, *Diatr.* 2.10.4–5; Dio Chrysostom, *Or.* 3.104–107; 9.2; 17.19; 33.16, 34; 34.32; 39.5; 40.21; 41.9; 50.3; Dionysius of Halicarnassus, *Ant. rom.* 6.86.4; Josephus, *J.W.* 4.406–407; and Philo, *Spec. Laws* 3.131. See also the references in Collins, *First Corinthians*, 458–60.

28. Martin comments that the use of body metaphor in political speeches was so common that they can be considered a genre unto themselves. See his *Corinthian Body*, 38.

anything for us or assisting us in accomplishing anything useful for the common good that you are actually a hindrance and a trouble to us and—a thing intolerable—compel us to serve you and to bring things to you from everywhere for the gratification of your desires. Come now, why do we not assert our liberty and free ourselves from the many troubles we undergo for the sake of this creature?' If, I say, they should decide upon this course and none of the parts should any longer perform its office, could the body possibly exist for any considerable time, and not rather be destroyed within a few days by the worst of all deaths, starvation? No one can deny it. Now consider the same condition existing in a commonwealth. For this also is composed of many classes of people not at all resembling one another, every one of which contributes some particular service to the common good, just as its members do to the body. For some cultivate the fields, some fight against the enemy in defence of those fields, others carry on much useful trade by sea, and still others ply the necessary crafts. If, then, all these different classes of people should rise against the senate, which is composed of the best men, and say, 'As for you, senate, what good do you do us, and for what reason do you presume to rule over others? Not a thing can you name. Well, then, shall we not now at least free ourselves from this tyranny of yours and live without a leader?' If, I say, they should take this resolution and quit their usual employment, what will hinder this miserable commonwealth from perishing miserably by famine, war and every other evil? Learn, therefore, plebeians, that, just as in our bodies the belly thus evilly reviled by the multitude nourishes the body even while it is itself nourished, and preserves it while it is preserved itself, and is a kind of feast, as it were, provided by joint contribution, which as a result of the exchange duly distributes that which is beneficial to each and all, so in commonwealth and senate, which administers the affairs of the public and provides what is expedient for everyone, preserves, guards, and corrects all things. Cease, then, uttering those invidious remarks about the senate, to the effect that you have been driven out of your country by it and that because of it you wander about like vagabonds and beggars. For it neither has done you any harm nor can do you any, but of its own accord calls you and entreats you, and opening all hearts together with the gates, is waiting to welcome you.[29]

29. Dionysius of Halicarnassus *Ant. rom.* 6.68.1–5. This story is also recounted in a slightly condensed version in Livy, *History of Rome* 2.32.7–2.33.1. Similar illustrations are also found in Cicero, *Off.* 3.5.22, Plutarch, *Cor.* 6.1–4; and Xenophon, *Mem.* 2.13.18. Garland, *1 Corinthians*, 593n5, thinks that references to this fable "is probably more

Menenius Agrippa's fable delivered the desired result when the plebeians stopped their rebellion and harmony was restored to the city council. By using the analogy of the body, Menenius Agrippa underscores the point that all parts of the body performed a necessary function for the good of the whole. This story emphasized that the stomach, a reference to the ruling classes, played a very crucial role in processing the food it received from the various members of the body, a reference to the masses. While the ruling elites appeared to be taking from the masses all the time, they were in fact essential to the wellbeing of society, a fact that other members of the body failed to recognize. This fable was effective and became a primary means by which Menenius Agrippa persuaded the people to submit to the ruling elites. His intention was to drive home the point that the human body had many parts and that these parts could not live without the stomach. Likewise, the Commonwealth had many kinds of people who all contributed to the common good, and it could not survive without the senate which was dominated by the ruling elites. In the final analysis, Menenius Agrippa's fable emphasized the importance of the ruling classes and further enhanced their elevated position in the eyes of the masses, while the masses and the poor had no choice but to serve the purpose of the elites.

Other writers also used the body metaphor and related it to the ruling elites. Seneca used the body metaphor to describe the relationship between Nero and the state and between the soul and the body.[30] Like Menenius Agrippa, Seneca began with a general description of the mind's relationship to the body and the Emperor's to the state. He then developed the relationship to the point where he established Rome as the body of Nero. Seneca's purpose was to persuade Nero to be merciful to the state for in so doing, he would be showing mercy to himself.

Aelius Aristides also likened any political unrest to a disease, to a tearing apart of the body, and to the folly of cutting off one's own feet.[31] The need for concord and harmony was often emphasized in using the body imagery within the context of the common good of life in the Commonwealth, as elaborated by Dio Chrysostom:

> When a city has concord, as many citizens as they are, so many are the eyes with which to see that city's interest, so many the

---

familiar to commentators that it was to the original recipients of the letter." However given the frequency of the references to body imagery in Greco-Roman literature, it would be surprising that it is not well known. Plutarch, who referred to this fable, described it as a "celebrated fable" (*Cor.* 6.2).

30. Seneca, *Clem.* 1.3.5–1.5.3.

31. Aelius Aristides, *Orat.* 17.9; 23.31; 24.18, 38–39; 26.43.

ears with which to hear, so many the tongues to give advice, so many the minds concerned in its behalf... Conversely neither abundance of riches nor number or men nor any other element of strength is of advantage to those who are divided, but all these things are rather on the side of loss, and the more abundant they are, so much the greater and more grievous the loss. Just so too, methinks, it is with human bodies—that body which is in sound health finds advantage in its height and bulk, while the body which is diseased and in poor condition finds a physical state of that kind to be most perilous and productive of severest risk.[32]

Similarly, Seneca further talked about the disparaging effect of injuring a fellow citizen in the commonwealth by using body imagery:

> To injure one's country is a crime; consequently, also, to injure a fellow-citizen—for he is a part of the country, and if we reverence the whole, the parts are sacred—consequently to injure any man is a crime, for he is your fellow-citizen in the greater commonwealth. What if the hands should desire to harm the feet, or the eyes the hands? As all the members of the body are in harmony one with another because it is to the advantage of the whole that the individual members be unharmed, so mankind should spare the individual man, because all are born for a life of fellowship, and society can be kept unharmed only by the mutual protection and love of its parts.[33]

This notion of a political reading of the body metaphor used by Paul has been favorably received by a number of scholars. Among those who vigorously defend this reading is Margaret Mitchell who commented: "The metaphor of the body for the social organism in ancient political tests, as we have seen, *is used to combat factionalism* ... That is the same application which Paul makes of his transferred metaphor 'the body of Christ.'"[34] In light of this, one can logically see the connection between the use of body metaphor and 1 Cor 12. Mitchell further argues that Paul reworked a common political metaphor in the Greco-Roman world and applied it to the church in Corinth. "There can be no doubt that 1 Cor 12, which employs the most common *topos* in ancient literature for unity, is a straightforward

---

32. Dio Chrysostom, *Or.* 39.5. Cf. Josephus, *J.W.* 5.278–279 who described how the rival Jewish factions came together as one body to fight the common enemy Rome (see also 3.102–105). This group was described as body when it set aside differences and quarrels and acted as a unified group.

33. Seneca, *Ira* 2.31.7.

34. Mitchell, *Paul and the Rhetoric of Reconciliation*, 157–64. Quotation is taken from page 161, emphasis hers.

response to the factionalism within the church community, which is the subject of the entire letter."[35] Other scholars like C. K. Barrett and Ciampa and Rosner also link Paul's body imagery to the Menenuis Agrippa fable with its political purpose.[36]

Moral Philosophical Image of the Body

Using the analogy of the body, Dio Chrysostom advised that one should not attempt to perform the function of others:

> (Eyes) believed themselves to be the most important organs of the body, and yet they observed that it was the mouth that got the benefit of most things and in particular of honey, the sweetest things of all. So they were angry and even found fault with their owner. But when he placed in them some of the honey, they smarted and wept and thought it a stinging, unpleasant substance. Therefore do not you yourselves seek to taste the words that philosophy has to offer, as the eyes tasted honey; if you do . . . not only will you be vexed when they cause a smart, but perhaps you will even say that such a thing cannot possibly be philosophy, but rather abuse and mischief.[37]

Epictetus also believed that being a member of the body had more implications than simply discharging one's function. One needs to consider how one's action may have an impact on others:

> If you regard yourself as a man and as a part of some whole, on account of that whole it is fitting for you now to be sick, and now to make a voyage and run risks, and now to be in want, and on occasion to die before your time . . . Well, would you go on a voyage, someone else die, someone else be condemned? For it is impossible in such a body as ours, in this universe that envelops us, among these fellow-creatures of ours, that such things should not happen, some to one man and some to another.[38]

The Stoics also believed that the body goes beyond its function—it gives identity to the person. Epictetus highlighted this fact when he raised

---

35. Ibid., 161.

36. Barrett, *First Epistle to the Corinthians*, 287; Ciampa and Rosner, *First Letter to the Corinthains*, 597–98; Garland, *1 Corinthians*, 593–94; and Witherington, *Conflict and Community*, 253–54.

37. Dio Chrysostom, *Or.* 33.16.

38. Epictetus, *Diatr.* 2.5.28.

a question, "Do you not know that the foot, if detached, will no longer be a foot, so you too, if detached will no longer be a human being?"[39] Similarly, Xenophon, in making reference to Dio Chrysostom, also compared the significance of friends to that of having eyes, ears, a tongue, and hands. Without these parts of the body, a man was nothing. So it is with the man who has no friends.[40]

Plato took the body metaphor even further by stating that the universe was like a body, being composed of the same elements.[41] Similarly, Cicero also described the universe as a body since it was a living organism that produced growth.[42] The oneness of the many parts made the universe a body, just as it did in the human being. The Stoic political/philosophical image of the cosmos or state as a body has also received wide scholarly support.[43]

To further reinforce his emphasis on honoring one another, Plutarch employed the human body as an analogy to describe the harmonious relationship between siblings.[44] Promoting unity in diversity, Plutarch reminded those who were superior that the fingers that wrote and played musical instruments were not superior to those who could not.[45] As such, one must be mindful of one's inferior brother. Plutarch also recalled:

> Nature has placed at no great distance from us; on the contrary, in the body itself she has contrived to make most of the necessary parts double and brothers and twins: hands, feet, eyes, ears, nostrils; and she has thus taught us that she has divided them in this fashion for mutual preservation and assistance, not for variance and strife.[46]

Plutarch's goal was that there should be concord and interdependence in the body by being mindful of one's weaker brother.[47]

39. Ibid., 2.5.24.
40. Xenophon, *Mem.* 2:3.18–19; 2:4.7.
41. Plato, *Phileb*, 29D–E; *Tim.* 69C, 92C.
42. Cicero, *Nat. d.* 2.33.86.
43. See Lee, *Paul*, 46–58.
44. Plutarch, *Frat. amor.* 485F–486A.
45. Hierocles also made reference to body parts to underscore the connection of siblings: "Brothers for more than parts of the body are adapted by nature to help each other. For the eyes, indeed being present with each other, see together, and one hand works together with the other that is present. But the cooperation of brothers with each other is much more varied, for they do things which by common consent are excellent even if they greatly separate from each other, and they greatly benefit each other if the distance that separates them is immense" (Stob. 4.27.20).
46. Plutarch, *Frat. amor.* 478D.
47. Cf. Cicero, *Off.* 3.5.22 and Plutarch, *Cor.* 6 where the interdependence of the

DIFFERENCES BETWEEN HELLENISTIC AND PAUL'S USE OF BODY METAPHOR

After examining the Hellenistic philosophical and political sources that received overwhelming support as possible backgrounds to Paul's use of body metaphor,[48] a proper comparison can now be made between these sources and 1 Cor 12:12–27. There are indeed some close similarities and parallels in the use of body imagery in Hellenistic literature and Paul's letters. Both talked about the various parts of the body—the hands, feet, eyes, and mouth. Both also referred to the fact that the parts were merely a part of the bigger whole, and stressed the importance of the whole and interdependence of the parts in which respect must be given to one another. Finally, both also used the body metaphor to overcome divisions and promote unity in the community.

However, on further analysis, a number of stark differences emerge. First of all, while the idea of common advantage is often stressed in Hellenistic literature, this is, without fail, used in favor of the strong, the elites, or the ruling power. In highlighting the interdependence of the various parts and the functions of each, what is often emphasized was that respect must be given to the ruling elites. Cooperation of the diverse parts of the body for the good of the whole was also often promoted for the benefit of the ruling elites. With Paul, the opposite is true.[49] Respect and honor must be given to the less honorable and weaker members of the community. This is one area that the Hellenistic moral philosophy omitted in its discourses.

Secondly, the hierarchical emphasis in the Hellenistic use of the body metaphor often underscored that the superior parts of the body deserve more honor and respect than the weaker parts. This is seen in the focus of Menenius Agrippa's speech where the masses were required to contribute to the ruling elites. The ultimate aim of this discourse was to preserve the existing social structures of the elites and the masses, and to suppress any form of rebellion by the lower class against the social elites. However, for Paul, it is the strong who were called to give honor and respect to the weaker

---

various parts of the body is mentioned.

48. For example, Mitchell, *Paul and the Rhetoric of Reconciliation*, 159, sees overwhelming close parallels: "Paul's uniformity of use of this metaphor with ancient political writers applies even to the details . . . Paul's rhetorical use of personification of the parts of the body speaking is also paralleled. This consistency in detail in the body metaphor by Paul is combined with a remarkable correspondence between 1 Cor 12 and ancient political theory in its application." See also Barrett, *First Epistle to the Corinthians*, 287; Ciampa and Rosner, *First Letter to the Corinthains*, 597–98; Garland, *1 Corinthians*, 593–94; and Witherington, *Conflict and Community*, 253–54.

49. Martin, *Corinthian Body*, 28–34; and Lee, *Paul*, 16.

parts of the body. This is seen in the graphic language used by Paul in 1 Cor 12:22–24 in referring to the weaker, less honorable, and less presentable members of the body. This is often thought to be a direct reference to the sexual organs or genitalia.[50] The genitalia may seem to be the most shameful part of the body with the constant care to cover them and shield them from public exposure, but the attention given to them demonstrated that they were important part of the body. It is also interesting that Paul claimed that the weaker members were ἀναγχαῖα (neseccary) parts of the body, going against the prevailing view that those of higher status were the most indispensable parts of the body. This is where "Paul admits that the genitals, the 'necessary' members, seem to be the weaker; but, by their very necessariness, they can demand high status."[51] Therefore, the weaker members had a claim to proper care and honor.

Finally, Paul attributes the diverse members of the body of Christ to a work of God. From the very beginning in 1 Cor 12, Paul has been emphasizing that it is through the Spirit of God that the apportionment of the diverse gifts in the body of Christ is carried out. This notion of divine activity is missing from the Hellenistic literature.

Based on these observations, it is very unlikely that Paul could have drawn from the Hellenistic political and philosophical sources. So the questions remain: Why did Paul focus on the weak and less honorable, a departure from the prevailing social convention? What was Paul trying to say in this passage? What was the message of Paul to the social elites?

THE WELL-BEING OF THE BODY

In order to answer these questions, I will examine two other sources that promote the well-being of the body as possible provenance of the body imagery: the religious cult of Asklepios, and the ancient world's medical understanding of the well-being of the body drawn from the writings of Hippocrates and Galen.

Disease, if not cured, has the potential to spread throughout the entire body, thereby affecting the health, well-being, and function of the affected

---

50. John Chrysostom believed that Paul referred to the genitalia (*Hom. 1 Cor.* 31.425–426). See also Fee, *First Epistle to the Corinthians*, 679; Martin, *Corinthian Body*, 95 and Ciampa and Rosner, *First Letter to the Corinthians*, 605: "Everyone agrees that the *unpresentable* parts which *are treated with special modesty* refer in the first place to the sexual organs" (emphasis original). Contra Martin, *Spirit and the Congregation*, 28 who believes that the less honourable members are the gastric organs, especially the stomach.

51. Martin, *Corinthian Body*, 95.

parts.⁵² Dio Chrysostom, in addressing the conflict of Tarsus with smaller neighboring towns, draws an analogy between the health of the body and the divisions in the Council:

> For, let me tell you, you must not think that there is harmony (ὁμονοεῖν) in the Council itself, nor yet among yourselves, the Assembly. At any rate, if one were to run through the entire list of citizens, I believe he would not discover even two men in Tarsus who think alike, but on the contrary, just as with certain incurable and distressing diseases which are accustomed to pervade the whole body, exempting no member of it from their inroads, so this state of discord, this almost complete estrangement of one from another, has invaded your entire body politic.⁵³

In light of this, there is some merit in looking at how the well-being of body was understood in the Greco-Roman world.

The Cult of Asklepios

One of the largest temple buildings found in Corinth was a major sanctuary of Asklepios, the god of healing.⁵⁴ Archaeological excavations carried out at the temple have discovered a large number of terracotta replicas of various parts of the human body. These life-sized terracotta replicas were offerings of gratitude made by the devotees to Asklepios to whom they attributed the healing of their bodies. Collins has remarked that more than seventy stories attributable to Asklepios were associated with the cult temples located in Epidaurus, Kos, and an island in the Tiber at Rome.⁵⁵ This indicates how popular the deity was. In addition, coins minted in the second and early third century CE in Corinth depicting Asklepios and Hygieia further suggest the popularity of this cult.⁵⁶ A display room in the museum at ancient Corinth contains examples of these anatomical votives including ears, feet, male genitalia, woman's breasts, hands, legs, and feet. These demonstrated not only the popularity and power of the Asklepios cult but also underscored that even the smaller parts of the body that were unwell could affect

52. See Philo, *Decalogue* 150.
53. Dio Chrysostom, *Or.* 34.20.
54. For an overview of Asklepios cult activity in Corinth, see Wickkiser, "Asklepios," 37–66; and Bookidis, "Sanctuaries of Corinth," 247–59.
55. Collins, *First Corinthians*, 462. See also Wickkiser, "Asklepios," 37–39 for the popularity and significance of the Asklepios cult.
56. Wickkiser, "Asklepios," 55. See also Fig. 6.21 on page 184 for a photograph of the coin.

a person's overall well-being. According to Collins, one of the interesting features of the collection of terracotta replicas is the inclusion of eighteen complete examples of male genitalia.[57] The fact that many of the replicas are genitalia, which were described by Paul as parts of the body that were weaker, less honorable, and inferior, clearly underscored the importance of this member of the body.

Andrew Hill has suggested that the cult of Asklepios could be a possible source for Paul's understanding of body imagery.[58] Paul lived eighteen months in Corinth and addressed many issues related to the social reality of the city, so it is not unreasonable to conjecture that the inspiration for his body imagery in 1 Cor 12 could be derived from within the city of Corinth itself. The fact that the Asklepios cult was extremely popular not only in Corinth but also the Mediterranean world coupled with the evidence drawn from extensive archaeological excavations make for a convincing case that Paul would have been at least familiar with the cult's practices. At the least, the votive offerings that placed emphasis on the individual dismembered body parts were probably a contributory influence on the thought and language of Paul who refers to such dismembered parts in 1 Cor 12:14–25.[59]

If the cult of Asklepios was operative in Paul's mind, then he was essentially saying that the pagans knew better how to care for their body. If any parts of their body were not functioning well and if the prevailing medical science was unable to provide adequate care, they would not have hesitated to seek for divine healing in the temple of Asklepios. This would have been with the promise that they would offer up terracotta replicas of those parts of the body as an acknowledgement that the healing came from Asklepios. The large number of male genitalia and women's breasts showed that ancient people knew better when it came to the well-being and treatment of the lesser, inferior, and weak parts of their bodies.[60]

---

57. Collins, *First Corinthians*, 462.

58. Hill, "Temple of Asclepius," 437–39. Cf. Fee, *First Epistle to the Corinthians*, 667, who is too quick to dismiss Hill's suggestion without assigning any valid reasons.

59. Hill, "Temple of Asclepius," 438.

60. While it has been common suggestion that the high number of male genitalia as displayed in the archaeological museum in Corinth attested to the licentious lifestyle of the Corinthians in which the offerings were made after the healing of some venereal disease by Asklepios, Collins suggests that these are more likely thank offerings made to the cult for the cure of impotence (Collins, *First Corinthians*, 462).

Honoring the Weak and Inferior: Lessons from Galen and Hippocrates

Timothy Carter takes into serious consideration Paul's admonition to the strong to honor the weaker members of the body by drawing from the writings of Hippocrates and Galen on physiology.[61] Sociologically, while the "weaker members of the body" may refer to the social standing of the members, the same can also be said of the human body. Carter argues that if "the physical body has 'weaker members' then the term needs to be understood firstly in terms of its physiological meaning and then secondarily in terms of its metaphorical meaning as applied to the social body of the church."[62]

In the human body, organs such as the heart, lungs, and liver are recognized as vital. Hippocrates suggested that there was a correlation between unity of the various parts of the body and the health of the person: "I hold that if man were a unity he would never feel pain, as there would be nothing from which a unity could suffer pain. And even if he were to suffer, the cure too would have to be one."[63]

But Hippocrates was quick to add that in reality this was not always the case.

> But as a matter of fact cures are many. For in the body are many constituents, which by heating, by cooling, by drying, or by wetting one another contrary to nature, engender diseases; so that both the forms of diseases are many and the healing of them is manifold.[64]

According to Hippocrates, there were four humors that made up a person: blood, phlegm, yellow bile, and black bile, and it was through these that a person felt pain or enjoyed health.[65] A person was healthy if there was balance among these humors. However, when there was excess or defect among these elements, then a person would feel pain. Hippocrates acknowledged that a human body had stronger and weaker parts. Diseases were most dangerous when they moved from the strongest part of the body to the weakest:

> Those diseases are most dangerous which arise in the strongest part of the body. For should the disease remain where it began,

---

61. Carter, "Looking at the Metaphor," 93–115.
62. Ibid., 100.
63. Hippocrates, *Nat. hom.* 2.11–15.
64. Ibid., 2.15–20.
65. Ibid., 4.1–4.

the whole body, as the strongest limb in it feels pain, must be in pain; while should the disease move from a stronger part to one of the weaker parts, the riddance of it proves difficult. But when diseases move from weaker parts to stronger parts, it is easier to get rid of them, as the strength of the stronger part will easily consume the humours that flow into them.[66]

Hippocrates did not mention what constituted the stronger or weaker parts of the body. Since the diseases that originated from the strongest parts and moved to the weakest parts were the deadliest, and the stronger parts were able to deal with any humors from the weakest parts, the questions that arise are: Who were the most essential parts of the body? Were they the stronger parts?

Assuming that it was better for the humors to move from the weaker parts to the stronger parts, then the latter would seem to be more important. However, this made no sense, as suggested by Galen. He described this argument as false and argued that on the contrary, the reverse was true.[67] Following Galen, Carter argues: "If the Hippocratic writer is correct in saying that it is better for humors to move from the weaker to the stronger parts of the body, it follows that the stronger parts of the body cannot be the most essential."[68] Since the weaker parts required the cooperation from the stronger parts to draw the humors away in order to neutralize them, it would seem that the weaker parts were the parts that should be given more care and protection. In this respect, the weaker parts of the body were the most essential parts after all.[69]

If Carter is correct, this insight would contribute significantly to understanding Paul's use of body imagery. Although there is no evidence that Paul drew his understanding of body imagery from Hippocratic writings as suggested by Carter,[70] it nevertheless sheds light on the interpretation of 1 Cor 12:12–27, and further enhances Paul's exhortation to the strong to care for the weak. Therefore by using body imagery, Paul turns the social convention upside down and emphasizes the vital role the weak played in the body. The well-being of the body as a whole demands that more care should be given to the weaker members. As seen in the Hippocratic model,

---

66. Ibid., 10.1–10.
67. Galen, *On Hippocrates'* 128–30.
68. Carter, "Looking at the Metaphor," 104.
69. Ibid., 104–5.

70. Ibid., 105. However, Carter speculates that perhaps Luke the Evangelist as a doctor could be a source of Paul's claim in 1 Cor 12:22. See Carter, "Looking at the Metaphor," 104n42.

the stronger members had the power to draw excess humors away from the weaker and vulnerable members and neutralize them before finally expelling them. Hence, the stronger members had the duty to ensure the well-being of the weaker ones by protecting them from harmful humors.

Health and Social Status

Galen, in his writings, made an interesting observation between a person's social status and the maintenance of health. He assumed that people of lower socioeconomic status, due to their lack of education, would have a more difficult time warding off disease and maintaining their health.[71] They were the weaker members of the body. This is not surprising as the body was a direct expression of social status in Greco-Roman culture and higher status was assigned to the visible parts. This was conveniently framed within an upper-class ideology. The rich were always portrayed as having natural beauty and were often positioned close to the gods.[72] Furthermore, Martin also suggests that since illness was portrayed by ancient medical writers as a disruption of the natural harmony and balance of the body's essence, humors, and states (hot/cold, moist/dry), so discord was envisaged as the disruption of the natural concord of the different groups and classes that made up the body politic.[73] In this respect, even in the medical field, the emphasis remains firmly rooted in social hierarchy. Therefore it is not surprising that the Corinthian church echoed how the weak, the less honorable, and the inferior were despised by those of higher social status. To them, the weaker members of the congregation simply did not deserve any respect or honor.

BODY METAPHOR AND SOCIAL IDENTITY FORMATION

The body metaphor is a powerful expression and symbol of a society and its culture. Its representation in literature contemporaneous with Paul constitutes a reflection of society's attitude towards itself and others. Likewise, Paul's use of body metaphor was also a powerful expression of what the Christ-community should be. Drawing inspiration from the medical sources for the promotion of well-being of the body, Paul uses the body

---

71. Galen, *Hygiene* as quoted in Martin, *Corinthian Body*, 31–32.

72. For further discussion, see Martin, *Corinthian Body*, 34–37.

73. Ibid., 39. See also Isocrates, *De pace* 109; Dio Chrysostom *Or.* 34.17, 20, 22; 38.12.14; and Aelius Aristides *Orat.* 24.16, 18.

metaphor to focus on the weak and less honorable, a departure from the prevailing social convention. He did not seem to be interested in enforcing the social conventions marked by hierarchy that favored the elites of the Christ-community.

Re-socialization that Includes a Voice for the Other

Paul uses body metaphor in the re-socialization process of the Corinthians in the formation of social identity. As we have seen, the division in the Corinthian church was not only along the lines of rich and poor, higher-status and lower status believers, and elites and the masses, but also according to the type of manifestation of spiritual gifts.[74] By using the body metaphor, Paul was able to address these issues. He not only exhorted the Corinthians to social harmony, but exposed the folly of their thoughts and actions.

What sort of unity did Paul envision in the formation of social identity? Meeks argues that Paul used the image of body as the moral philosophers did to suggest that differentiation does not compromise but promotes the unity of the group, so long as the interdependence of the members is recognized.[75] But Meeks' insistence fails to take cognizance of the fact that in Hellenistic writings, the weak and the marginalized were never given a place or hearing in the body. Interdependence was promoted only if this benefited the elites or the ruling class. Likewise, unity was promoted not for the benefit of those of lower social status, but the ruling elites.[76] It was often forged by silencing the voice of the poor, the weak, and the marginalized whose only option was to comply with the ruling elites for the sake of survival.

On the other hand, Kim argues that reading Paul's use of body metaphor as functioning *only* for a call for unity is, without doubt, missing the point.[77] Not only would this condone Paul as advocating "a dominant ideol-

74. See Banks, *Paul's Idea of Community*, 58–61.

75. Meeks, *First Urban Christians*, 90.

76. Contra Mitchell where she argues that appeal for harmony and concord (*homonoia*) is made at the price of diversity, Mitchell, *Paul and Rhetoric of Reconciliation*, 20–64. Kim has offered his critique for Mitchell's work where her reading only hears the voice of the elites but not the voice of the women, slaves, the weak, and other marginalized groups of people. See Kim, *Christ's Body in Corinth*, 24. See also Barrett, *First Epistle to the Corinthians*, 292–93; Dunn, "'The Body of Christ'," 146–62; Witherington, *Conflict and Community*, 261.

77. Kim, *Christ's Body in Corinth*, 1–5. See also Robinson, *Body*, 60, who argues that Paul's use of the body language goes beyond unity and that multiplicity is always expressed in the language of the body as in 1 Cor 10:17; 12:12; Rom 12:5; Gal 3:28. See also 1 Cor 12:4–31; Rom 12:3–8; Eph 4:1–16.

ogy of hierarchical unity" which is promoted by the Greco-Roman rhetoric of concord, it would also silence the voice of those who are being marginalized in the community.[78] For Paul, unity was not the exclusion of others. In 1 Cor 12:22–26, Paul defends the weak and views them as indispensable (1 Cor 12:22), regards the less honorable with honor (1 Cor 12:23), and treats the parts that are not presentable with special modesty (1 Cor 12:23). Paul further mentions that God is the one who puts together various members of the body and gave greater honor to those that lacked it (1 Cor 12:24). This is hardly a case of forcing the marginalized or weaker members of the body to submit to the strong or to conform to the wishes of the more honorable ones. Instead, Paul seems to advocate that unity should not be promoted at the dictation of the stronger members, but by recognizing the needs of the weak. Read in this light, Paul seems to go against the Greco-Roman conventions of his days where honoring and promoting the strong were the norms.

The imagery of the body used by Paul allowed the Corinthians to see how in their own physical body, they could not afford to ignore those inferior and less honorable parts. Instead, they ought to take greater care for these weaker parts. Likewise, the inferior and weaker members of the body of Christ were not only worthy of respect and honor, it would be a disgrace to the wider community if these sub-groups were to be despised. Paul did this by allowing his audience to listen to the talking feet, ears, and eyes, and to reflect on their own situation of how they had repudiated those weaker and less honorable members of their body. In Paul's vision of the body, the strong was responsible to protect the weak and to ensure that no harm will befall them. In this respect, Paul urged the Corinthians to use the spiritual gifts given by God for the common good of the body and building up the community, rather than forcing the subordination of some members to others in the name of unity.

The body also speaks of a community that not only embraces but celebrates diversity and solidarity. The image of Christ crucified demonstrates that Jews and gentiles, slave and free were not only welcome but were to become this one body. The Corinthian community was to be defined not by wealth or status, but based on one's identity in Christ. Whether a community of Christ lives up to its calling depends on how it offers sacrificial love to and stands in solidarity with those who are broken and marginalized in society. This is where Paul's vision of the social identity of a united Christ-community—where weaker sub-groups are given proper recognition and honor—differentiates it from other communities. Paul's understanding of the gospel of Christ "challenges the whole notion of the community based

---

78. Kim, *Christ's Body in Corinth*, 1.

on 'either/or' language of belonging and exclusion and makes possible a new formation of the community of *all* in diversity."[79] In this respect, Gerd Theissen's "love patriarchalism," an ethos of interpersonal warmth which functioned to allow a few rich or upper class people to maintain the Pauline communities, may not have worked in Paul's vision for the Corinthians.[80] Theissen's "love patriachalism" endorses the hierarchy deeply entrenched within the Greco-Roman world, with some slight modifications where sacrificial love now rules the community. This approach fails to take into consideration Paul's exhortation to honor the weak and less honorable within the community, and Kim rightly questions whether the voice of the marginalized has been properly heard in the reading of body metaphor.[81]

Social Hierarchy Relativized in Christ

Dale Martin argues that the body is commonly used to reinforce the traditional hierarchy reflected in the social reality in which the head was often used to represent the most divine part of the body where it ruled the rest.[82] Martin makes reference to Artemidorus who in his *Dream Handbook* pointed out that the different parts of the body had different status significance. The head represented one's father, the foot a slave; the right hand male family members, and the left hand female family members. Artemidorus also described the eyes as representing one's daughter and the feet one's slave. While the interpretation of the different parts of the body may be fluid, Martin argues that without exception, hierarchy is always assumed.[83] Similarly, Philo called the virtuous person the "head" of the human race, the one from whom all other people drew their life force.[84] Plato also made attribution to the human head as the most divine part of the body, ruling the rest. The body was a mere vehicle for the head, designed to carry it around and to keep it from rolling on the ground.[85]

Since there is some form of social hierarchy attached to the use of body imagery, it is not surprising that this metaphor is used to argue for the

79. Kim, *Christ's Body in Corinth*, 21, emphasis his.

80. See Theissen, *Social Setting*, 36–37, 96–99, 121–40. See Kim, *Christ's Body in Corinth*, 16–18.

81. See Kim, *Christ's Body in Corinth*, 39–63, and his treatment on the politics of the hegemonic body.

82. Martin, *Corinthian Body*, 29–47. See also Lee, *Paul*, 143–50.

83. Martin, *Corinthian Body*, 31.

84. Philo, *Rewards* 125.

85. Plato, *Tim.* 44D.

cessation of dissensions through the acceptance of one's place in the body in Hellenistic literature. The typical argument is for the strong or elites to rule while the weak or marginalized submit to them to ensure harmony and concord are maintained for the common good. The lower class is often forced to accommodate the demands of the higher class in order to protect the interests of those lower down the social scale. This form of relationship is labeled by Martin as "benevolent patriarchalism."[86] Martin defines benevolent patriarchalism as offering a middle way between two political extremes. He explains:

> In Greco-Roman political writings and speeches, democracy is portrayed as the excessive freedom of the masses and the enslavement of the upper class (the "natural leaders") to the lower class, resulting in chaos. Tyranny, at the other extreme, is portrayed as excessively harsh and unbending rule whereby the upper class, an oligarchic faction, or a dictator rules without taking into account sufficiently the interests of the entire political body, including the masses. But when the stronger rules the weaker with restraint and the weaker submits to the stronger in self-control, the interests of the entire city are protected, and everybody lives happily ever after.[87]

While Martin's proposal is attractive, it remains rooted in some form of promotion of social hierarchy. What Paul clearly advocates is that the strong is to honor the less honorable, inferior, and weaker members of the body. This appeal stands in sharp contrast to the traditional understanding of societal hierarchy,[88] and would have been scandalous to the strong or elites in the community. Instead of promoting and defending the strong and elite, Paul adopts a status reversal approach by focusing on the weak, and eventually elevates the status of the weak. This is where Carson, who argues that Paul is not interested in the varied social strata that made up the community but in the perceived stratification of the gifts, misses the point.[89] If one takes the language that Paul uses in 1 Cor 12:22–24—ἀσθενέστερα (weaker); ἀτιμότερα (less honourable); τιμὴν περισσοτέραν περιτίθεμεν (bestowed with abundant honour); τὰ ἀσχήμονα (the shameful/unpresentable ones); εὐσχημοσύνην περισσοτέραν ἔχει (with greater respect); τὰ . . . εὐσχήμονα (the respectable ones)—the focus on social strata is unmistakably apparent, but unfortunately lost in translation. There is even a high likelihood of a

---

86. Martin, *Corinthian Body*, 42. See his wider discussion in 38–68.
87. Ibid., 42.
88. Lee, *Paul*, 144–45.
89. Cf. Carson, *Showing the Spirit*, 49,

close correlation between social stratification and the stratification of gifts.[90] Witherington rightly points out that the Romans divided society into two groups with regard to honor: "... the *honestiores*, or priviledged and 'honorable' strata of society, and the *humiliores*, who did not qualify for reasons of birth, lack of wealth, or possibly education to be among the elite."[91] In this respect, gifts such as tongues, wisdom, and knowledge would have been perceived to be of higher status.

This reversal of status can be further seen in 1 Cor 14:18–19 where Paul identifies himself with the strong first by declaring that he speaks in tongues more than anyone. But he immediately switches his tone by reiterating that he would give up speaking in tongues and instead, speaking in intelligible words so that the rest of the church may understand the message of exhortation (1 Cor 14:18–19). In declaring this, Paul is also instructing those who perceived that they might have higher social status because of the possession of the gift of tongues to give up their rights to speak for the sake of the weaker brother so that there would be no schism in the body (1 Cor 12:25).

This status reversal changed the way the Corinthians were to look at themselves and the world around them. By using body imagery, Paul goes beyond maintaining order within the assembly where the less honorable, inferior, and weaker members of the body were expected to submit to the ruling elites. Here Paul redefines the boundaries of the Christ-followers. He challenges the strong and the elites to a self-lowering status reversal to serve and care for the weak, the inferior, and the less honorable. It is in doing so that the body of Christ is built up and edified. This argument flies in the face of the prevailing culture, and would have evoked strong emotional response from the elites. This is the main point of departure that Paul takes in building up the community and in the creation of Christian identity. Essentially, Paul is not just offering his criticism of the prevailing culture with its value and status system, he is countering it with the message of his gospel. The values that Paul is propagating would have seriously undermined the social systems and values that he finds incompatible with his understanding of the gospel of Christ. As such, the identity of the community as the body of Christ provides group boundaries that distinguished the Corinthian Christ-followers from the wider society. In light of this, Paul's letter not only reflects what the Christ-community was like but what it should be. The constant emphasis that the poor and weak should be honored shows that

---

90. Ciampa and Rosner, *First Letter to the Corinthians*, 605.
91. Witherington, *Conflict and Community*, 259–60.

they not only belonged to the body of Christ, but their presence made the community a true body of Christ.

Solidarity with the Weak

To add to the element of surprise and shock for his audience, Paul introduces the theme of solidarity in suffering with the weaker members of the body: "If one member suffers, all suffer together with it; if one member is honored, all rejoice together with it" (1 Cor 12:26). While the notion of solidarity in suffering is present in Hellenistic writings, it is hardly used in direct reference to the weaker members of the body. Dio Chrysostom commented:

> For is that man not most blessed who has many bodies with which to be happy when he experiences a pleasure, many souls with which to rejoice when he is fortunate? And if glory be the high goal of the ambitions, he may achieve it through the eulogies of his friend.[92]

Plutarch was once asked by Menemachus, a young man, for advice concerning public life. In his replies, Plutarch commented that there should be "sharing the griefs of those who fail and the joys of those who succeed."[93] The understanding of co-suffering and co-rejoicing often pointed towards the good of the community, but at the same time, the idea of the strong caring and suffering together with the weak was almost unheard of.

At the same time, Paul also advocates the interdependence of all members of the body. The body of Christ is a single body. This was in accordance with the divine ordinance in arranging the different parts of the body together. Because of this, practices such as hierarchy where certain members of the community were granted special status and one party was honored more than another were to be rejected. The gifts of God were given freely by the Spirit of God and were not based on one's social status. As such, possession of these gifts was not reason to boast. Those who were blessed with the seemingly greater gifts were to use them for the community as a whole, not for themselves and certainly not for the enhancement of their status within and without the community.

---

92. Dio Chrysostom, *Or.* 3.108–109.
93. Plutarch, *Praec. ger. rei publ.* 823A.

Rituals to Solidify the Social Identity of the Corinthians

Paul also draws on the baptism rites in 1 Cor 12:13 to reinforce his point that the Christ-community was to be a single body where social hierarchy was relativized. Each person, after having been baptized into the one body, and having the same spirit, should not be subjected to any form of distinction based on social status when the church gathered together for worship. Earlier on in 1 Cor 11:17–34, Paul had evoked the Eucharistic meal where he established the bonds of a fictive family—all members of this family shared the same meal, and ate together. By evoking another rite—the ritual of baptism—Paul further reminds the Corinthian of their identity in Christ (see also 1 Cor 1:14–15; Gal 3:27–28; and Rom 6:3–11).

The use of religious rites was to prompt the Corinthians to evaluate whether what they had been practicing corresponded with the symbolic meaning of these rites. By baptizing each member of the Christ-community into the body of Christ, Paul's concern was that the members of the community acknowledge and respect diversity and embrace those who were marginalized. Those who insisted on maintaining hierarchical boundaries of power, honor, wealth, and status would find no room in Paul's vision of the Christ-community. Through the use of body metaphor, Paul challenges the Corinthians' narrow vision of the community based on their social norms. For the community to be a body of Christ—a Christ that is crucified (cf. 1 Cor 1:23; 2:2)—it needed to learn to embrace diversity. In this respect, Paul's voice has not only become the voice of the marginalized, but one that was deeply rooted in his vision of the cross. Kim rightly argues:

> Christ's body imagined through Christ crucified gives hope to the weak and marginalized in the community, even in the midst of their limited, marginal experience—just as Christ necessarily did. Christ crucified is a symbol and the power of God reaching out to the downtrodden, the dregs of the world. In short, accounting for the crucified body as a dimension of the "body of Christ" provides us with a vision of the "body of Christ" in radical association with the broken bodies of the world.[94]

Those marginalized—the weak, who were invisible and hidden behind the powerful and elite and the strong—had now been given a voice, a face, a place of belonging, and a sense of identity. Paul's vision of social identity for the Christ-community is nothing short of radical. In inter-group comparison, the norm is that the lower the status of a group in comparison to other

---

94. Kim, *Christ's Body in Corinth*, 31. See also Barton, *Life Together*, and Barton, "Paul's Sense of Place," 225–46.

groups, the less this lower status group would have to contribute to positive social identity formation.[95] But in the Pauline community, the reverse was true.

A body can only function normally and properly if it is healthy and whole. Paul feared for the mutilation of the body if the Corinthians continued to disregard other parts of the body. It is because of this that he emphasized the body as a whole and yet retained the individuality of the body where the hand remained a hand, and the feet remained the feet. But now that they are in Christ, both the rich and poor are on equal ground. It is in this new body that all members acknowledge their complementarity and mutuality. It is in this new body that they are to respect, honor, and cooperate with one another. The metaphor of body provides this body with an identity that served as a model for the larger community in the city.

SUMMARY

Paul's use of body imagery did not merely serve as a foundation for his exhortation. It also served to give the Christ-community a sense of identity that governed their ethical and social behavior. In the context of the Corinthian correspondence, the body imagery functions as the very theological conviction that undergirds Paul's exhortations and ethical instructions to honor, nurture, and care for the weaker and vulnerable members of the body. It is these theological convictions that shape Paul's response to questions related to proper conduct that would eventually characterize those belonging to the Christ-community. What starts off as seemingly similar to the Greco-Roman discourses on body imagery ends up being a radical critique of the prevailing social conventions. Paul is socially subversive in his use of body imagery, challenging many assumptions and self-understanding of the Corinthians. At the same time, he creatively re-imagines the Corinthians' ideas associated with body metaphor. The church, comprising both strong and weak members, relied on the former to protect the latter and ensured its survival. The strong had a duty to look out for the welfare of the weak and not merely their own interests. Caring only for themselves and despising the weak would have disastrous consequences for the body of Christ. Therefore, all members of Christ's body must stand united in honoring those who were weaker, less honorable, and less presentable parts. In the body of Christ, social stratification of the Greco-Roman culture was radically and profoundly subverted by the rich serving the poor and the master honoring the slave.

95. See Tajfel and Turner, "An Integrative Theory," 43.

Part III

7

Paul, Metaphors, and Social Identity Formation in the Corinthian Letters

THROUGHOUT THIS BOOK, I have argued that carefully and skillfully chosen metaphors are not mere linguistic tools or rhetorical devices that enhance the literary beauty of Paul's rhetoric, but also cognitive devices that could shape the thinking, change the behavior, and construct new realities among the Christ-followers in their social identity formation.

In chapter 1, I highlighted that the study of Paul's use of metaphors had been neglected, particularly the range of metaphors in his letters to the Corinthians that would shape the social identity of the recipients. I suggested that the power of metaphor to communicate largely depends on the capacity of these images to encompass and condense a range of meanings and convey the intended message. In order for a metaphor to be understood and its message transmitted, both author and audience must understand it in the same manner. If there is discrepancy between the two parties, then the message of the metaphor may be lost or misunderstood. In light of this, I argued that the metaphors Paul used to address his predominantly gentile audience were largely drawn from the Greco-Roman world. To understand Paul's use of metaphors, we need to discern the culture and worldviews of the Corinthians and his understanding of the gospel. As such, identifying the source domain and target domain for metaphors is necessary to understand how they function as effective communication tools and cognitive devices.

Drawing from Conceptual Metaphor Theory, I argued that Paul's use of metaphors is not only calculated but a deliberate attempt at persuading the Christ-followers to remember the preaching of his gospel of Christ, adhere to certain behavioral patterns and ethical norms, and observe certain rituals in the formation of a distinct Christian social identity. What makes a metaphor meaningful is the frequency and thematic coherence of its use together with other metaphors. In the case of the Corinthian correspondence, there are several notable observations. First of all, in using metaphors, Paul is not simply attempting to appeal to his readers' rational intellect by advancing his ideas and arguments. His intention is to move, transform, and direct them to the authentic path of his gospel, and demonstrate how life within a community could possible reflect that. Secondly, Paul is also appealing to the imagination, conscience, and worldviews of his recipients. He tries to draw them into exploring these familiar images in new dimensions that were rooted in their social reality as Christ-followers. Finally, Paul also issues an invitation for the readers to unite the images conveyed by these metaphors—such as brothers and sisters, temple, body—with their own experience living as part of a community. It is when these images are united with the readers' experience that a shared repertoire emerges that will then have profound effects on the way the Christ-followers live and in the formation of their social identity.

To consider the process of identity formation as group phenomena, I turned to the application of Social Identity Theory (SIT) as the key contribution to this study in chapter 2. SIT provides a valuable conceptual framework to understand the process of forming and maintaining identity, and prepares the ground for a reading of the interplay between metaphors and social identity in the Corinthian letters. Group dynamics which influenced how people perceived themselves and other groups were ingrained in first-century Mediterranean society. As such, SIT serves our purpose well in understanding first-century Mediterranean society as well as Paul's letters, particularly the two canonical letters of Corinthians which deal with numerous problems and conflicts of real people. SIT focuses on how members of one group seek to differentiate themselves from other groups so as to achieve a positive social identity. It argues that humans function not as individuals, but as part of the wider socio-cultural domain. Differences and similarities among these groups are clearly reflected across a shared boundary. Members of a group are seen, perceived, and described in ways that emphasize their similarities that bind them together, while distinguishing them from other groups.

Chapters 3 through 6 contained my examination of four major clusters of metaphors used by Paul—sibling, familial, temple, and body metaphors—in the formation of Christian social identity of the Corinthian assembly. In using these metaphors, Paul was concerned not only with the salient identity of the community but also the cognitive transformation of the Christ-followers. Transformation of the cognitive process is part of the communal spiritual experience in the formation of their social identity.[1] I have attempted to show that many of the problems and conflicts within the Christ-movement in Corinth addressed by Paul were group-related issues. Thus, SIT is helpful in analyzing how Paul identified and addressed these issues. It is now time to bring together the results of my investigation on Paul's use of metaphors in social identity formation of the Corinthian assembly.

PROBLEMS IN SOCIAL IDENTITY FORMATION IN CORINTH

By the time 1 and 2 Corinthians were written, the Christ-community would have been in existence for at least five years.[2] In other words, Paul was not dealing with the initial formation of Christian social identity but that of the next stage of group formation.[3] During this period, the number of Christ-followers would have increased considerably, and possibly with subgroups meeting in various locations.[4] Diverse social groups also existed, comprising gentiles and Jews drawn from both upper and lower strata of

---

1. This nuanced understanding of Pauline anthropology finds support in Rom 12:1, and is often badly translated in the English translations. The translation of τὴν λογικὴν λατρείαν into "spiritual worship" (NRSV and ESV), "spiritual act of worship" (NIV 1984), "true worship" (TNIV), "true or proper worship" (NIV 2011), "reasonable service" (NET) amongst others, fails to bring up the cognitive dimension of τὴν λογικὴν. A more appropriate translation of τὴν λογικὴν λατρείαν is "rational worship" since λογικός carries with it the meaning of "being carefully thought through, *thoughtful*" (BDAG, s.v.). This underscores the importance of the cognitive faculties and is further supported in Rom 12:2 where the language related to cognitive functions is clearly employed: "Do not be conformed to this world, but be transformed (μεταμορφοῦσθε) by the renewing of your minds (τοῦ νοὸς), so that you may discern (δοκιμάζειν) what is the will of God—what is good and acceptable and perfect."

2. According to Acts 18:1–17, we could confidently date the founding visit of Paul around 50–51 CE based on the reference to Gallio, the Proconsul of Achaia. If 1 and 2 Corinthians were written in the years of 55–58 CE, the community would have been in existence for at least five years.

3. According to Malina, this stage of group formation would probably be labeled as "storming." In this stage, "(c)onflict among members emerges, with emotions getting free expression . . . with group members arguing with each other and heaping criticism on the leaders." See Malina, "Early Christian Groups," 104.

4. For the possibility of the Christ-community meeting in different locations, see Adams, *Earliest Christian Meeting Places*.

society. While there is no evidence of social elites in Corinth in the likes of the order of senators, *equites* or *decurions*, there are indications of rather well to do people.[5] At the same time, considerable conflict, tensions, and divisions existed, threatening the unity and cohesiveness of the group. If these problems were not adequately addressed, the solidarity of the group would be severely threatened, and undermined the sense of belonging. An exodus, most likely of those from the subordinate groups, remained a high possibility. All of the above suggest that intragroup differentiation existed in the community, further contributing to internal conflicts resulting in a poor social identity formation and a less than cohesive group.

The formation of Christian social identity in Corinth faced several major obstacles. The first was the deteriorating relationship between the various subgroups. The oral report from Chloe's household suggests that there were σχίσματα, (divisions) and ἔριδες (quarrels) among the members of the community (1 Cor 1:10–11), leading to competing claims of loyalty to different leaders (1 Cor 1:12). Earlier scholarship attributes the primary causes for these divisions among the different subgroups to theological or doctrinal differences.[6] However, a closer examination of the Corinthian letters does not yield much to support this claim. The rise of social-scientific studies that have dominated Pauline studies in the past two decades has convincingly pointed out that the primary cause of these divisions was largely due to the prevailing social phenomena rather than doctrinal differences.

One social characteristic that contributed to deep conflicts was the social norms of honor and shame in the Greco-Roman world. Mark Finney, in examining the notion of φιλοτιμία, the love of honor, in the Greco-Roman world argues that φιλοτιμία and conflicts in the Christ-movement in Corinth were closely related.[7] According to Finney, many of the Christ-followers continued to operate within their previous social realities even after becoming members of the Christ-movement. This led to interpersonal conflicts, tensions in the community, and crisis of social identity.

Almost every aspect of Greco-Roman life was closely tied to the notion of honor—one's birth, family, lineage, status and social position, friends and acquaintances, wealth and other material possessions, one's size of retinues

---

5. For further discussion on socio-economic profiling and the possible social status of the various names related to the Corinthian church including Gaius, Phoebe, Priscilla and Aquilla, Stephanus, Crispus, Erastus, Chloe, Archaicus and Fortunatus, and Tertius, see Brookins, *Corinthian Wisdom*, 107–19. Brookins lists them as people with some degree of wealth and social status.

6. See Thiselton, *First Epistle to the Corinthians*, 121–33, for a survey of the history of interpretation.

7. Finney, *Honour and Conflict*.

(clients, slaves, and soldiers), and power and power relations. All these were held in high esteem. Any attack on one's honor was tantamount to an attack on one's life and well-being. When honor was central to an individual's significance, it is not surprising that the fear of shame may drive one to defend honor "at all cost and even life itself was considered to be inconsequential in its preservation or augmentation."[8] It is therefore not surprising that conflicts and social tensions in Corinth were closely related to φιλοτιμία. All the jostling for recognition, maintenance of social status, and defending of personal honor were major contributions to the problems in Corinth, leading to divisions and quarrels.

The second major obstacle for the Corinthian community was the lack of salient social identity rooted in the gospel proclaimed by Paul. Despite the community having been in existence for some years, a strong and shared Christian social identity across all subgroups was not yet fully established. One of the plausible reasons for this was the result of cross-cutting identities, where the dominance of those of a higher social status exerted their influences in the community, as seen in many of the problems addressed by Paul. Furthermore, the lack of tension between the Christ-movement and civic society is rather apparent from Paul's letters.[9] In other words, the Corinthians' civic identity had taken precedence over their social identity as Christ-followers. In light of this, Tucker convincingly argues that one of the problems in the Corinthian church was a serious lack of salient "in Christ" social identity. This lack of salient "in Christ" identity affected the way the community related to and thought about one another, and thus their communal life, as evidenced by the numerous conflicts and problems that were directly related to social relationships. This is largely because the Christ-followers in Corinth remained well-integrated into Roman civic and social life and identity instead of their "in-Christ" identity.[10] According to Berger and Luckmann, the process of re-socialization takes place when the converts leave behind old ties and embrace new ones, where a new experience with its own knowledge, values, ethos, and social meaning occurs.[11] Unfortunately, this process of re-socialization had yet to take place successfully.

The third obstacle was the chaos and disorder that took place when the community gathered together in worship (1 Cor 11–14). Gender roles, social status, and cultural values collided when the community came together,

---

8. Ibid., 47.

9. See Barclay, "Thessalonica and Corinth," 49–74; Tucker, *You Belong to Christ*, 152–209; and Finney, *Honour and Conflict*, 221.

10. Tucker, *You Belong to Christ*, 152–209.

11. Berger and Luckmann, *Social Construction of Reality*, 176–82.

resulting in disorder and disruption. According to SIT, once members of the group identify with the social identity, their behavior changes to reflect the group norms and ethos. They begin to speak and behave in a way that conforms to the values and expectations of the group. This visible and public performance of social identity reflecting the group sense of belonging was what was glaringly lacking among the Corinthians.

All the above issues demonstrate that cultural beliefs and social pressures seem to have taken higher priority, resulting in the failure of the core expression of Christian social identity. As Meeks says, "Being or becoming religious in the Greco-Roman world did not entail either moral transformation or sectarian socialization."[12] In light of this, existing social identities that stood in contradiction to Paul's social vision of the gospel of Christ needed to be reevaluated and reprioritized. Paul's goal for the communities he planted was the formation of an alternative community with a distinct ethos that served as a visible manifestation of the transforming power of the gospel. But this did not mean the abandonment of all values and norms rooted in Roman civic identity. The fact that Paul used metaphors drawn from the Greco-Roman world is evidence that only specific values and ethos that contradicted or opposed their salient identity in Christ were to be reevaluated. Those that did not contradict Paul's social identity of the gospel were used to promote group identity and cohesiveness.

METAPHORS AND SOCIAL IDENTITY FORMATION

I examined a range of metaphors used by Paul from chapters 3 to 6. The sibling metaphor, ἀδελφός, was the most frequently used self-designation for members within the Christ-community. When a member of a Pauline community called another "brother" or "sister," that member was expressing a term of endearment that speaks of solidarity, affection, or friendship, indicating that the ἐκκλησία was a home to all. The sibling metaphor speaks of physical and emotional security, care and belonging, and mutuality and respect that existed only within the family and household. Family members must not be in conflict with one another. Paul's frequent use of sibling language clearly points to the fact that the Christ-followers should be a very close-knit group, a benchmark that the Corinthians had fallen short of.

Apart from sibling metaphor, Paul uses a range of familial metaphors in describing his relationship with the Corinthians. He was authoritative, yet filled with intimacy and love for them. As a father, he instructed and disciplined his children for their benefit. As a nursing mother, he loved, cared,

---

12. Meeks, *Origins of First Christian Morality*, 28.

and nurtured them towards maturity. As an infant, he was innocent and without any malicious intention to harm them. As a slave, he was humble in carrying out the task assigned for him. Taken together, this range of familial metaphors underscored the fact that Paul would do anything for the Corinthians to shape and build them.

The temple metaphor allows Paul to draw on the previous symbolic universe of the Christ-community and use it powerfully to address issues concerning community identity, the building-up of community, and the appearance of the community to the outsiders. For Paul, the Christ-community was to be a unified community, a holy community, and a community set apart and distinct from the society around them.

The body metaphor is a collective and corporate language used to stress the unity, concord, and togetherness of the community. The well-being of the body could only be promoted if the various parts, whether strong or weak, rich or poor, presentable or unpresentable, functioned properly. This metaphor undergirds Paul's exhortations and ethical instructions to honor, nurture, and care for the weaker and vulnerable members of the body.

Collectively, these metaphors point to a powerful symbolic construction of social identity in a number of ways.[13] First of all, these metaphors speak of a sense of shared belonging. As members of the Christ-community in Corinth, these Christ-followers organized their lives and understood their social locations in which they lived. Their relationships with one another were now defined by their salient "in Christ" identity and this governed their deep sense of belonging to the community. Though strangers and unrelated, they were now considered brothers and sisters in the family of God when the sibling metaphor was evoked. They were now a body with different parts, and constituted a temple in which God dwelt. This demanded a complete reordering of human relationships. Paul uses sibling imagery whose literal meaning were people who shared the same birth parents. He applies this to the Corinthians who did not share the same birth parents, but who had in common their baptism into and union in Christ. In this context, Paul substitutes the idea of being "in Christ" for the idea of sharing the same parents and suggests that the Corinthians were now siblings, sharing the same duties and responsibilities, and carrying with it ethical consequences. These metaphors collectively called forth the bonds of affection that Paul had for the Corinthians, and also the ties that bound the members of the community together in goodwill, interdependence, friendship, protection, provision, honor, respect, love, kinship and glory. Every member had a

---

13. For further discussion, see Cohen, *Symbolic Construction of Community*.

place in this community and was important. No one was a stranger. All were welcome.

Secondly, Paul used these metaphors to exhort members of the Christ-community to act in the best interests of the community and evaluate their relationship with outsiders. Collectively, these metaphors transmitted not only shared assumptions about the community but also a collective consciousness of the social bond that defines and shapes the community's identity. An individual's identity was redefined, then woven and knit together with the identity of the group. The boundary lines were drawn between the "in-Christ" group and outsiders, and the Corinthians were reminded that in this new family, all social, economic, and ethnic boundaries established by Greco-Roman society were now eliminated. New expectations were now imposed on them in the way they were to think and act. They could no longer view others through the lens of ethnicity and socio-economic status. They were to increase the honor of everyone in this family, particularly those who were poorer and weaker. The social identity formed transcended social status and ethnic identity. These metaphors were used to shape, guide, and govern how they behaved towards one another.

Thirdly, as a community, the Corinthians shared and participated in a common identity narrative involving the group's social memory of history and tradition rooted in the story of Jesus. The recollection of the shared identity memory not only recounted the shared social vision of what the group was to be, but also provided newer group members a platform to understand and deepen their social identification. This shared narrative also provided a sense of collective continuity, and contributed to group stability and cohesiveness. It also allowed the group to envision how they might change their thinking and the way they behaved so that a consistent group social identity could be maintained. In the context of the Corinthians, Paul emphasized rituals such as Eucharist (1 Cor 11:17–34), baptism (1 Cor 12:13), and collection for the poor in Jerusalem (1 Cor 16:1–4; 2 Cor 8–9) to reinforce the communal sense of belonging. That the divisions were publicly displayed during times of public gathering for worship reflected a fundamental misunderstanding of their social identity.

Finally, metaphors are used to restructure the social reality to match the social vision of the gospel and to realign the values of the Corinthians to the foundational beliefs of the gospel. The explicit reference of the body metaphor to Christ (1 Cor 12:27) serves as a reminder to the Corinthians of the body of Christ crucified. Taken together, the body of Christ and Christ crucified both pointed to the cross where shame and humiliation collided with the pride, boasting, and honor-centric culture of the Corinthians. By using the sibling metaphor to address the various issues related to divisions, sexual immorality, civil litigation, food sacrificed to idols, the operation of spiritual gifts, amongst others, Paul convinced the Corinthians to reconsider their treatment of those who were considered the weaker or poorer siblings in their midst. In this respect, metaphors were not mere cognitive devices to shape and govern the way one thinks and behaves but were also an integral part of Paul's proclamation of the gospel aiming to realign the Corinthians to the fundamental truth of his gospel of Christ crucified.

SOCIAL IDENTITY AND TEMPORAL CONSIDERATION

I have suggested elsewhere that identify formation is not static but a dynamic and continuous process.[14] Identity is formed and shaped, reinforced and strengthened, and modified and reshaped in the continuous dialectic process between the individual and society, and between social relations and social structures. Throughout this process, the individual's patterns of thoughts, symbolic universe, feelings, and actions are shaped, whether consciously or unconsciously, and attributed to the group in which he or she belongs. In view of this, the temporal aspect of social identity formation needs to be taken into account. The context of Corinthians allows further reflection on social identity formation as we have the benefit of subsequent letters written to the Corinthians post-Pauline era that enables temporal comparison to be made.

The letter of 1 Clement, widely accepted to be written at the turn of the second century CE by the Bishop of Rome, offers insights into the temporal aspects of social identity formation. Some of the issues addressed by Paul in his Corinthian letters were similarly picked up by Clement. This leads Horrell to suggest that there is "clearly a good deal of continuity between Paul's Corinthian correspondence and 1 Clement, both in terms of purpose—to restore unity to the Corinthian congregation—and of content, for Clement took up a number of rules and resources which were used within 1 Corinthians."[15]

Divisions and conflicts in the community were among the main problems that continued to plague the Corinthians. This issue had been extensively addressed by Paul in 1 Corinthians (see 1 Cor 1–4; 11:18 and 12:25) and the same is seen in 1 Clement. According to 1 Clem 3:2–3, jealousy and envy (ζῆλος καὶ φθόνος), strife and sedition (ἔρις καὶ στάσις), persecution and tumult (διωγμὸς καὶ ἀκαταστασία), and war and captivity (πόλεμος καὶ αἰχμαλωσία) occurred in the community. This was due to those of lower

---

14. See Lim, "If Anyone Is in Christ," 289–310.
15. Horrell, *Social Ethos*, 278,

status reacting against the rich. Clement specifically labeled this action as the dishonored against the honorable (οἱ ἄτιμοι ἐπὶ τοὺς ἐντίμους), the ill reputed against the highly reputed (οἱ ἄδοξοι ἐπὶ τοὺς ἐνδόξους), the foolish against the wise (οἱ ἄφρονες ἐπὶ τοὺς φρονίμους), and the young against the elder (οἱ νέοι ἐπὶ τοὺς πρεσβυτέρους). This conflict was regarded by Clement as "sedition" (στάσις). In 1 Clem 47:6, the nature of στάσις was described as rebellion carried out by one or two people against the presbyters, possible due to the competition for power. This struggle for power subsequently led to divisions and the wrongful removal of some faithful presbyters from their ministry (see 1 Clem 44:3–6). Clement described this act as "abominable and unholy sedition" (μιαρᾶς καὶ ἀνοσίου στάσεως) that was "alien and foreign to the elect of God" (ἀλλοτρίας καὶ ξένης τοῖς ἐκλεκτοῖς τοῦ Θεοῦ) (1 Clem 1:1), resulting in the name of God being blasphemed and causing many others to stumble (1 Clem 46:9).

Close parallels to Paul's exhortation to peace and order in the assembly (see 1 Cor 14:33, 40) are also reflected in Clement's appeal to the Corinthians. Instead of sedition and strife, the Corinthians were exhorted to pursue peace and harmony (εἰρήνη καί ὁμόνοια), a theme that permeates throughout the letter (see 1 Clem 20:11; 60:4; 61:1; 63:2; 65:1).[16] Like Paul's admonition to the Corinthians, Clement also insisted that the weaker members in the assembly were to be cared for, and they were to reciprocate as well by respecting and being subordinate to the leaders.

Clement also used metaphors in addressing the Corinthians. In demonstrating why division and sedition were so destructive, Clement, like Paul, appealed to the body metaphor. For Clement, it was madness if one rebelled against his or her own body (1 Clem 46:7). Like Paul, Clement also emphasized the unity of and diversity in the body, and the need for cooperation and interdependence where all parts of the body worked together for the good of the whole.[17] Clement also used the sibling metaphor extensively. The word ἀδελφός appears a total of twenty one times, fourteen of which were used in addressing the Corinthians.[18] There is also reference to family

---

16. By using rhetorical analysis, Bakke argues that 1 Clement is a letter promoting concord and peace in the community, where the author urged the Christ-followers in Corinth to cease from strife and sedition and re-establish peace and harmony (εἰρήνη καί ὁμόνοια). See Bakke, *Concord and Peace*. See also Horrell, *Social Ethos*, 238–80.

17. See 1 Clem 46:5–7. See also 1 Clem 37:1–5; 38:1–5; 46:6 where body metaphor is used. Interestingly, 1 Clem 37:5 closely parallels 1 Cor 12:21–22.

18. See 1 Clem 1:1; 13:1; 14:1; 33:1; 37:1; 38:3; 41:1, 2, 4; 45:1, 6; 48:1; 51:1; 62:1. Other references to ἀδελφός appear in 4:6–8 (four times); 31:4; 35:8; 43:4, and once appears as "brotherhood" (ἀδελφότης) in 2:4.

in 1 Clem 21:6–8 although it parallels more closely the Household Codes found in the Deutero-Pauline letters.

Centuries after 1 Clement, tensions, divisions, and conflicts continued to confront the Corinthian church. In the early fifth century CE, the church took matters into its own hands in the appointment of bishops, ignoring canonical law of the Council of Nicaea.[19] While there were rebellions, the hagiography of Corinth as reflected in the lives of St Kodratos and St Leonidas together with their companions revealed a city that saw itself "as a thoroughly Christian city, bearing witness *locally* to the Christian life."[20]

Subsequent evidence and letters in the post-Pauline era to the Corinthian church suggest that the formation of social identity was not static but a continual process. While Paul's vision for social identity formation was clear, it appears this was not adequately translated to the communities, at least by the turn of the second century CE. One may ask why this was so. Either the pull of the civic identity was too strong or Paul's instructions were inadequate for the Christ-community. However, the issue in the Corinthian assembly is not unique. We see similar misunderstanding elsewhere in Galatians on the issue of observance of the Torah and the works of the Law; Thessalonians on the misunderstanding of the parousia and the nature of the resurrection of the body; and Philippians on the presence of Judaizers and divisions in the church. In his letters, we see Paul's attempt to address these issues. This probably suggests that the social implications of the gospel's radical message on the formative communities may not have been adequately reflected upon by Paul. Many of the problems that arose were not anticipated. Paul's directive, according to Finney, appears to be "reactive rather than proactive,"[21] suggesting that the apostle might not have fully anticipated most of these problems, and at the same time, grossly underestimating the strong attachment of his converts to the prevailing civic identity.

CONCLUDING REMARKS

Paul employed metaphors as powerful rhetorical tools to shape the thinking and behavior of the Corinthians. This study has demonstrated the ways in which the sibling, familial, temple and body metaphors were concerted attempts to influence the way the Corinthians think in relation to Paul, his gospel, one another, and subsequently the way they behave and treat each other. As such, Paul's diverse use of metaphors was not accidental but intentional,

19. See Limberis, "Ecclesiastical Ambiguities," 443–547.
20. Ibid., 457, emphasis hers. See also her wider discussion in pages 449–57.
21. Finney, *Honour and Conflict*, 222.

as seen in the thematic coherence of these metaphors in the formation of Christian identity. With the use of these metaphors, Paul creatively tapped into the everyday reality of the ancient world of Corinth. Therefore, membership in the Christ-community depended on the symbolic construction and significance of the similarities that all members could identify with, an umbrella of solidarity under which all could take shelter, whether rich or poor, strong or weak, Jews or gentiles, where diversity is robustly defended, affirmed and celebrated. Taken together, these metaphors functioned powerfully in the formation of social identity rooted in the gospel proclaimed by Paul. At the same time, they served as a foundation for the community's ethos, behavior, and ongoing Christian life and experience.

Bibliography

Aasgaard, Reidar. "Brotherhood in Plutarch and Paul: Its Role and Character." In *Constructing Early Christian Families: Family as Social Reality and Metaphor*, edited by Halvor Moxnes, 166–82. London: Routledge, 1997.
———. "Like a Child: Paul's Rhetorical Uses of Childhood." In *The Child in the Bible*, edited by Marcia J. Bunge, Terence E. Fretheim, and Beverly Roberts Gaventa, 249–77. Grand Rapids: Eerdmans, 2008.
———. *"My Beloved Brothers and Sisters!": Christian Siblingship in Paul.* JSNTSup 265. London: T. & T. Clark, 2004.
———. "Paul as a Child: Children and Childhood in the Letters of Paul." *JBL* 126 (2007) 129–59.
———. "'Role Ethics' in Paul: The Significance of the Sibling Role for Paul's Ethical Thinking." *NTS* 48 (2002) 513–30.
Abrams, Dominic, and Michael A. Hogg, eds. *Social Identity and Social Cognition*. Oxford: Blackwell, 1999.
———, eds. *Social Identity Theory: Constructive and Critical Advances*. New York: Harvester-Wheatsheaf, 1990.
Adams, Edward. *The Earliest Christian Meeting Places: Almost Exclusively Houses?* LNTS 450. London: Bloomsbury T. & T. Clark, 2013.
Adewuya, J. Ayodeji. *Holiness and Community in 2 Cor 6:14–7:1: Paul's View of Communal Holiness in the Corinthian Correspondence*. StBibLit 40. New York: Peter Lang, 2001.
Arzt-Grabner, P. "'Brothers' and 'Sisters' in Documentary Papyri and in Early Christianity." *RivB* 50 (2002) 185–204.
Asano, Atsuhiro. *Commuity-Identity Construction in Galatians*. JSNTSup 285. London: T. & T. Clark, 2005.
Aune, David E. *The New Testament and Its Literary Environment*. LEC 8. Philadelphia: Westminster, 1987.
Aus, Roger David. *Imagery of Triumph and Rebellion in 2 Corinthians 2:14–17 and Elsewhere in the Epistle: An Example of the Combination of Greco-Roman and Judaic Traditions in the Apostle Paul*. Lanham, MD: University Press of America, 2005.
Austin, W. C., and S. Worchel, eds. *The Social Psychology of Intergroup Relations*. Monterey, CA: Brooks/Cole, 1979.
Aymer, Margaret. "'Mother Knows Best': The Story of Mother Paul Revisited." In *Mother Goose, Mother Jones, Mommie Dearest: Biblical Mothers and Their Children*, edited

by Cheryl A. Kirk-Dunggan and Tina Pippin, 187–98. Semeia 61. Atlanta: Society of Biblical Literature, 2009.

Baker, Coleman A. *Identity, Memory, and Narrative in Early Christianity: Peter, Paul, and Recategorization in the Book of Acts*. Eugene, OR: Pickwick, 2011.

Bakke, Odd Magne. *"Concord and Peace": A Rhetorical Analysis of the First Letter of Clement with an Emphasis on the Language of Unity and Sedition*. WUNT 2/143. Tübingen: Mohr Siebeck, 2001.

Balch, David L. *Let Wives Be Submissive: The Domestic Code in 1 Peter*. SBLMS 26. Chico, CA: Scholars, 1981.

———. "Rich Pompeiian Houses, Shops for Rent, and the Huge Apartment Building in Herculaneum as Typical Spaces for Pauline House Churches." *JSNT* 27 (2004) 27–46.

Balch, David L., Everett Ferguson, and Wayne A. Meeks, eds. *Greeks, Romans, and Christians: Essays in Honor of Abraham J. Malherbe*. Minneapolis: Fortress, 1990.

Balch, David L., and Carolyn Osiek, eds. *Early Christian Families in Context: An Interdisciplinary Dialogue*. Grand Rapids: Eerdmans, 2003.

Balla, Peter. *The Child-Parent Relationship in the New Testament and Its Environment*. WUNT I/155. Tübingen: Mohr Siebeck, 2003.

Banks, Robert. *Paul's Idea of Community: The Early House Churches in their Historical Setting*. Rev. ed. Peabody, MA: Hendrickson, 1994.

Barclay, John M. G. "'Because He was Rich He Became Poor': Translation, Exegesis and Hermeneutics in the Reading of 2 Cor 8.9." In *Theologizing in the Corinthian Conflict: Studies in the Exegesis and Theology of 2 Corinthians*, edited by Reimund Bieringer et al., 331–44. BTS 16. Leuven: Peeters, 2013.

———. "The Family as the Bearer of Religion in Judaism and Early Christianity." In *Constructing Early Christian Families: Family as Social Reality and Metaphor*, edited by Halvor Moxnes, 66–72. London: Routledge, 1997.

———. *Pauline Churches and Diaspora Jews: Studies in the Social Formation of Christian Identity*. WUNT 275. Tübingen: Mohr Siebeck, 2010.

———. "Poverty in Pauline Studies: A Response to Steven Friesen." *JSNT* 26 (2004) 363–66.

———. "Thessalonica and Corinth: Social Contrasts in Pauline Christianity." *JSNT* 47 (1992) 49–72.

Barentsen, Jack. *Emerging Leadership in the Pauline Mission: A Social Identity Perspective on Local Leadership Development in Corinth and Ephesus*. PTMS 168. Eugene, OR: Pickwick, 2011.

Barfoot, C. C., ed. *Beyond Pug's Tour: National and Ethnic Stereotyping in Theory and Literary Practice*. Amsterdam: Rodopi, 1997.

Barnett, Paul. *The Second Epistle to the Corinthians*. NICNT. Grand Rapids: Eerdmans, 1997.

Barrett, C. K. *A Commentary on the First Epistle to the Corinthians*. 2nd ed. London: A. & C. Black, 1971.

Bartchy, S. Scott. "Undermining Ancient Patriarchy: The Apostle Paul's Vision of a Society of Siblings." *BTB* 29 (1999) 68–78.

———. "Who Should Be Called 'Father'? Paul of Tarsus between the Jesus Tradition and *Patria Potestas*." In *The Social World of the New Testament: Insights and Models*, edited by Jerome H. Neyrey and Eric C. Steward, 163–80. Peabody, MA: Hendrickson, 2008.

Barth, Markus, and Helmut Blanke. *Colossians: A New Translation with Introduction and Commentary*. AB 34B. New Haven, CT: Yale University Press, 1994.
Barton, Stephen C., ed. *The Family in Theological Perspective*. Edinburgh: T. & T. Clark, 1996.
———. *Life Together: Family Sexuality and Community in the New Testament and Today*. Edinburgh: T. & T. Clark, 2001.
———. "Paul's Sense of Place: An Anthropological Approach to Community Formation in Corinth." *NTS* 32 (1986) 225–46.
Beale, G. K. *The Temple and the Church's Mission: A Biblical Theology of the Dwelling Place of God*. NSBT 17. Downers Grove, IL: InterVarsity, 2004.
Bell, G. K. A., and Adolf Deissmann, eds. *Mysterium Christi*. London: Longmans, 1930.
Belleville, Linda. "'Imitate Me, Just as I Imitate Christ': Discipleship in the Corinthian Correspondence." In *Patterns of Discipleship in the New Testament*, edited by Richard N. Longenecker, 120–42. Grand Rapids: Eerdmans, 1996.
Berge, Mary Katherine. *The Language of Belonging: A Rhetorical Analysis of Kinship Language in First Corinthians*. CBET 31. Leuven: Peeters, 2004.
Berger, Peter L., and Thomas Luckmann. *The Social Construction of Reality: A Treatise in the Sociology of Knowledge*. London: Penguin, 1967.
Best, Ernest. *One Body in Christ: A Study in the Relationship of the Church to Christ in the Epistles of the Apostle Paul*. London: SPCK, 1955.
Bieringer, Reimund, et al., eds. *Theologizing in the Corinthian Conflict: Studies in the Exegesis and Theology of 2 Corinthians*. BTS 16. Leuven: Peeters, 2013.
Birge, Mary Katherine. *The Language of Belonging: A Rhetorical Analysis of Kinship Language in First Corinthians*. CBET 31. Leuven: Peeters, 2002.
Bitner, Bradley J. *Paul's Political Strategy in 1 Corinthians 1–4: Constitution and Covenant*. SNTSMS 163. New York: Cambridge University Press, 2015.
Black, Max. *Models and Metaphors: Studies in Language and Philosophy*. Ithaca, NY: Cornell University Press, 1962.
Blasi, Anthony J., Jean Duhaime, and Paul-Andre Turcotte, eds. *Handbook of Early Christianity: Social Science Approaches*. Walnut Creek, CA: Altamira, 2002.
Bookidis, Nancy. "Religion in Corinth: 146 B.C.E. to 100 C.E." In *Urban Religion in Roman Corinth: Interdisciplinary Approaches*, edited by Daniel N. Schowalter and Steven J. Friesen, 141–64. HTS 53. Cambridge, MA: Harvard University Press, 2005.
———. "The Sanctuaries of Corinth." In *Corinth, The Centenary 1896–1996*, edited by Charles K. Williams II and Nancy Bookidis, 20:247–59. Athens: American School of Classical Studies at Athens, 2003.
Bossman, David. "Paul's Fictive Kinship Movement." *BTB* 26 (1996) 163–71.
Bradley, Keith R. *Discovering the Roman Family: Studies in Roman Social History*. Oxford: Oxford University Press, 1991.
———. "Wet-nursing at Rome: A Study in Social Relations." In *The Family in Ancient Rome: New Perspectives*, edited by Beryl Rawson, 201–29. Ithaca, NY: Cornell University Press, 1986.
Bray, Gerald, ed. *1–2 Corinthians*. ACCS 7. Downers Grove, IL: InterVarsity 1999.
Brenner, Athalya, and Jan Willem van Henten, eds. *Families and Family Relations as Represented in Early Judaisms and Early Christianities: Texts and Fictions: Papers Read as Noster Colloquium in Amsterdam, June 9–11, 1988*. Leiden: Deo, 2000.

Brewer, Marilynn B. "The Psychology of Prejudice: Ingroup Love or Outgroup Hate?" *JSI* 55 (1999) 429–44.

———. "When Contact Is Not Enough: Social Identity and Intergroup Cooperation." *IJIR* 20 (1996) 291–303.

Brewer, Marilynn B., and Norman Miller. "Beyond the Contact Hypothesis: Theoretical Perspectives on Desegregation." In *Groups in Contact: The Psychology of Desegregation*, edited by N. Miller and M. B. Brewer, 281–302. Orlando: Academic, 1984.

Breytenbach, Cilliers. *Grace, Reconciliation, Concord: The Death of Christ in Graeco-Roman Metaphors*. NovTSup 135. Leiden: Brill, 2010.

Breytenbach, Cilliers, Johan C. Thom, and Jeremy Punt, eds. *New Testament Interpreted: Essays in Honour of Bernard C. Lategan*. Leiden: Brill, 2006.

Briones, David E. *Paul's Financial Policy: A Socio-Theological Approach*. LNTS 494. London: Bloomsbury T. & T. Clark, 2013.

Brookins, Timothy A. *Corinthian Wisdom, Stoic Philosophy, and the Ancient Economy*. SNTSMS 159. New York: Cambridge University Press, 2014.

Brown, Rupert J. *Group Processes: Dynamics within and between Groups*. 2nd ed. Malden, MA: Blackwell, 2000.

———. "Social Identity Theory: Past Achievements, Current Problems, and Future Challenges." *EJSP* 30 (2000) 745–78.

Brown, Rupert J., and G. F. Ross, "The Battle for Acceptance: An Exploration into the Dynamics of Intergroup Behaviours." In *Social Identity and Intergroup Relations*, edited by Henri Tajfel, 155–78. Cambridge: Cambridge University Press, 1982.

Buell, D. K. *Why This New Race: Ethnic Reasoning in Early Christianity*. GTR. New York: Columbia University Press, 2005.

Buitenwerf, Rieuwerd, Haram W. Hollander, and Hohannes Tromp, eds. *Jesus, Paul, and Early Christianity: Studies in Honour of Henk Jan de Jonge*. NovTSup 130. Leiden: Brill, 2008.

Bultmann, Rudolf. *Theology of the New Testament*. Vol. 1. London: SCM, 1952.

Bunge, Marcia J., ed. *The Child in Christian Thought*. Grand Rapids: Eerdmans, 2001.

Bunge, Marcia J., Terence E. Fretheim, and Beverly Roberts Gaventa, eds. *The Child in the Bible*. Grand Rapids: Eerdmans, 2008.

Burke, Trevor J. *Adopted into God's Family: Exploring A Pauline Metaphor*. NSBT 22. Downers Grove, IL: InterVarsity, 2006.

———. *Family Matters: A Socio-Historical Study of Kinship Metaphors in 1 Thessalonians*. JSNTSup 247. London: T. & T. Clark, 2003.

———. "Pauline Adoption: A Sociological Approach." *EvQ* 73/2 (2001) 119–34.

———. "Pauline Paternity in 1 Thessalonians." *TynB* 51 (2000) 59–80.

———. "Paul's New Family in Thessalonica." *NovT* 54 (2012) 269–87.

———. "Paul's Role as 'Father' to his Corinthian 'Children' in Socio-Historical Context (1 Corinthians 4:14–21)." In *Paul and the Corinthians: Studies on a Community in Conflict*, edited by Trevor J. Burke and James Keith Elliott, 95–113. NovTSup 109. Leiden: Brill, 2003.

Burke, Trevor J., and James Keith Elliott, eds. *Paul and the Corinthians: Studies on a Community in Conflict*. NovTSup 109. Leiden: Brill, 2003.

Burkett, Walter. *Ancient Mystery Cults*. Cambridge, MA: Harvard University Press, 1987.

———. "The Meaning and Function of the Temple in Classical Greek." In *Temple in Society*, edited by Michael V. Fox, 27–47. Winona Lake, IN: Eisenbrauns, 1988.
Byatt, Anthony. *New Testament Metaphors: Illustrations in Word and Phrase*. Durham: Pentland, 1995.
Byron, John. *Slavery Metaphors in Early Judaism and Pauline Christianity: A Traditio-Historical and Exegetical Examination*. WUNT 2/162. Tübingen: Mohr Siebeck, 2003.
Caird, G. B. *The Language and Imagery of the Bible*. London: Duckworth, 1980.
Campbell, William S. *Paul and the Creation of Christian Identity*. LNTS 322. London: T. & T. Clark, 2006.
Canavan, Rosemary. *Clothing the Body of Christ at Colossae: A Visual Construction of Identity*. WUNT 2/334. Tübingen: Mohn Siebeck, 2012.
Capozza, Dora, and Rupert Brown, eds. *Social Identity Process*. London: Sage, 2000.
Carson, D. A. *Showing the Spirit: A Theological Exposition of 1 Corinthians 12–14*. Grand Rapids: Baker, 1987.
Carter, Timothy L. "Looking at the Metaphor of Christ's Body in 1 Corinthians 12." In *Paul: Jew, Greek, and Roman*, edited by Stanley E. Porter, 93–115. PAST 5. Leiden, Brill, 2008.
Carter, Warren. *Matthew and the Margins: A Socio-Political and Religious Reading*. JSNTSup 204. Sheffield: Sheffield Academic Press: 2000.
Cartledge, J. Mark. *Charismatic Glossolalia*. Aldershot: Ashgate, 2002.
Castelli, Elizabeth A. *Imitating Paul: A Discourse on Power*. Louisville: Westminter/John Knox, 1991.
Cerfaux, L. *The Church in the Theology of St Paul*. New York: Herder, 1959.
Cheung, Alex T. *Idol Food in Corinth: Jewish Background and Pauline Legacy*. JSNTSup 176. Sheffield: Sheffield Academic Press, 1999.
Chiu, José Enrique Aguilar. *1 Cor 12–14: Literary Structure and Theology*. AnBib 166. Rome: Editrice Pontificia Instituto Biblico, 2007.
Chow, John K. *Patronage and Power: A Study on Paul's Social Networks in Corinth*. JSNTSup 75. Sheffield: JSOT, 1992.
Christophersen, Alf, et al., eds. *Paul, Luke and the Graeco-Roman World: Essays in Honour of Alexander J.M. Wedderburn*. JSNTSup 217. Sheffield: Sheffield Academic Press, 2002.
Ciampa, Roy E., and Brian S. Rosner. *The First Letter to the Corinthians*. PNTC. Grand Rapids: Eerdmans, 2010.
Cinnirella, Marco. "Exploring Temporal Aspects of Social Identity: The Concept of Possible Social Identities." *EJSP* 28 (1998) 227–48.
Clark, Donald Lemen. "Imitation: Theory and Practice in Roman Rhetoric." *QJS* 37 (1951) 11–22.
Clarke, Andrew D. "Another Corinthian Erastus Inscription." *TynBul* 42 (1991) 146–51.
———. "'Be Imitators of Me': Paul's Model of Leadership." *TynBul* 49 (1998) 329–60.
———. *Secular and Christian Leadership in Corinth: A Socio-Historical and Exegetical Study of 1 Corinthians 1–6*. Leiden: Brill, 1993.
———. *Secular and Christian Leadership in Corinth: A Socio-Historical and Exegetical Study of 1 Corinthians 1–6*. 2nd ed. PBM. Milton Keynes: Paternoster, 2006.
———. *Serve the Community of the Church: Christians as Leaders and Ministers, First-Century Christians in the Graeco-Roman World*. Grand Rapids: Eerdmans, 2000.
Cohen, Anthony. *The Symbolic Construction of Community*. London: Tavistock, 1985.

Cohen, Shaye J. D., ed. *The Jewish Family in Antiquity*. Atlanta: Scholars, 1993.
Colish, Marcia L. "Stoicism and the New Testament: An Essay in Historiography." *ANRW* 26 (1992) 334–79.
———. *Stoicism in Christian Latin Thought through the Sixth Century*. Leiden: Brill, 1990.
Collins, Adela Yarbro, and Margaret M. Mitchell. *Antiquity and Humanity: Essays on Ancient Religion and Philosophy Presented to Hans Dieter Betz on His 70th Birthday*. Tübingen: Mohr Siebeck, 2001.
Collins, Raymond F. "Constructing A Metaphor: 1 Corinthians 3,9b–17 and Ephesians 2,19–22." In *Paul et l'unité des chrétiens*, edited by Jacques Schlosser, 193–216. COP 19. Leuven: Peeters, 2010.
———. *First Corinthians*. SP. Collegeville, MN: Liturgical, 1999.
———. *The Power of Images in Paul*. Collegeville, MN: Liturgical, 2008.
Condor, Susan. "Having History: A Social Psychological Exploration of Anglo-British Autostereotypes." In *Beyond Pug's Tour: National and Ethnic Stereotyping in Theory and Literary Practice*, edited by C. C. Barfoot, 213–53. Amsterdam: Rodopi, 1997.
———. "Social Identity and Time." In *Social Groups and Identity: Developing the Legacy of Henri Tajfel*, edited by W. Peter Robinson, 285–316. Boston: Butterworth-Heinemann, 1996.
———. "Temporality and Collectivity: Diversity, History and the Rhetorical Construction of National Entitativity." *BJSP* 45 (2006) 657–82.
Conway, Collen W. *Behold the Man: Jesus and Greco-Roman Masculinity*. Oxford: Oxford University Press, 2008.
Conzelmann, Hans. *1 Corinthians*. Hermeneia. Philadelphia: Fortress, 1975.
———. *An Outline of the Theology of the New Testament*. London: SCM, 1969.
Corbier, Mireille. "Child Exposure and Abandonment." In *Childhood, Class and Kin in the Roman World*, edited by Suzanne Dixon, 58–73. London: Routledge, 2001.
Coutsoumpos, Panayotis. *Paul and the Lord's Supper: A Socio-Historical Investigation*. StBibLit 84. New York: Peter Lang, 2005.
———. "Paul, the Cults in Corinth and the Corinthian Correspondence." In *Paul's World*, edited by Stanley E. Porter, 171–80. PAST 4. Leiden: Brill, 2008.
Cox, Cheryl Anne. *Household Interests: Property, Marriage Strategies, and Family Dynamics in Ancient Athens*. Princeton: Princeton University Press, 1998.
Crone, Theodore M. *Early Christian Prophecy: A Study of Its Origin and Function*. Baltimore: St Mary's University Press, 1973.
Crouch, J. E. *The Origin and Intention of the Colossian Haustafeln*. Göttingen: Vandenhoeck & Ruprecht, 1972.
D'Angelo, Mary R. "Εὐσέβεια: Roman Imperial Family Values and the Sexual Politics of 4 Maccabees and the Pastorals." *BibInt* 11 (2003) 139–65.
Daines, B. "Paul's Use of the Analogy of the Body of Christ—With Special Reference to 1 Corinthians 12." *EvQ* 50 (1978) 71–78.
Darko, Daniel K. "Adopted Siblings in the Household of God: Kinship Lexemes in the Social Identity Construction of Ephesus." In *T. & T. Clark Handbook to Social Identity in the New Testament*, edited by J. Brian Tucker and Coleman A. Baker, 333–46. London: T. & T. Clark 2014.
———. *No Longer Living as the Gentiles: Differentiation and Shared Ethical Values in Ephesians 4.17—6.9*. LNTS 375. London: T. & T. Clark, 2008.

Daube, D. "Paul a Hellenistic Schoolmaster?" In *Studies in Rationalism, Judaism, and Universalism in Memory of Leon Roth*, edited by R. Loewe, 67–71. London: Routledge, 1966.

Davies, W. D. *Paul and Rabbinic Judaism*. Philadelphia: Fortress, 1980.

Dawes, Gregory W. *The Body in Question: Metaphor and Meaning in the Interpretation of Ephesians 5:21–33*. Leiden: Brill, 1998.

De Lacey, D. R. "οἵτινές ἐστε ὑμεῖς: The Function of A Metaphor in St Paul." In *Templum Amicitiae: Essays on the Second Temple Presented to Ernst Bammel*, edited by William Horbury, 391–409. JSNTSup 48. Sheffield: Sheffield Academic Press, 1991.

DeMaris, Richard. *The New Testament and Its Ritual World*. London: Routledge, 2008.

deSilva, David. *Honor, Patronage, Kinship and Purity: Unlocking New Testament Culture*. Downers Grove, IL: InterVarsity, 2000.

Dixon, Suzanne, ed. *Childhood, Class and Kin in the Roman World*. London: Routledge, 2001.

———. *The Roman Family*. Baltimore: The John Hopkins University Press, 1992.

———. "The Sentimental Ideal of the Roman Family." In *Marriage, Divorce and Children in Ancient Rome*, edited by Beryl Rawson, 99–113. Oxford: Clarendon, 1991.

Douglas, Mary. *Purity and Danger: An Analysis of Concepts of Pollution and Taboo*. London: Routledge, 1966.

Downs, David J. *The Offering of the Gentiles: Paul's Collection for Jerusalem in Its Chronological, Cultural, and Cultic Contexts*. WUNT 2/248. Tübingen: Mohr Siebeck, 2008.

Dunn, James D. G. "'The Body of Christ' in Paul." In *Worship, Theology and Ministry in the Early Church: Essays in Honor of Ralph P. Martin*, edited by Michael J. Wilkins and Terence Paige, 146–162. JSNTSup 87. Sheffield: Sheffield Academic Press, 1992.

———. *Christology in the Making: A New Testament Inquiry into the Origins of the Doctrine of the Incarnation*. 2nd ed. London: SCM, 1989.

———. "The Household Rules in the New Testament." In *The Family in Theological Perspective*, edited by Stephen C. Barton, 43–63. Edinburgh: T. & T. Clark, 1996.

———. *The Theology of Paul the Apostle*. Grand Rapids: Eerdmans, 1998.

Dutch, Robert S. *The Educated Elite in 1 Corinthians: Education and Community Conflict in Graeco-Roman Context*. JSNTSup 271. London: T. & T. Clark, 2005.

Ehrensperger, Kathy. "'Be Imitators of Me as I am of Christ': A Hidden Discourse of Power and Domination in Paul?" *LTQ* 38 (2003) 241–61.

———. *Paul and the Dynamics of Power: Communication and Interaction in the Early Christ-Movement*. LNTS 325. London: T. & T. Clark, 2007.

———. *Paul at the Crossroads of Cultures: Theologizing in the Space Between*. LNTS 456. London: Bloomsbury T. & T. Clark, 2013.

———. "To Eat or Not to Eat—Is This the Question? Table Disputes in Corinth." In *Decisive Meals: Table Politics in Biblical Literature*, edited by Kathy Ehrensperger, Nathan MacDonald, and Luzia Sutter Rehmann, 114–33. LNTS 449. New York: T. & T. Clark, 2012.

Ehrensperger, Kathy, Nathan MacDonald, and Luzia Sutter Rehmann, eds. *Decisive Meals: Table Politics in Biblical Literature*. LNTS 449. New York: T. & T. Clark, 2012.

Ehrensperger, Kathy, and J. Brian Tucker, eds. *Reading Paul in Context: Explorations in Identity Formation, Essays in Honour of William S. Campbell*. LNTS 428. London: T. & T. Clark, 2010.

Elliott, Neil, and Mark Reasoner, eds. *Documents and Images for the Study of Paul*. Philadelphia: Fortress, 2010.

Engberg-Pedersen, Troel. *Paul and the Stoics*. Louisville: Westminster John Knox, 2000.

Engels, Donald. *Roman Corinth: An Alternative Model for the Classical City*. Chicago: University of Chicago Press, 1990.

Esler, Philip F. *Conflict and Identity in Romans: The Social Setting of Paul's Letter*. Minneapolis: Ausgburg Fortress 2003.

———. "Family Imagery and Christian Identity in Gal 5:13 to 6:10." In *Constructing Early Christian Families: Family as Social Reality and Metaphor*, edited by Halvor Moxnes, 121–49. London: Routledge, 1997.

———. *The First Christians in Their Social Worlds: Social-Scientific Approaches to New Testament Interpretation*. London: Routledge, 1994.

———. *Galatians*. NTR. London: Routledge, 1998.

———. "Keeping It in the Family: Culture, Kinship and Identity in 1 Thessalonians and Galatians." In *Families and Family Relations as Represented in Early Judaisms and Early Christianities: Texts and Fictions: Papers Read at Noster Colloquium in Amsterdam, June 9–11, 1988*, edited by Athalya Brenner and Jan Willem van Henten, 145–84. Leiden: Deo, 2000.

———. "Paul and the *Agon:* Understanding a Pauline Motif in Its Cultural and Visual Context." In *Picturing the New Testament, Studies in Ancient Visual Images*, edited by Annette Weissenrieder, Friederike Wendt, and Petra von Gemünden, 356–84. WUNT 2/193. Tübingen: Mohr Siebeck, 2005.

———, ed. *Modelling Early Christianity: Social Scientific Studies of the New Testament in Its Context*. London: Routledge, 1995.

Evans, Craig A., ed. *The World of Jesus and the Early Church: Identity and Interpretation in Early Communities of Faith*. Peabody, MA: Hendrickson, 2011.

Eyben, Emiel. "Fathers and Sons." In *Marriage, Divorce, and Children in Ancient Rome*, edited by Beryl Rawson, 114–43. Oxford: Clarendon, 1991.

———. *Restless Youth in Ancient Rome*. London: Routledge, 1993.

Fatum, Lone. "Brotherhood in Christ: A Gender Hermeneutical Reading of 1 Thessalonians." In *Constructing Early Christian Families: Family as Social Reality and Metaphor*, edited by Halvor Moxnes, 183–97. London: Routledge, 1997.

Fay, Ron C. "Greco-Roman Concepts of Deity." In *Paul's World*, edited by Stanley E. Porter, 51–79. PAST 4. Leiden: Brill, 2008.

Fee, Gordon D. *The First Epistle to the Corinthians*. 2nd ed. NICNT. Grand Rapids: Eerdmans, 2014.

———. *Pauline Christology: An Exegetical-Theological Study*. Peabody, MA: Hendrickson, 2007.

Feyaerts, Kurt, ed. *The Bible through Metaphor and Translation: A Cognitive Semantic Perspective*. Bern: Peter Lang, 2003.

Finlan, Stephen. *The Background and Content of Paul's Cultic Atonement Metaphors*. AnBib 19. Atlanta: SBL, 2004.

Finney, Mark T. "Christ Crucified and the Inversion of Roman Imperial Ideology in 1 Corinthians." *BTB* 35 (2005) 20–33.

———. *Honour and Conflict in the Ancient World: 1 Corinthians in its Greco-Roman Social Setting.* LNTS 460. London: T. & T. Clark, 2012.

———. "Social Identity and Conflict in Corinth: 1 Corinthians 11.17–34 in Context." In *T. & T. Clark Handbook to Social Identity in the New Testament*, edited by J. Brian Tucker and Coleman A. Baker, 273–87. London: T. & T. Clark, 2014.

Fiore, Benjamin. "Paul, Exemplification, and Imitation." In *Paul in the Greco-Roman World: A Handbook*, edited by J. Paul Sampley, 228–57. Harrisburg, PA: Trinity, 2003.

Fitzgerald, John T. *Cracks in an Earthen Vessel: An Examination of the Catalogues of Hardships in the Corinthian Correspondence.* Atlanta: Scholars, 1988.

Fitzmyer, Joseph A. *First Corinthians.* AB 32. New Haven, CT: Yale University Press, 2008.

Forbes, Christopher. "Early Christian Inspired Speech and Hellenistic Popular Religion." *NovT* 28 (1986) 257–70.

———. *Prophecy and Inspired Speech in Early Christianity and Its Hellenistic Environment.* WUNT 2/75. Tübingen: Mohr Siebeck, 1995.

Fotopoulos, John. *Food Offered to Idols in Roman Corinth: A Social-rhetorical Reconsideration of 1 Corinthians 8:1—11:1.* WUNT 2/151. Tübingen: Mohr Siebeck, 2003.

Fox, Michael V., ed. *Temple in Society.* Winona Lake, IN: Eisenbrauns, 1988.

Francis, James. "'As Babes in Christ': Some Proposals Regarding 1 Cor 3:1–3." *JSNT* 7 (1980) 41–60.

———. "Children and Childhood in the New Testament." In *The Family in Theological Perspective*, edited by Stephen C. Barton, 65–85. Edinburgh: T. & T. Clark, 1996.

Friesen, Steven J. "Poverty in Pauline Studies: Beyond the So-called New Consensus." *JSNT* 26 (2004) 323–61.

———. "Prospects for a Demography of the Pauline Mission: Corinth among the Churches." In *Urban Religion in Roman Corinth: Interdisciplinary Approaches*, edited by Daniel N. Schowalter and Steven J. Friesen, 352–70. HTS 53. Cambridge, MA: Harvard University Press, 2005.

———. "The Wrong Erastus: Ideology, Archaeology and Exegesis." In *Corinth in Context: Comparative Studies on Religion and Society*, edited by James C. Walters, Daniel N. Schowalter, and Steven J. Friesen, 231–56. NovTSup 134. Leiden: Brill, 2010.

Friesen, Steven J., Daniel N. Schowalter, and James C. Walters, eds. *Corinth in Context: Comparative Studies on Religion and Society.* NovTSup 134. Leiden: Brill, 2010.

Frilingos, Chris. "'For My Child, Onesimus': Paul and Domestic Power in Philemon." *JBL* 119 (2000) 91–104.

Furnish, Victor Paul. *II Corinthians.* AB. New York: Doubleday, 1984.

Gaertner, Samuel L., et al. "The Common Ingroup Identity Model: Recategorization and the Reduction of Intergroup Bias." *ERSP* 4 (1993) 1–26.

Gale, Herbert M. *The Use of Analogy in the Letters of Paul.* Philadelphia: Westminster, 1964.

Garland, David E. *1 Corinthians.* BECNT. Grand Rapids: Baker Academic, 2003.

Garnsey, Peter, and Richard Saller. *The Roman Empire: Economy, Society, and Culture.* Berkerly: University of California Press, 1987.

Gärtner, Bertil. *The Temple and the Community in Qumran and the New Testament: A Comparative Study in the Temple Symbolism of the Qumran Texts and the New Testament*. SNTSMS 1. Cambridge: Cambridge University Press, 1965.

Gaventa, Beverly Roberts. "Finding a Place for Children in the Letters of Paul." In *The Child in the Bible*, edited by Marcia J. Bunge, Terence E. Fretheim, and Beverly Roberts Gaventa, 233–48. Grand Rapids: Eerdmans, 2008.

———. "Mother's Milk and Ministry in 1 Corinthians 3." In *Theology and Ethics in Paul and His Interpreters: Essays in Honor of Victor Paul Furnish*, edited by Eugene H. Lovering Jr. and Jerry L. Sumney, 101–13. Nashville: Sbingdon, 1996.

———. *Our Mother Saint Paul*. Louisville: Westminster John Knox, 2007.

———. "'You Proclaim the Lord's Death': 1 Corinthians 11:26 and Paul's Understanding of Worship." *RevExp* 80 (1983) 377–87.

Gentry, L. "Beyond Remembering: Proclaiming the Death in the Supper." *ResQ* 41 (1999) 241–43.

Georgi, Dieter. *Remembering the Poor: The History of Paul's Collection for Jerusalem*. Nashville: Abingdon, 1992.

Gill, D. W. "Erastus the Aedile." *TynBul* 40 (1989) 293–300.

———. "In Search of the Social Elite in the Corinthian Church." *TynBul* 44 (1993) 323–37.

Gleason, Maud W. *Making Men: Sophists and Self-Presentation in Ancient Rome*. Princeton: Princeton University Press, 1995.

Golden, Mark. *Children and Childhood in Classical Athens*. Ancient Society and History. Baltimore: Johns Hopkins University Press, 1990.

Goodrich, John K. "Erastus of Corinth (Romans 16.23): Responding to Recent Proposals on his Rank, Status, and Faith." *NTS* 57 (2011) 583–93.

———. "Erastus, Quaestor of Corinth: The Administrative Rank of Ὁ Οἰκονόμος Τῆς Πόλεως (Rom 16.23) in an Achaean Colony." *NTS* 56 (2010) 90–115.

———. *Paul as an Administrator of God in 1 Corinthians*. SNTSMS 152. Cambridge: Cambridge University Press, 2012.

Goulder, Michael D. *Paul and the Competing Mission in Corinth*. LPS. Peabody, MA: Hendrickson, 2001.

Gundry-Volf, Judith M. "The Least and the Greatest: Children in the New Testament." In *The Child in Christian Thought*, edited by M. J. Bunge, 29–60. Grand Rapids: Eerdmans, 2001.

Gundry, Robert H. *Sōma in Biblical Theology with Emphasis on Pauline Anthropology*. Cambridge: Cambridge University Press, 1976.

Gupta, Nijay K. "Towards a Set of Principles for Interpreting Metaphors in Paul." *ResQ* 51/3 (2009) 169–81.

———. "Whose Body Was a Temple (1 Cor 6.19)? Paul Beyond the Individualism/Communalism Divide." *CBQ* 72 (2010) 518–36.

———. *Worship that Makes Sense to Paul: A New Approach to the Theology and Ethics of Paul's Cultic Metaphors*. BZNW 175. Berlin: De Gruyter, 2010.

Guthrie, George H. *2 Corinthians*. BECNT. Grand Rapids: Baker, 2015.

Hall, David R. *The Unity of the Corinthian Correspondence*. JSNTSup 251. London: T. & T. Clark, 2003.

Hansen, Bruce. *All of You are One: The Social Vision of Galatians 3.28, 1 Corinthians 12.13 and Colossians 3.11*. LNTS 409. London: T. & T. Clark, 2010.

Hansen, K. C. "Kinship." In *The Social Sciences and the New Testament Interpretation*, edited by R. L. Rohrbaugh, 62–79. Peabody, MA: Hendrickson, 1996.

Harland, Philip A. *Dynamics of Identity in the World of the Early Christians: Associations, Judeans, and Cultural Minorities*. New York: T. & T. Clark, 2009.

———. "Familial Dimensions of Group Identity: 'Brothers' (ἀδελφοί) in Associations of the Greek East." *JBL* 124 (2005) 491–513.

Harmon, Matthew S., and Jay E. Smith, eds. *Studies in the Pauline Epistles: Essays in Honor of Douglas J. Moo*. Grand Rapids: Zondervan, 2014.

Harrill, J. Albert. "Invective against Paul (2 Cor 10:10), the Physiognomics of the Ancient Slave Body, and the Greco-Roman Rhetoric of Manhood." In *Antiquity and Humanity: Essays on Ancient Religion and Philosophy Presented to Hans Dieter Betz on His 70th Birthday*, edited by Adela Yarbro Collins and Margaret M. Mitchell, 189–213. Tübingen: Mohr Siebeck, 2001.

———. *Slaves in the New Testament: Literary, Social, and Moral Dimensions*. Minneapolis: Fortress, 2006.

Harris, Murray J. *The Second Epistle to the Corinthians*. NIGTC. Grand Rapids: Eerdmans, 2005.

———. *Slave of Christ: A New Testament Metaphor for Total Devotion to Christ*. NSBT 8. Downers Grove, IL: InterVarsity, 1999.

Harrison, James R. "Paul the 'Paradoxical' Parent: The Politics of Family Benefience in First-century Context (2 Cor 12:14–16)." In *Theologizing in the Corinthian Conflict: Studies in the Exegesis and Theology of 2 Corinthians*, edited by Reimund Bieringer et al., 399–425. BTS 16. Leuven: Peeters, 2013.

———. *Paul's Language of Grace in Its Graeco-Roman Context*. WUNT 2/172. Tübingen: Mohr Siebeck, 2003.

Hays, Richard B. *First Corinthians*. IBC. Louisville: Westminster John Knox, 1997.

Heil, J. P. *The Rhetorical Role of Scripture in 1 Corinthians*. SBLStBL. Atlanta: Society of Biblical Literature, 2005.

Hellerman, Joseph H. *The Ancient Church as Family*. Minneapolis: Fortress, 2001.

Henderson, Suzanne Watts. "'If Anyone Hungers . . .': An Integrated Reading of 1 Cor 11.17–34." *NTS* 48 (2002) 295–308.

Hering, James P. *The Colossian and Ephesian Haustafeln in Theological Context: An Analysis of Their Origins, Relationship, and Message*. TR 260. New York: Peter Lang, 2007.

Hewtone, Miles, and Rupert Brown. "Contact Is Not Enough: An Intergroup Perspective on the Contact Hypothesis." In *Contact and Conflict in Intergroup Encounters*, edited by Miles Hewstone and Rupert Brown, 1–44. Oxford: Blackwell, 1986.

———, eds. *Contact and Conflict in Intergroup Encounters*. Oxford: Blackwell, 1986.

Hill, Andrew E. "The Temple of Asclepius: An Alternative Source for Paul's Body Theology?" *JBL* 99 (1980) 437–39.

Hiu, Elim. *Regulations Concerning Tongues and Prophecy in 1 Corinthians 14.26–40: Relevance Beyond the Corinthian Church*. LNTS 406. London: T. & T. Clark, 2010.

Hock, Ronald F. "Paul and Greco Roman Education." In *Paul in the Greco-Roman World: A Handbook*, edited by J. Paul Sampley, 198–227. Harrisburg, PA: Trinity, 2003.

Hodge, Caroline Johnson. *If Sons, Then Heirs: A Study of Kinship and Ethnicity in the Letters of Paul*. Oxford: Oxford University Press, 2007.

Hoehner, Harold W. *Ephesians: An Exegetical Commentary.* Grand Rapids: Baker Academic, 2002.

Hogeterp, Albert L. A. "Community as a Temple in Paul's Letters: The Case of Cultic Terms in 2 Corinthians 6:14–7:1." In *Anthropology and Biblical Studies: Avenues of Approach*, edited by Louise J. Lawrence and Mario I. Aguilar, 281–95. Leiden: Leo, 2004.

———. *Paul and God's Temple: A Historical Interpretation of Cultic Imagery in the Corinthian Correspondence.* BTS 2. Leuven: Peeters, 2006.

Hogg, Michael A., and Dominic Abrams. *Social Identifications: A Social Psychology of Intergroup Relations and Group Process.* London: Routledge, 1988.

Holmberg, Bengt, ed. *Exploring Christian Identity.* WUNT 1/226. Tübingen: Mohr Siebeck, 2008.

———. *Paul and Power: The Structure of Authority in the Primitive Church as Reflected in the Pauline Epistles.* Philadelphia: Fortress, 1978.

———. *Sociology and the New Testament: An Appraisal.* Minneapolis: Fortress, 1990.

———. "Understanding the First Hundred Years of Christian Identity." In *Exploring Christian Identity*, edited by Bengt Holmberg, 1–32. WUNT 1/226. Tübingen: Mohr Siebeck, 2008.

Holmberg, Bengt, and Mikael Winninge, eds. *Identity Formation in the New Testament.* WUNT 1/227. Tübingen: Mohr Siebeck, 2008.

Hölscher, Tonio. *The Language of Images in Roman Art.* Translated by Anthony Snodgrass and Annemarie Kunzl-Snodgrass. Cambridge: Cambridge University Press, 2004.

Hooker, Morna. "Hard Sayings: 1 Corinthians 3:1." *Theology* 69 (1966) 19–22.

———. "Interchange in Christ." *JTS* 22/2 (1971) 349–61.

Horbury, William, ed. *Templum Amicitiae: Essays on the Second Temple Presented to Ernst Bammel.* JSNTSup 48. Sheffield: Sheffield Academic Press, 1991.

Horrell, David G. *Becoming Christian: Essays on 1 Peter and the Making of Christian Identity.* LNTS 394. London: Bloomsbury T. & T. Clark, 2013.

———. "Domestic Space and Christian Meetings at Corinth: Imagining New Contexts and the Building East of the Theatre." *NTS* 50 (2004) 349–69.

———. "From ἀδελφοί to οἶκος θεοῦ: Social Transformation in Pauline Christianity." *JBL* 120 (2001) 83–114.

———. *The Social Ethos of the Corinthian Correspondence: Interests and Ideology from 1 Corinthians to 1 Clement.* Edinburgh: T. & T. Clark, 1996.

———. *Solidarity and Difference: A Contemporary Reading of Paul's Ethics.* London: T. & T. Clark, 2005.

Horsley, G. H. R. *New Documents Illustrating Early Christianity: A Review of the Greek Inscriptions and Papyri published in 1976.* Vol. 1. North Ryde: Macquarie University, 1981.

———. *New Documents Illustrating Early Christianity: A Review of the Greek Inscriptions and Papyri Published in 1979.* Vol. 4. North Ryde: Macquarie University, 1987.

Horsley, Richard A. *1 Corinthians.* ANTC. Nashville: Abingdon, 1998.

———. "Paul's Assembly in Corinth: An Alternative Society." In *Urban Religion in Roman Corinth: Interdisciplinary Approaches*, edited by Daniel N. Schowalter and Steven J. Friesen, 369–95. HTS 53. Cambridge, MA: Harvard University Press, 2005.

Hovenden, Gerald. *Speaking in Tongues: The New Testament Evidence in Context.* London: Sheffield Academic Press, 2002.
Howell, Brian C. *In the Eyes of God: A Contextual Approach to Biblical Anthropomorphic Metaphors.* PTMS 192. Eugene, OR: Pickwick, 2013.
Hunt, A. R. *The Inspired Body: Paul, the Corinthians, and Divine Inspiration.* Macon, GA: Mercer University Press, 1996.
Imber, Margaret. "Life Without Father: Declamation and the Construction of Paternity in the Roman Empire." In *Role Models in the Roman World: Identity and Assimilation,* edited by Sinclair Bell and Inge Lyse Hansen, 161–69. Supplements to the Memoirs of the American Academy in Rome 7. Ann Arbor: University of Michigan Press, 2008.
Jamir, Lanuwabang. *Exclusion and Judgment in Fellowship Meals: The Socio-Historical Background of 1 Corinthians 11:17–34.* Eugene, OR: Pickwick, 2016.
Jenkins, Richard. *Social Identity.* London: Routledge, 1996.
Jewett, Robert. *Paul's Anthropological Terms: A Study of Their Use in Conflict Settings.* Leiden: Brill, 1971.
Jongkind, Dirk. "Corinth in the First Century A.D.: The Search for Another Class." *TynBul* 52 (2001) 139–48.
Joubert, Stephen J. "Managing the Household: Paul as *Paterfamilias* of the Christian Household Group in Corinth." In *Modelling Early Christianity: Social Scientific Studies of the New Testament in Its Context,* edited by Philip F. Esler, 213–23. London: Routledge, 1995.
———. *Paul as Benefactor: Reciprocity, Strategy and Theological Reflection in Paul's Collection.* WUNT 2/124. Tübingen: Mohr Siebeck, 2000.
Judge, Edwin A. "The Conflict of Educational Aims in the New Testament." In *The First Christians in the Roman World: Augustan and New Testament Essays,* edited by James R. Harrison, 693–708. WUNT 229. Tübingen: Mohr Siebeck, 2008.
———. "The Social Identity of the First Christians: A Question of Method in Religious History." *JRH* 11 (1980) 201–17.
Judge, Edwin A., and David Scholer, *Social Distinctives of the Christians in the First Century: Pivotal Essays.* Peabody, MA: Hendrickson, 2008.
Kahl, Brigitte. *Galatians Re-imagined: Reading with the Eyes of the Vanquished.* Minneapolis: Fortress, 2010.
Käsemann, Ernst. *Perspectives on Paul.* Translated by Margaret Kohl. Philadelphia: Fortress, 1971.
Keener, Craig S. *1–2 Corinthians.* NCBC. Cambridge: Cambridge University Press, 2005.
Keesing, Roger M. *Kin Groups and Social Structure.* New York: Holt, Rinehart and Winston, 1975.
Kempthorne, R. "Incest and the Body of Christ: A Study on 1 Corinthians VI. 12–20." *NTS* 14 (1978–88) 568–74.
Kertzer, David I., and Richard P. Saller. *The Family in Italy from Antiquity to the Present.* New Haven, CT: Yale University Press, 1991.
Kim, Jung Hoon. *The Significance of Clothing Imagery in the Pauline Corpus.* JSNTSup 268. London: T. & T. Clark, 2004.
Kim, Seyoon. *The Origin of Paul's Gospel.* 2nd ed. WUNT 2/4. Tübingen: Mohr Siebeck, 1984.

Kim, Yung Suk. *Christ's Body in Corinth: The Politics of A Metaphor*. Minneapolis: Fortress, 2008.

———. "'Imitators' (*Mimetai*) in 1 Cor. 4:16 and 11:1: A New Reading of Threefold Embodiment." *HBT* 33 (2011) 147–70.

Kirk-Dunggan, Cheryl A., and Tina Pippin, eds. *Mother Goose, Mother Jones, Mommie Dearest: Biblical Mothers and Their Children*. Semeia 61. Atlanta: SBL, 2009.

Klauck, Hans-Josef. "Brotherly Love in Plutarch and in 4 Maccabees." In *Greeks, Romans, and Christians: Essays in Honor of Abraham J. Malherbe*, edited by David L. Balch, Everett Ferguson, and Wayne A. Meeks, 144–56. Minneapolis: Fortress, 1990.

Kloppenborg, John S. "Edwin Hatch, Churches, and *Collegia*." In *Origins and Methods: Towards a New Understanding of Judaism and Christianity: Essays in Honour of John C. Hurd*, edited by B. H. McLean, 212–38. JSNTSup 86. Sheffield: JSOT, 1993.

Kloppenborg, John S., and Stephen G. Wilson, eds. *Voluntary Associations in the Greco-Roman World*. London: Routledge, 1996.

Konsmo, Erik. *The Pauline Metaphors of the Holy Spirit: The Intangible Spirit's Tangible Presence in the Life of the Christian*. StBibLit 130. New York: Peter Lang, 2010.

Kuecker, Aaron. *The Spirit and the "Other": The Identity, Ethnicity and Intergroup Reconciliation in Luke-Acts*. LNTS 444. London: T. & T. Clark, 2011.

Lacey, W. K. *The Family in Classical Greece*. London: Thames & Hudson, 1968.

———. "Patria Potestas." In *The Family in Ancient Rome: New Perspectives*, edited by Beryl Rawson, 121–44. Ithaca, NY: Cornell University Press, 1986.

Lakoff, George, and Mark Johnson. *Metaphors We Live By*. Chicago: University of Chicago Press, 2003.

Lampe, Peter. "The Corinthian Eucharistic Dinner Party: Exegesis of a Cultural Context (1 Cor. 11:17–34)." *Affirmation* 4 (1991) 1–15.

———. "The Eucharist: Identifying with Christ on the Cross." *Int* 48 (1994) 36–49.

Lanci, John R. *A New Temple for Corinth: Rhetorical and Archaeological Approaches to Pauline Imagery*. StBibLit 1. New York: Peter Lang, 1997.

Lassen, Eva Marie. "The Roman Family: Ideal and Metaphor." In *Constructing Early Christian Families: Family as Social Reality and Metaphor*, edited by Halvor Moxnes, 103–20. London: Routledge, 1997.

———. "The Use of the Father Image in Imperial Propaganda and 1 Corinthians 4:14–21." *TynBul* 42 (1991) 127–136.

Lawler, Edward J., ed. *Advances in Group Processes*. Greenwich, CT: JAI, 1985.

Lee, Michelle V. *Paul, The Stoics, and the Body of Christ*. SNTSMS 137. Cambridge: Cambridge University Press, 2006.

Lee, Min Choon. *Freedom of Religion in Malaysia*. Petaling Jaya: Kairos, 1999.

Levison, John R. "The Spirit and the Temple in Paul's Letters to the Corinthians." In *Paul and His Theology*, edited by Stanley E. Porter, 189–215. PAST 3. Leiden: Brill, 2006.

Lietaert Peerbolte, Bert Jan. "Paul and the Practice and Paidea." In *Jesus, Paul, and Early Christianity: Studies in Honour of Henk Jan de Jonge*, edited by Rieuwerd Buitenwerf, Haram W. Hollander, and Hohannes Tromp, 261–80. NovTSup 130. Leiden: Brill, 2008.

Lietaert Peerbolte, Bert Jan, and Leendert Groenendijk. "Family Discourse, Identity Formation, and the Education of Children in Earliest Christianity." *ASE* 33 (2016) 129–49.

Lieu, Judith. *Christian Identity in the Jewish and Graeco-Roman World*. Oxford: Oxford University Press, 2004.
Lim, Kar Yong. "'If Anyone is in Christ, New Creation: The Old has Gone, the New has Come' (2 Cor 5.17): New Creation and Temporal Comparison in Social Identity Fomration in 2 Corinthians." In *T. & T. Clark Handbook to Social Identity in the New Testament*, edited by J. Brian Tucker and Coleman A. Baker, 289–310. London: Bloomsbury Academic, 2014.
———. "Generosity from Pauline Perspective: Insight from Paul's Letters to the Corinthians." *ERT* 37 (2013) 20–33.
———. "Paul the Economist? Economic Principles in Pauline Literature with the Jerusalem Collection as a Test Case." *ERT* 41 (2017) 19–31.
———. "Paul's Use of Temple Imagery in the Corinthian Correspondence: The Creation of Christian Identity." In *Reading Paul in Context: Explorations in Identity Formation: Essays in Honour of William S. Campbell*, edited by Kathy Ehrensperger and J. Brian Tucker, 189–205.LNTS 428. London: T. & T. Clark, 2010.
———. *"The Sufferings of Christ Are Abundant in Us": A Narrative Dynamics Investigation of Paul's Sufferings in 2 Corinthians*. LNTS 399. London: T. & T. Clark, 2009.
Limberis, Vasiliki. "Ecclesiastical Ambiguities: Corinth in the Fourth and Fifth Centuries." In *Urban Religion in Roman Corinth: Interdisciplinary Approaches*, edited by Daniel N. Schowalter and Steven Friesen, 443–547. HTS 53. Cambridge, MA: Harvard University Press, 2005.
Liu, Yulin. *Temple Purity in 1–2 Corinthians*. WUNT 2/343. Tübingen: Mohr Siebeck, 2013.
Lockwood, Gregory J. *1 Corinthians*. ConC. St. Louis: Concordia, 2000.
Loewe, R., ed. *Studies in Rationalism, Judaism, and Universalism in Memory of Leon Roth*. London: Routledge, 1966.
Long, Adrian. *Paul and Human Rights: A Dialogue with the Father of the Corinthian Community*. Sheffield: Sheffield Phoenix, 2009.
Longenecker, Bruce W. "Exposing the Economic Middle: A Revised Economy Scale for the Study of Early Urban Christianity." *JSNT* 31 (2009) 243–78.
———. *Remembering the Poor: Paul, Poverty, and the Greco-Roman World*. Grand Rapids: Eerdmans, 2010.
Longenecker, Richard N., ed. *Patterns of Discipleship in the New Testament*. Grand Rapids: Eerdmans, 1996.
Lopez, Davina C. *Apostle to the Conquered: Reimagining Paul's Mission*. Minneapolis: Fortress, 2008.
Lovacs, Judith L. "Echoes of Valentinian Exegesis in Clement of Alexandria and Origen: The Interpretation of 1 Cor 3, 1–3." In *Origeniana Octava: Origen and the Alexandrian Tradition*, edited by L. Perrone, 317–29. BETL 164. Leuven: Leuven University Press, 2003.
Lovering, Eugene H., Jr., and Jerry L. Sumney, eds. *Theology and Ethics in Paul and His Interpreters: Essays in Honor of Victor Paul Furnish*. Nashville: Abingdon, 1996.
Luomanen, Petri, Ilkka Pyysiäinen, and Risto Uro, eds. *Explaining Christian Origins and Early Judaism: Contributions from Cognitive and Social Science*. BibInt 89. Leiden: Brill, 2007.
MacDonald, Margaret Y. "Beyond Identification of the Topos of Household Management: Reading the Household Codes in Light of Recent Methodologies

and Theoretical Perspectives in the Study of the New Testament." *NTS* 57 (2010) 65–90.

———. "Children in House Churches in Light of New Research on Families in the Roman World." In *The World of Jesus and the Early Church: Identity and Interpretation in Early Communities of Faith*, edited by Craig A. Evans, 69–85. Peabody, MA: Hendrickson, 2011.

———. "Kinship and Family in the New Testament World." In *Understanding the Social World of the New Testament*, edited by Dietmer Neufeld and Richard E. DeMaris, 29–43. London: Routledge 2010.

———. *The Pauline Churches: A Socio-Historical Study of Institutionalisation in the Pauline and Deutero-Pauline Writings*. SNTSMS 60. Cambridge: Cambridge University Press, 1988.

———. "A Place of Belonging: Perspectives on Children from Colossians and Ephesians." In *The Child in the Bible*, edited by Marcia J. Bunge, Terence E. Fretheim, and Beverly Roberts Gaventa, 278–304. Grand Rapids: Eerdmans, 2008.

Macky, Peter W. *The Centrality of Metaphors to Biblical Thought: A Method for Interpreting the Bible*. SBEC 19. Lampeter: Edwin Mellen, 1990.

Maier, Harry O. "Barbarians, Scythians and Imperial Iconography in the Epistle to the Colossians." In *Picturing the New Testament, Studies in Ancient Visual Images*, edited by Annette Weissenrieder, Friederike Wendt, and Petra von Gemünden, 385–406. WUNT 2/193. Tübingen: Mohr Siebeck, 2005.

———. *Picturing Paul in Empire: Imperial Image, Text and Persuasion in Colossians, Ephesians and the Pastoral Epistles*. London: Bloomsbury T. & T. Clark, 2013.

Malherbe, Abraham J. "Antisthenes and Odysseus, and Paul at War." *HTR* 76 (1983) 143–73.

———. "'Gentle as a Nurse': The Cynic Background to I Thess II." *NovT* 12 (1970) 203–17.

———. "Hellenistic Moralists and the New Testament." *ANRW* 26 (1992) 267–333.

———. *Paul and the Popular Philosophers*. Minneapolis: Fortress, 1989.

———. *Social Aspects of Early Christianity*. Philadelphia: Fortress, 1983.

Malina, Bruce J. "Collectivism in Mediterranean Culture." In *Understanding the Social World of the New Testament*, edited by Dietmar Neufeld and Richard E. DeMaris, 17–28. Abingdon, UK: Routledge, 2010.

———. "Early Christian Groups: Using Small Group Formation Theory to Explain Christian Organisations." In *Modelling Early Christianity: Social-Scientific Studies of the New Testament in Its Context*, edited by Philip F. Esler, 96–113. London: Routledge, 1995.

———. *The New Testament World: Insights from Cultural Anthropology*. 3rd ed. Louisville: Westminster John Knox, 2001.

Malina, Bruce J., and John J. Pilch. *Social Science Commentary on the Letters of Paul*. Minneapolis: Augsburg, 2006.

Marohl, Matthew J. *Faithfulness and the Purpose of Hebrews: A Social Identity Approach*. PTMS 82. Eugene, OR: Pickwick, 2008.

Marshall, Peter. *Enmity in Corinth: Social Conventions in Paul's Relation with the Corinthians*. WUNT 2/23. Tübingen: J.C.B. Siebeck, 1987.

Martin, Dale B. *The Corinthian Body*. New Haven, CT: Yale University Press, 1995.

———. "Tongues of Angels and Other Status Indicator." *JAAR* 59 (1991) 547–89.

―――. *Slavery as Salvation: The Metaphor of Slavery in Pauline Christianity*. New Haven, CT: Yale University Press, 1990.
Martin, Ralph P. *2 Corinthians*. 2nd ed. WBC 40. Grand Rapids: Zondervan, 2014.
―――. *The Spirit and the Congregation: Studies in 1 Corinthians 12–15*. Grand Rapids: Eerdmans, 1984.
May, Alistair Scott. *"The Body for the Lord": Sex and Identity in 1 Corinthians 5–7*. JSNTSup 278. London: T. & T. Clark, 2004.
McCready, Wayne O. "EKKLEĒSIA and Voluntary Associations." In *Voluntary Associations in the Greco-Roman World*, edited by John S. Kloppenborg and Stephen G. Wilson, 59–73. London: Routledge, 1996.
McGrath, Joseph E., and Franziska Tschan. *Temporal Matters in Social Psychology: Examining the Role of Time in the Lives of Groups and Individuals*. Washington, DC: American Psychological Association, 2004.
McKelvey, R. J. *The New Temple: The Church in the New Testament*. Oxford: Oxford University Press, 1969.
McLean, B. H. *Origins and Methods: Towards a New Understanding of Judaism and Christianity: Essays in Honour of John C. Hurd*. JSNTSup 86. Sheffield: JSOT, 1993.
McNeel, Jennifer Houston. *Paul as Infant and Nursing Mother: Metaphor, Rhetoric, and Identity in 1 Thessalonians 2:5–8*. ECL 12. Atlanta: SBL, 2014.
Meeks, Wayne A. *The First Urban Christians: The Social World of the Apostle Paul*. 2nd ed. New Haven, CT: Yale University Press, 2003.
―――. *The Origins of First Christian Morality: The First Two Centuries*. New Haven, CT: Yale University Press, 1993.
Meggitt, Justin J. *Paul, Poverty and Survival*. Edinburgh: T. & T. Clark, 1998.
―――. "The Social Status of Erastus (Rom. 16:23)." *NovT* 38 (1996) 218–23.
Mengestu, Abera M. *God as Father in Paul: Kinship Language and Identity Formation in Early Christianity*. Eugene, OR: Pickwick, 2013.
Miller, N., and M. B. Brewer, eds. *Groups in Contact: The Psychology of Desegregation*. Orlando: Academic, 1984.
Mitchell, Alan C. "Friends Do Not Wrong Friends: Friendship and Justice in 1 Corinthians 6.8." In *The Impartial God: Essays in Biblical Studies in Honor of Jouette M. Bassler*, edited by Calvin J. Roetzel and Robert L. Foster, 134–44. NTM 22. Sheffield: Sheffield Phoenix, 2007.
―――. "Rich and Poor in the Courts of Corinth: Litigiousness and Status in 1 Cor 6:1–11." *NTS* 39 (1993) 562–86.
Mitchell, Margaret M. *Paul and the Rhetoric of Reconciliation: An Exegetical Investigation of the Language and Composition of 1 Corinthians*. Louisville: Westminster/John Knox, 1991.
―――. "New Testament Envoys in the Context of Greco-Roman Diplomatic and Epistolary Conventions: The Example of Timothy and Titus." *JBL* 111 (1992) 641–62.
Mitchell, Matthew W. "Reexamining the 'Aborted Apostle': An Exploration of Paul's Self-Description in 1 Corinthians 15.8." *JSNT* 25 (2002–3) 469–85.
Moo, Jonathan. "Of Parents and Children: 1 Corinthians 4:15–16 and Life in the Family of God." In *Studies in the Pauline Epistles: Essays in Honor of Douglas J. Moo*, edited by Matthew S. Harmon and Jay E. Smith, 57–73. Grand Rapids: Zondervan, 2014.
Morris, Leon. *The First Epistle of Paul to the Corinthians*. Tyndale New Testament Commentaries. Grand Rapids: Eerdmans, 1985.

Moscovici, S., ed. *Introduction à la Psychologie Sociale*. Vol 1. Paris: Larousse, 1972.
Moxnes, Halvor. "Body, Gender and Social Space: Dilemmas in Constructing Early Christian Identities." In *Identity Formation in the New Testament*, edited by Bengt Holmberg and Mikael Winninge, 163–81. WUNT 1/227. Tübingen: Mohr Siebeck, 2008.

———. "What Is Family? Problems in Constructing Early Christian Families." In *Constructing Early Christian Families: Family as Social Reality and Metaphor*, edited by Halvor Moxnes, 13–41. London: Routledge, 1997.

———, ed. *Constructing Early Christian Families: Family as Social Reality and Metaphor*. London: Routledge, 1997.

Mummendey, Amélie, Andreas Klink, and Rupert Brown. "Nationalism and Patriotism: National Identification and Out-Group Rejection." *BJSP* 40 (2001) 159–72.

Murphy-O'Connor, Jerome. *St. Paul's Corinth: Texts and Archaeology*. 3rd ed. Collegeville, MN: Liturgical, 2002.

Nathan, Emmanuel. "Fragmented Theology in 2 Corinthians: The Unresolved Puzzle of 6:14–7:1." In *Theologizing in the Corinthian Conflict: Studies in the Exegesis and Theology of 2 Corinthians*, edited by Reimund Bieringer et al., 211–28. BTS 16. Leuven: Peeters, 2013.

Nathan, Geoffrey S. *The Family in Late Antiquity: The Rise of Christianity and the Endurance of Tradition*. London: Routledge, 2000.

Nebreda, Sergio Rosell. *Christ Identity: A Social-Scientific Reading of Philippians 2.5–11*. FRLANT 240. Göttingen: Vandenhoeck & Ruprecht, 2011.

Neils, Jennifer, and John H. Oakley, eds. *Coming of Age in Ancient Greece: Images of Childhood from the Classical Past*. New Haven, CT: Yale University Press, 2003.

Neufeld, Dietmar, and Richard E. DeMaris, eds. *Understanding the Social World of the New Testament*. Abingdon, UK: Routledge, 2010.

Newton, Derek. *Deity and Diet: The Dilemma of Sacrificial Food at Corinth*. JSNTSup 169. Sheffield: Sheffield Academic, 1998.

Newton, Michael. *The Concept of Purity At Qumran and in the Letters of Paul*. SNTSMS 53. Cambridge: Cambridge University Press, 1985.

Neyrey, Jerome H. "God, Benefactor and Patron: The Major Cultural Model for Interpreting the Deity in Greco-Roman Antiquity." *JSNT* 27 (2005) 465–92.

———. "Loss of Wealth, Loss of Family and Loss of Honour." In *Modelling Early Christianity: Social Scientific Studies of the New Testament in its Context*, edited by Philip F. Esler, 139–58. London: Routledge, 1995.

———. *Paul, in Other Words: A Cultural Reading of his Letters*. Louisville: Westminster John Knox, 1990.

Neyrey, Jerome H., and Eric C. Steward, eds. *The Social World of the New Testament: Insights and Models*. Peabody, MA: Hendrickson, 2008.

Nguyen, V. Henry T. *Christian Identity in Corinth: A Comparative Study of 2 Corinthians, Epictetus and Valeruis Maximus*. WUNT 2/243. Tübingen: Mohr Siebeck, 2008.

Nicholson, G. C. "Houses for Hospitality: 1 Cor 11:17–34." *Colloq* 19 (1986) 1–6.

Nickelsburg, George W. E. "An *Ektroma*, Though Appointed from the Womb: Paul's Apostolic Self-Description in 1 Corinthians and Galatians 1." *HTR* 79 (1986) 198–205.

Oakes, Peter. *Reading Romans in Pompeii*. Minneapolis: Fortress, 2009.

Öhler, Markus. "Cultic Meals in Associations and the Early Christian Eucharist." *EC* 5/4 (2014) 475–502.

Orlin, Eric M. *Temples, Religion and Politics in the Roman Republic.* Leiden: Brill, 1997.
Orr, William F., and James Arthus Walther. *1 Corinthians.* AB. New York: Doubleday, 1976.
Osiek, Carolyn. "The Family in Early Christianity: 'Family Values' Revisited." *CBQ* 58 (1996) 1–24.
Osiek, Carolyn, and David L. Balch. *Families in the New Testament World: Households and House Churches.* Louisville: Westminster John Knox, 1997.
Papahatzis, Nicos. *Ancient Corinth: The Museums of Corinth, Isthmia and Sicyon.* Athens: Ekdotike Athenon, 1977.
Parsons, Mikeal C. *Body and Character in Luke and Acts: The Subversion of Physiognomy in Early Christianity.* Grand Rapids: Baker Academic, 2006.
Patterson, Cynthia B. *The Family in Greek History.* Cambridge, MA: Harvard University Press, 1998.
Patterson, Jane Lancaster. *Keeping the Feast: Metaphors and Sacrifice in 1 Corinthians and Philippians.* ECL 16. Atlanta: SBL, 2015.
Paul, Ian. "Metaphor." In *Dictionary of Theological Interpretation of the Bible*, edited by Kevin J. Vanhoozer et al., 507–10. Grand Rapids: Baker Academic, 2005.
Pedley, John. *Sanctuaries and the Sacred in the Ancient Greek World.* Cambridge: Cambridge University Press, 2005.
Peppard, Michael. "Brother against Brother: *Controversiae* about Inheritance Disputes and 1 Corinthians 6:1–1." *JBL* 133 (2014) 179–92.
Perdue, Leo G., et al., eds. *Families in Ancient Israel.* FRC. Louisville: Westminster John Knox, 1997.
Perrone, L., ed. *Origeniana Octava: Origen and the Alexandrian Tradition.* BETL 164. Leuven: Leuven University Press, 2003.
Pickett, Raymond. *The Cross in Corinth: The Social Significance of the Death of Jesus.* JSNTSup 143. Sheffield: Sheffield Academic Press, 1997.
Plummer, Alfred. *A Critical and Exegetical Commentary on the Second Epistle of St. Paul to the Corinthians.* ICC. Edinburgh: T. & T. Clark, 1915.
Plummer, Robert L. "Imitation of Paul and the Church's Missionary Role in 1 Corinthians." *JETS* 444 (2001) 219–35.
Pogoloff, Stephen M. *Logos and Sophia: The Rhetorical Situation of 1 Corinthians.* SBLDS 134. Atlanta: Scholars, 1992.
Poirier, John C. *The Tongues of Angels: The Concept of Angelic Languages in Classical Jewish and Christian Texts.* WUNT 2/287. Tübingen: Mohr Siebeck, 2010.
Polaski, Sandra Hack. *Paul and the Discourse of Power.* GCT 8, The Biblical Seminar 62. Sheffield: Sheffield Academic Press, 1999.
Porter, Stanley E. "How Do We Define Pauline Social Relations?" In *Paul and His Social Relations*, edited by Stanley E. Porter and Christopher D. Land, 7–33. PAST 7. Leiden: Brill, 2013.
———. "Paul and His Bible: His Education and Access to the Scriptures of Israel." In *As It Is Written: Studying Paul's Use of Scripture*, edited by Stanley E. Porter and Christopher D. Stanley, 97–125. SBLSymS 50. Leiden: Brill, 2008.
———, ed. *Paul and His Theology.* PAST 3. Leiden: Brill, 2006.
———, ed. *Paul: Jew, Greek, and Roman.* PAST 5. Leiden, Brill, 2008.
———, ed. *Paul's World.* PAST 4. Leiden: Brill, 2008.
Porter, Stanley E., and Christopher D. Land, eds. *Paul and His Social Relations.* PAST 7. Leiden: Brill, 2013.

Porter, Stanley E., and Andrew W. Pitts, eds. *Christian Origins and Greco-Roman Culture: Social and Literary Contexts for the New Testament.* TENTS 9/ECIHC. Leiden: Brill, 2013.

Price, Susan R. F. *Rituals and Power: The Roman Imperial Cult in Asia Minor.* Cambridge: Cambridge University Press, 1984.

Punt, Jeremy. "He is Heavy . . . He's My Brother: Unravelling Fraternity in Paul (Galatians)." *Neot* 46 (2012) 153–71.

Rabens, Volker. "Paul's Rhetoric of Demarcation: Separation from 'Unbelievers' (2 Cor 6:14–7:1) in the Corinthian Conflict." In *Theologizing in the Corinthian Conflict: Studies in the Exegesis and Theology of 2 Corinthians*, edited by Reimund Bieringer et al., 229–53. BTS 16. Leuven: Peeters, 2013.

Rawlinson, A. E. J. "Corpus Christi." In *Mysterium Christi*, edited by G. K. A. Bell and Adolf Deissmann, 225–54. London: Longmans, 1930.

Rawson, Beryl. *Children and Childhood in Roman Italy.* Oxford: Oxford University Press, 2003.

———. "The Roman Family." In *The Family in Ancient Rome: New Perspectives*, edited by Beryl Rawson, 1–57. Ithaca, NY: Cornell University Press, 1986.

———. "'The Roman Family' in Recent Research: State of the Question." *BibInt* 11/2 (2003) 119–38.

———, ed. *The Family in Ancient Rome: New Perspectives.* Ithaca, NY: Cornell University Press, 1986.

———, ed. *Marriage, Divorce, and Children in Ancient Rome.* Oxford: Clarendon, 1991.

Rawson, Beryl, and Paul Weaver, eds. *The Roman Family in Italy: Status, Sentiment, Space.* Canberra: Humanities Research Centre, 1997.

Reumann, John. "Oikonomia-Terms in Paul and in Comparison with Lucan Heilsgeschichte." *NTS* 13 (1967) 147–67.

———. "'Stewards of God': Pre-Christian Religious Application of *Oikonomos* in Greek." *JBL* 77 (1958) 339–49.

Richards, I. A. *The Philosophy of Rhetoric.* London: Oxford University Press, 1936.

Ricoeur, Paul. *The Role of Metaphor: Multi-Disciplinary Studies of the Creation of Meaning in Language.* Toronto: University of Toronto Press, 1977.

Robbins, Vernon K. *The Tapestry of Early Christian Discourse: Rhetoric, Society and Ideology.* London: Routledge, 1996.

Robertson, Archibald, and Alfred Plummer. *A Critical and Exegetical Commentary on the First Epistle of St. Paul to the Corinthians.* 2nd ed. ICC. Edinburgh: T. & T. Clark, 1929.

Robinson, John A. T. *The Body: A Study in Pauline Theology.* London: SCM, 1952.

Robinson, W. Peter, ed. *Social Groups and Identity: Developing the Legacy of Henri Tajfel.* Oxford: Butterworth-Heinemann, 1996.

Roetzel, Calvin J., and Robert L. Foster, eds. *The Impartial God: Essays in Biblical Studies in Honor of Jouette M. Bassler.* NTM 22. Sheffield: Sheffield Phoenix Press, 2007.

Rohrbaugh, R. L., ed. *The Social Sciences and the New Testament Interpretation.* Peabody, MA: Hendrickson, 1996.

Roitto, Rikard. "Act as a Christ-Believer, as a Household Member or as Both? A Cognitive Perspective on the Relationship between the Social Identity in Christ and Household Identities in Pauline and Deutero-Pauline Texts." In *Identity Formation in the New Testament*, edited by Bengt Holmberg and Mikael Winninge, 141–61. WUNT 1/227. Tübingen: Mohr Siebeck, 2008.

———. *Behaving as A Christ-Believer: A Cognitive Perspective on Identity and Behavior Norms in Ephesians*. CBNTS 46. Winona Lake, IN: Eisenbrauns, 2011.
Rosner, Brian S. *Greed as Idolatry: The Origin and Meaning of a Pauline Metaphor*. Grand Rapids: Eerdmans, 2007.
———. "Temple Prostitution in 1 Corinthians 6:12-20." *NovT* 40 (1998) 336-51.
Saller, Richard P. "Corporal Punishment, Authority, and Obedience in the Roman Household." In *Marriage, Divorce and Children in Ancient Rome*, edited by Beryl Rawson, 144-65. Oxford: Clarendon, 1991.
———. "*Familia, Domus,* and the Roman Conception of Family." *Phoenix* 38 (1984) 336-55.
———. "*Pater Familias, Mater Familias,* and the Gendered Semantics of the Roman Household." *CP* 94 (1999) 182-97.
———. *Patriarchy, Property and Death in the Roman Family*. CSPESPT 25. Cambridge: Cambridge University Press, 1994.
Sampley, J. Paul, ed. *Paul in the Greco-Roman World: A Handbook*. Harrisburg, PA: Trinity, 2003.
Sanders, Boykin. "Imitating Paul: 1 Cor 4:16." *HTR* 74 (1981) 353-63.
Sandnes, Karl Olav. *Belly and Body in the Pauline Epistles*. SNTSMS 120. Cambridge: Cambridge University Press, 2002.
———. "Equality within Patriarchal Structures: Some New Testament Perspectives on the Christian Fellowship as a Brother-or Sisterhood and a Family." In *Constructing Early Christian Families: Family as Social Reality and Metaphor*, edited by Halvor Moxnes, 150-65. London: Routledge, 1997.
———. *A New Family: Conversion and Ecclesiology in the Early Church with Cross-Cultural Comparisons*. SIHC 91. Berne: Lang, 1994.
Savage, Timothy B. *Power through Weakness: Paul's Understanding of the Christian Ministry in 2 Corinthians*. SNTSMS 86. Cambridge: Cambridge University Press, 1996.
Schlosser, Jacques, ed. *Paul et l'unité des chrétiens*. COP 19. Leuven: Peeters, 2010.
Schmidt, Francis. *How the Temple Thinks: Identity and Social Cohesion in Ancient Judaism*. Sheffield: Sheffield Academic Press, 2001.
Schottroff, Luise. "Holiness and Justice: Exegetical Comments on 1 Corinthians 11.17-34." *JSNT* 79 (2000) 51-60.
Schowalter, Daniel N. "Seeking Shelter in Roman Corinth: Archaeology and the Placement of Paul's Communities." In *Corinth in Context: Comparative Studies on Religion and Society*, edited by Steven J. Friesen, Daniel N. Schowalter, and James C. Walters, 327-41. NovSup 134. Leiden: Brill, 2010.
Schowalter, Daniel N., and Steven J. Friesen, eds. *Urban Religion in Roman Corinth: Interdisciplinary Approaches*. HTS 53. Cambridge, MA: Harvard University Press, 2005.
Schüssler Fiorenza, Elizabeth. *In Memory of Her: A Feminist Theological Reconstruction of Christian Origins*. New York: Crossroad, 1983.
Schweitzer, Albert. *The Mysticisicm of Paul the Apostle*. Translated by William Montgomery. New York: Holt, 1931.
Shanor, Jay. "Paul as Master Builder: Construction Terms in First Corinthians." *NTS* 33 (1988) 461-71.
Shen, Michael. *Canaan to Corinth: Paul's Doctrine of God and the Issue of Food Offered to Idols in 1 Corinthians 8:1—11:1*. StBibLit 83. New York: Peter Lang, 2010.

Shkul, Minna. *Reading Ephesians: Exploring Social Entrepreneurship in the Text.* LNTS 408. London: T. & T. Clark, 2009.
Smith, Dennis E. *From Symposium to Eucharist: The Banquet in the Early Christian World.* Minneapolis: Fortress, 2003.
———. *Meals and Morality in Paul and his World.* Chico, CA: Scholars, 1981.
Snyder, Graydon F. *First Corinthians: A Faith Community Commentary.* Macon, GA: Mercer University Press, 1992.
Son, Sang-Won (Aaron). *Corporate Elements in Pauline Anthropology: A Study of Selected Terms, Idioms, and Concepts in the Light of Paul's Usage and Background.* AnBib 148. Rome: Editrice Pontificio Istituto Biblico, 2001.
Soskice, Janet Martin. *The Kindness of God: Metaphor, Gender, and Religious Language.* Oxford: Oxford University Press, 2007.
———. *Metaphor and Religious Language.* Oxford: Clarendon, 1985.
Stacey, W. David. *The Pauline View of Man: In Relation to Its Judaic and Hellenistic Background.* London: MacMillan, 1956.
Stienstra, Nelly. *YHWH is the Husband of His People: Analysis of a Biblical Metaphor with Special Reference to Translation.* Kampen: Kok Pharos, 1993.
Still, Todd D., and David G. Horrell, eds. *After the First Urban Christians: The Social-Scientific Study of Pauline Christianity Twenty-Five Years Later.* New York: T. & T. Clark, 2009.
Strange, William A. *Children in the Early Church: Children in the Ancient World, the New Testament and the Early Church.* Carlisle: Paternoster, 1996.
Swift, E. H. "A Group of Roman Imperial Portraits at Corinth." *AJA* 25/2 (1921) 142–59.
Tajfel, Henri. *Differentiation between Social Groups: Studies in the Social Psychology of Intergroup Relations.* EMSP 14. London: Academic, 1978.
———. *Human Groups and Social Categories: Studies in Social Psychology.* Cambridge: Cambridge University Press, 1981.
———. "La catégorisation sociale." In *Introduction à la Psychologie Sociale*, edited by S. Moscovici, 1:272–302. Paris: Larousse, 1972.
———. "Social Categorization, Social Identity and Social Comparison." In *Differentiation Between Social Groups: Studies in the Social Psychology of Intergroup Relations*, edited by Henri Tajfel, 61–76. EMSP 14. London: Academic, 1978.
———, ed. *Social Identity and Intergroup Relations.* Cambridge: Cambridge University Press, 1982.
Tajfel, Henri, and John Turner. "An Integrative Theory of Group Conflict." In *The Social Psychology of Intergroup Relations*, edited by W. C. Austin and S. Worchel, 33–47. Monterey, CA: Brooks/Cole, 1979.
Talbott, Rick F. *Jesus, Paul, and Power: Rhetoric, Ritual, and Metaphor in Ancient Mediterranean Christianity.* Eugene, OR: Cascade, 2010.
Tellbe, Mikael. *Christ-Believers in Ephesus: A Textual Analysis of Early Christian Identity Formation in a Local Perspective.* WUNT 1/242. Tübingen: Mohr Siebeck, 2009.
Theissen, Gerd. *Psychological Aspects of Pauline Theology.* Edinburgh: T. & T. Clark, 1987.
———. "Social Conflicts in the Corinthian Community: Further Remarks on J.J. Meggitt, Paul, Poverty and Survival." *JSNT* 25 (2003) 371–391.
———. *The Social Setting of Pauline Christianity.* Edinburgh: T. & T. Clark, 1982.
———. "The Social Structure of Pauline Communities: Some Critical Remarks on J.J. Meggitt, Paul, Poverty and Survival." *JSNT* 84 (2001) 65–84.

Thiselton, Anthony C. *The First Epistle to the Corinthians.* NIGTC. Grand Rapids: Eerdmans, 2000.
Thrall, Margaret E. *A Critical and Exegetical Commentary on the Second Epistle to the Corinthians.* Vol.1. ICC. Edinburgh: T. & T. Clark, 1994.
———. "The Initial Attraction of Paul's Mission in Corinth and of the Church He Founded There." In *Paul, Luke and the Graeco-Roman World: Essays in Honour of Alexander J. M. Wedderburn*, edited by Alf Christophersen et al., 59–73. JSNTSup 217. Sheffield: Sheffield Academic Press, 2002.
Tibbs, Clint. *Religious Experience of the Pneuma: Communicating with the Spirit World in 1 Corinthians 12 and 14.* WUNT 2/230. Tübingen: Mohr Siebeck, 2007.
Tidball, Derek J. *In Christ, In Colossae: Sociological Perspectives on Colossians.* Milton Keynes: Paternoster, 2011.
Tribilco, Paul R. *Self-Designations and Group Identity in the New Testament.* Cambridge: Cambridge University Press, 2012.
Tsang, Sam. *From Slaves to Sons: A New Rhetoric Analysis on Paul's Slave Metaphors in His Letters to the Galatians.* New York: Peter Lang, 2005.
Tucker, J. Brian. *Remain in Your Calling: Paul and the Continuation of Social Identities in 1 Corinthians.* Eugene, OR: Pickwick, 2011.
———. *"You Belong to Christ": Paul and the Formation of Social Identity in 1 Corinthians 1–4.* Eugene, OR: Pickwick, 2010.
Tucker, J. Brian, and Coleman A. Baker, eds. *T. & T. Clark Handbook to Social Identity in the New Testament.* London: Bloomsbury T. & T. Clark 2014.
Tuckett, Christopher. "The Church as the Body of Christ." In *Paul et l'unité des chrétiens*, edited by Jacques Schlosser, 161–91. COP 19. Leuven: Peeters, 2010.
Turner, John C. "Social Categorization and the Self-Concept: A Social Cognitive Theory." In *Advances in Group Processes*, edited by Edward J. Lawler, 77–122. Greenwich, CT: JAI, 1985.
Turner, John C., et al. *Rediscovering the Social Group: A Self-Categorization Theory.* Oxford: Blackwell, 1987.
Turner, Max. *The Holy Spirit and Spiritual Gifts in the New Testament.* Rev. ed. Peabody, MA: Hendrickson, 1998.
———. "A Response to the Responses of Menzies and Chan." *AJPS* 2 (1999) 297–308.
Tyler, Ronald L. "First Corinthians 4:6 and Hellenistic Pedagogy." *CBQ* 60 (1998) 97–103.
Van der Watt, Jan G. *Family of the King: Dynamics of Metaphor in the Gospel according to John.* Leiden: Brill, 1999.
Van Henten, Jan Willem, and Athalya Brenner, eds. *Families and Family Relations as Represented in Early Judaisms and Early Christianities: Texts and Fictions.* STAR 2. Leiden: Deo, 2000.
Van Oudenhouven, J. P., J. T. Groenewoud, and M. Hewstone. "Co-operation Ethnic Salience and Generalization of Inter-ethnic Attitudes." *EJSP* 1996 (26) 649–62.
Vanhoye, A., ed. *L'Apôtre Paul: Personnalité, style et conception du ministère.* BETL 73. Leuven: Leuven University Press, 1986.
Verbrugge, Veryn D., and Keith R. Krell. *Paul and Money: A Biblical and Theological Analysis of the Apostle's Teachings and Practices.* Grand Rapids: Zondervan, 2015.
Verner, D. C. *The Household of God: The Social World of the Pastoral Epistles.* SBLDS 71. Chico, CA: Scholars, 1983.

Walbank, Mary E. Hoskins. "Image and Cult: The Coinage of Roman Corinth." In *Corinth in Context: Comparative Studies on Religion and Society*, edited by Steven J. Friesen, Daniel N. Schowalter, and James C. Walters, 151–97. NovSup 134. Leiden: Brill, 2010.

Walters, James C. "Civic Identity in Roman Corinth and Its Impact on Early Christianity." In *Urban Religion in Roman Corinth: Interdisciplinary Approaches*, edited by Daniel N. Schowalter and Steven J. Friesen, 397–417. HTS 53. Cambridge, MA: Harvard University Press, 2005.

———. "Paul and the Politics of Meals in Roman Corinth." In *Corinth in Context: Comparative Studies on Religion and Society*, edited by Steven J. Friesen, Daniel N. Schowalter, and James C. Walters, 343–64. NovTSup 134. Leiden: Brill, 2010.

Wanamaker, Charles. "Metaphor and Morality: Examples of Paul's Moral Thinking in 1 Corinthians 1–5." *Neot* 39/2 (2005) 409–33.

———. "The Power of the Absent Father: A Socio-rhetorical Analysis of 1 Corinthians 4:14—5:13." In *New Testament Interpreted: Essays in Honour of Bernard C. Lategan*, edited by Cilliers Breytenbach, Johan C. Thom, and Jeremy Punt, 339–64. Leiden: Brill, 2006.

Wardle, Timothy. *The Jerusalem Temple and Early Christian Identity*. WUNT 2/291. Tübingen: Mohr Siebeck, 2010.

Wedderburn, A. J. M. "Paul's Collection: Chronology and History." *NTS* 48 (2002) 95–110.

Weima, Jeffrey A. D. "Infants, Nursing Mother, and Father: Paul's Portrayal of a Pastor." *CTJ* 37 (2002) 209–29.

Weissenrieder, Annette, Friederike Wendt, and Petra von Gemünden, eds., *Picturing the New Testament: Studies in Ancient Visual Images*. WUNT 2/193. Tübingen: Mohr Siebeck, 2005.

Westfall, Cynthia Long. "'This is A Great Metaphor!': Reciprocity in the Ephesian Household Code." In *Christian Origins and Greco-Roman Culture: Social and Literary Contexts for the New Testament*, edited by Stanley E. Porter and Andrew W. Pitts, 561–98. TENTS 9/ECIHC. Leiden: Brill, 2013.

White, Adam G. *Where is the Wise Man? Graeco-Roman Education as a Background to the Divisions in 1 Corinthians 1–4*. LNTS 536. London: Bloomsbury T. & T. Clark, 2015.

White, John L. "God's Paternity as Root Metaphor in Paul's Conception of Community." *Forum* 8 (1992) 271–95.

———. *Light from Ancient Letters*. Philadelphia: Fortress, 1986.

White, L. Michael. "Paul and Pater Familias." In *Paul in the Greco-Roman World: A Handbook*, edited by J. Paul Sampley, 457–87. Harrisburg, PA: Trinity, 2003.

White, L. Michael, and O. Larry Yarbrough, eds. *The Social World of the First Christians: Essays in Honor of Wayne A. Meeks*. Minneapolis: Fortress, 1995.

Wickkiser, Bronwen L. "Asklepios in Greek and Roman Corinth." In *Corinth in Context: Comparative Studies on Religion and Society*, edited by Steven J. Friesen, Daniel N. Schowalter, and James C. Walters, 37–66. NovTSup 134. Leiden: Brill, 2010.

Wiedemann, Thomas. *Adults and Children in the Roman Empire*. New Haven, CT: Yale University Press, 1989.

Wilkins, Michael J., and Terence Paige, eds. *Worship, Theology and Ministry in the Early Church: Essays in Honor of Ralph P. Martin*. JSNTSup 87. Sheffield: Sheffield Academic, 1992.

Williams, Charles K., II, and Nancy Bookidis, eds. *Corinth: The Centenary 1896–1996*. Vol. 20. Athens: American School of Classical Studies at Athens, 2003.

Williams, David J. *Paul's Metaphors: Their Context and Character*. Peabody, MA: Hendrickson, 1999.

Willis, Wendell Lee. *Idol Meat in Corinth: The Pauline Argument in 1 Corinthians 8 and 10*. SBLDS. Chico, CA: Scholars, 1985.

Winter, Bruce W. *After Paul Left Corinth: The Influence of Secular Ethics and Social Change*. Grand Rapids: Eerdmans, 2001.

———. "Civil Litigation in Secular Corinth and the Church." *NTS* 37 (1991) 559–72.

———. *Philo and Paul Among the Sophists: Alexandrian and Corinthian Responses to a Julio-Claudian Movement*. 2nd ed. Grand Rapids: Eerdmans, 2002.

———. *Seek the Welfare of the City: Christians as Benefactors and Citizens*. Grand Rapids: Eerdmans, 1994.

Witherington, Ben, III. *Conflict and Community in Corinth: A Socio-Rhetorical Commentary on 1 and 2 Corinthians*. Grand Rapids: Eerdmans, 1995.

Worchel, Stephen, et al., eds. *Social Identity: International Perspectives*. London: Sage, 1998.

Wuellner, William. "Paul as Pastor: The Function of Rhetorical Questions in First Corinthians." In *L'Apôtre Paul: Personnalité, style et conception du ministère*, edited by A. Vanhoye, 49–77. BETL 73. Leuven: Leuven University Press, 1986.

Yarbrough, O. Larry. "Parents and Children in the Jewish Family of Antiquity." In *The Jewish Family in Antiquity*, edited by Shaye J. D. Cohen, 49–55. Atlanta: Scholars, 1993.

———. "Parents and Children in the Letters of Paul." In *The Social World of the First Christians: Essays in Honor of Wayne A. Meeks*, edited by L. Michael White and O. Larry Yarbrough, 126–41. Minneapolis: Fortress, 1995.

Young, Norman H. "Paidagogos: The Social Setting of a Pauline Metaphor." *NovT* 29 (1987) 150–76.

Zanker, Paul. *The Power of Images in the Age of Augustus*. Translated by Alan Shapiro. Ann Arbor: University of Michigan Press, 1988.

Author Index

Aasgaard, Reidar, 6, 52, 61, 63, 64, 96, 97, 118, 127, 128, 129, 130
Abrams, Dominic, 31
Adams, Edward, 81, 193
Adewuya, J. Ayodeji, 142
Arzt-Grabner, P., 70
Aus, Roger David, 6
Aymer, Margaret, 122, 123

Baker, Coleman A., 39
Bakke, Odd Magne, 200
Balch, David L., 52, 81, 95, 96
Balla, Peter, 52, 71, 97, 98, 101, 107, 111, 127
Banks, Robert, 58, 59, 73, 180
Barclay, John M. G., 39, 57, 88, 89, 111, 195
Barentsen, Jack, 37
Barnett, Paul, 154
Barrett, C. K., 164, 166, 171, 173, 180
Bartchy, S. Scott, 58, 59, 60, 95, 116
Barth, Markus, 163
Barton, Stephen C., 80, 186
Beale, G. K., 144, 146
Belleville, Linda, 113
Berge, Mary Katherine, 6
Berger, Peter L., 195
Best, Ernest, 164
Birge, Mary Katherine, 62, 63
Bitner, Bradley J., 141
Black, Max., 18, 19
Blanke, Helmut, 163
Blasi, Anthony J., 27
Bookidis, Nancy, 137, 175
Bossman, David, 74, 134

Bradley, Keith R., 99, 122
Brenner, Athalya, 52, 99
Brewer, M. B., 37, 38
Breytenbach, Cilliers. 6
Briones, David E., 86
Brookins, Timothy A., 194
Brown, Rupert J., 35, 36, 37
Bultmann, Rudolf, 165
Burke, Trevor J., 6, 61, 64, 71, 96, 97, 98, 107
Burkett, Walter, 73
Byatt, Anthony, 6, 22
Byron, John, 6, 130, 131

Caird, G. B., 6
Canavan, Rosemary, 43, 44
Carson, D. A., 183
Carter, Timothy L., 164, 177, 178
Carter, Warren, 45
Cartledge, J. Mark, 159
Castelli, Elizabeth A., 95, 112, 113
Cerfaux, L., 164
Cheung, Alex T., 138
Chiu, José Enrique Aguilar, 159, 162
Chow, John K., 74
Ciampa, Roy E., 79, 115, 122, 128, 161, 162, 171, 173, 174, 184
Cinnirella, Marco, 35
Clarke, Andrew D., 47, 56, 57, 76, 101, 113
Cohen, Anthony, 197,
Collins, Raymond F., 7, 127, 129, 147, 161, 167, 175, 176
Condor, Susan, 35, 36
Conway, Collen W., 124

Author Index

Conzelmann, Hans, 81, 164, 166
Corbier, Mireille, 128
Coutsoumpos, Panayotis, 81, 84, 137, 138
Cox, Cheryl Anne, 99
Crone, Theodore M., 159
Crouch, J. E., 52, 95

D'Angelo, Mary R., 110
Daines, B., 162
Darko, Daniel K., 39
Daube, D., 115
Davies, W. D., 166
Dawes, Gregory W., 163
De Lacey, D. R., 142
deSilva, David., 165
Dixon, Suzanne, 99, 101. 112
Downs, David J., 87
Dunn, James D. G., 87, 95, 166, 180
Dutch, Robert S., 111, 115

Ehrensperger, Kathy, vii, 83, 86, 113, 114
Elliot, Neil, 155
Engels, Donald, 137
Esler, Philip F., 39, 41, 42, 90, 134, 135
Eyben, Emiel, 99, 101, 107, 111, 116

Fatum, Lone, 52, 96, 112
Fay, Ron C., 149
Fee, Gordon D., 79, 80, 81, 87, 115, 140, 142, 161, 164, 166, 174, 176
Feyaerts, Kurt, 8
Finlan, Stephen, 6
Finney, Mark T., 27, 56, 57, 76, 78, 81, 84, 165, 194, 195, 201
Fiore, Benjamin, 113
Fitzmyer, Joseph A., 142
Forbes, Christopher, 159, 161
Fotopoulos, John, 138
Francis, James, 97, 121
Friesen, Steven J., 57, 82, 137
Frilingos, Chris, 95
Furnish, Victor Paul, 87, 88, 142

Gaertner, Samuel L., 37
Gale, Herbert M., 5, 6

Garland, David E., 111, 115, 138, 150, 162, 168, 171, 173
Garnsey, Peter, 100,
Gärtner, Bertil, 143
Gaventa, Beverly Roberts, 6, 71, 97, 98, 121, 122, 126, 127
Georgi, Dieter, 87
Gill, D. W., 57
Gleason, Maud W., 124, 125
Golden, Mark, 99,
Goodrich, John K., 6, 57, 130, 131, 132
Goulder, Michael D., 56
Groenendijk, Leendert, 111
Groenewoud, J. T., 38
Gundry-Volf, Judith M., 97
Gundry, Robert H., 162, 164, 165
Gupta, Nijay K., 6, 8, 22, 23, 140, 141, 142, 154
Guthrie, George H., 117, 153, 154, 156

Hall, David R., xviii
Hansen, Bruce, 27
Harland, Philip A, 70, 71
Harrill, J. Albert, 125, 130
Harris, Murray J., xviii, 6, 87, 117, 130, 131, 142, 153, 156
Harrison, James R., 118
Hays, Richard B., 82, 120
Hellerman, Joseph H., 60, 72, 73, 74, 95, 96
Henderson, Suzanne Watts, 79, 83
Hering, James P., 52, 95
Hewstone, M., 38
Hill, Andrew E., 138, 176
Hiu, Elim, 159, 161, 162
Hodge, Caroline Johnson, 27
Hoehner, Harold W, 163
Hogeterp, Albert L. A., 6, 145, 150, 156
Hogg, Michael A., 31
Holmberg, Bengt, 27, 39
Hölscher, Tonio, 44
Hooker, Morna, 87, 121
Horrell, David G., 26, 27,
Horsley, G. H. R., 102, 106, 155
Horsley, Richard A., 139

Hovenden, Gerald, 159

Jamir, Lanuwabang, 80, 82, 85
Jenkins, Richard, 31
Jewett, Robert, 166
Johnson, Mark, 19, 20, 21, 22
Jongkind, Dirk, 57
Joubert, Stephen J., 95, 101, 110
Judge, Edwin A, 27, 47, 59

Kahl, Brigitte, 43, 47
Käsemann, Ernst, 165
Keener, Craig S., 156
Keesing, Roger M., 133
Kempthorne, R., 142
Kertzer, David I., 99
Kim, Jung Hoon, 6
Kim, Seyoon, 166
Kim, Yung Suk, 114, 180, 181, 182, 186
Klauck, Hans-Josef, 64
Kloppenborg, John S., 72
Konsmo, Erik, 6, 140, 145, 157
Krell, Keith R., 87

Lacey, W. K., 99, 100, 110
Lakoff, George, 19, 20, 21, 22
Lampe, Peter, 81
Lanci, John R., 6, 137, 140, 145, 149, 150, 155
Lassen, Eva Marie, 101, 109, 110, 115, 116, 128, 133
Lee, Michelle V., 162, 164, 165, 166, 172, 173, 182, 183
Lee, Min Choon, 30
Levison, John R., 140, 149, 150
Lietaert Peerbolte, 111
Lieu, Judith, 29, 45
Lim, Kar Yong, xviii, 35, 58, 86, 114, 125, 138, 142, 199
Limberis, Vasiliki, 201
Liu, Yulin, 137, 154, 155
Lockwood, Gregory J., 115
Long, Adrian, 97, 119
Longenecker, Bruce W., 57, 82
Lopez, Davina C., 42, 43
Lovacs, Judith L., 120
Luckmann, Thomas, 195

MacDonald, Margaret Y., 95, 97, 98, 127
Macky, Peter W., 6
Maier, Harry O., 41, 42
Malherbe, Abraham J., 122
Malina, Bruce J., 26, 28, 29, 145, 193
Martin, Dale B., 78, 79, 124, 130, 131, 160, 161, 167, 173, 174, 179, 182, 183
Martin, Ralph P., 87, 145, 174
May, Alistair Scott, 39
McCready, Wayne O., 72
McKelvey, R. J., 143, 144, 145
McNeel, Jennifer Houston, 6, 44, 97, 99, 120, 121, 127, 128
Meeks, Wayne A., 26, 27, 57, 59, 60, 61, 71, 72, 81, 85, 180, 196
Meggitt, Justin J., 57
Miller N., 37
Mitchell, Alan C., 75, 77
Mitchell, Margaret M., 56, 78, 112, 142, 150, 165, 170, 171, 173, 180
Mitchell, Matthew W., 129
Moo, Jonathan, 127
Moxnes, Halvor, 52, 93, 96
Mummendey, Amélie, 36
Murphy-O'Connor, Jerome, 81

Nathan, Emmanuel, 142, 146
Nathan, Geoffrey S., 99
Nebreda, Sergio Rosell, 47
Neils, Jennifer, 99
Newton, Derek, 138
Newton, Michael, 142, 143, 154
Neyrey, Jerome H., 94, 95, 156
Nguyen, V. Henry T., 27, 47, 56
Nickelsburg, George W. E., 128

Oakes, Peter, 81
Oakley, John H., 99
Öhler, Markus, 84
Orlin, Eric M., 148
Orr, William F., 78, 85
Osiek, Carolyn, 52, 81, 96

Papahatzis, Nicos, 138
Parsons, Mikeal C., 124, 125
Patterson, Cynthia B., 99

Author Index

Patterson, Jane Lancaster, 6
Paul, Ian, 5
Pedley, John, 148, 149
Peppard, Michael, 74
Pickett, Raymond, 156
Pilch, John J., 145
Plummer, Alfred, 87, 120, 140, 145, 148
Pogoloff, Stephen M., 57
Poirier, John C., 159,
Polaski, Sandra Hack, 95, 113
Punt, Jeremy, 62

Rabens, Volker, 156
Rawlinson, A. E. J., 166
Rawson, Beryl, 52, 99, 116, 128
Reasoner, Mark, 155
Reumann, John, 130
Richards, I. A., 18
Ricoeur, Paul, 9
Robbins, Vernon K., 95
Robertson, Archibald, 120, 140, 148
Robinson, John A. T., 164, 180
Rosner, Brian S., 6, 79, 115, 122, 128, 138, 161, 162, 171, 173, 174, 184
Ross, G. F., 35, 36, 37

Saller, Richard P., 93, 99, 100, 101, 102, 104, 105, 116
Sandnes, Karl Olav, 59, 60, 61, 63, 82, 96, 135
Savage, Timothy B., 56
Scholer, David, 27
Schottroff, Luise, 84
Schowalter, Daniel N., 81, 137
Schüssler Fiorenza, Elizabeth, 61
Schweitzer, Albert, 164, 166
Shanor, Jay, 150
Shen, Michael, 138
Smith, Dennis E., 81, 82
Smith, Dennis, 81
Snyder, Graydon F., 145
Son, Sang-Won (Aaron), 162, 165, 166
Soskice, Janet Martin, 8, 9
Still, Todd D., 26, 27,
Strange, William A., 97
Swift, E. H., 116

Tajfel, Henri, 30, 31, 32, 33, 35, 48, 187
Talbott, Rick F., 114
Tellbe, Mikael, 27
Theissen, Gerd, 57, 80, 81, 85, 161, 182
Thiselton, Anthony C., 81, 83, 111, 113, 140, 152, 194
Thrall, Margaret E., 73, 142
Tibbs, Clint, 159, 161
Trebilco, Paul R., 52, 91
Tsang, Sam, 6, 130
Tucker, J. Brian, vii, 27, 28, 38, 39, 45, 47, 139, 195
Tuckett, Christopher, 164
Turner, John, 31, 32, 34, 187
Turner, John C., 34
Turner, Max, 159, 161

Van der Watt, Jan G., 9, 11
Van Henten, Jan Willem, 52, 99
Van Oudenhouven, J. P., 38
Verbrugge, Veryn D., 87
Verner, D. C., 95

Walbank, Mary E. Hoskins, 149
Walters, James C., 80, 86
Walther, James Arthus, 78, 85
Wanamaker, Charles, 8, 115, 155
Wardle, Timothy, 142, 144, 145
Weaver, Paul, 99
Weima, Jeffrey A. D., 96
Weissenrieder, Annette, 41
Westfall, Cynthia Long, 95
White, Adam G., 115, 127
White, John L., 95, 100
White, L. Michael, 27
Wickkiser, Bronwen L., 175
Wiedemann, Thomas, 99
Williams, David J., 6, 7
Willis, Wendell Lee, 138
Winter, Bruce W., xviii, xix, 56, 75, 76, 79, 80, 138, 139
Witherington, Ben, 166, 171, 173, 180, 184
Wuellner, William, 147

Yarbrough, O. Larry, 27, 71, 97, 111, 117, 118, 119, 121
Young, Norman H., 114

Zanker, Paul, 39, 40, 41, 44

Ancient Document Index

HEBREW BIBLE

Exodus
20:5	117
25:8	154
34:14	117

Leviticus
26:11–12	154

Numbers
11:12	122
12:12	128
25:11–13	117

2 Samuel
7:14	115, 154

Job
3:16	128

Proverbs
13:24	111
19:18	111
22:15	115
23:13–14	115
26:3	115

Ecclesiastes
6:3	128

Isaiah
43:6	154
52:11	154

Ezekiel
20:41	154
37:27	154

APOCRYPHA

Sirach
7:23–25	111
22:3–6	111
30:1–13	111

4 Maccabees
18:10–19	111

NEW TESTAMENT

Matthew
27:5	140

Mark
5:26	118

Luke
15:14	118

John
2:20	140

Acts
18:1–17	193
18:1–2	121
18:1	xvii, xviii
18:11	138
19:8–41	148

Acts (continued)

19:23–25	148
20:31	111

Romans

6:3–11	186
6:16	147
8:22	122
8:29	63
9:3	91
12:1	193
12:2	193
12:3–8	180
12:3	163
12:4–5	162
12:5	180
12:6–8	163
12:9–13	63
14:15	63
15:14	111
16:1	52
16:15	52
16:23	57

1 Corinthians

1–4	56, 115, 131, 141, 199
1:1–9	55
1:10–13	151
1:10–12	141
1:10–11	194
1:10	xv, 53, 56, 79
1:11–12	32
1:11	53, 55
1:12	55, 194
1:13	164
1:14–15	186
1:16	52
1:17—2:5	139
1:23	186
1:29	151
2:1–5	125
2:2	83, 186
3–6	62
3:1–13	127
3:1–4	122
3:1–3	71, 120, 121, 123, 126
3:1–2	94, 120
3:1–2a	xv
3:2	25, 52
3:3	55, 123, 151
3:5–23	141
3:5–9a	141
3:9–10	4
3:9b–15	141
3:10–15	150, 152
3:16–17	xv, 3, 8, 10, 139, 141, 143, 147, 150
3:16	140
3:17	140, 148, 150
3:21	151
4	130
4:1–2	94, 130, 131
4:1	130
4:7	151
4:9–13	114
4:14–21	71, 93, 110
4:14–17	52, 119
4:14–15	4, 110
4:14	78, 111, 120
4:15	xv, 111, 122
4:16–21	95
4:16	52, 112–13
4:17	52, 112, 114
4:18—7:40	115
4:18–21	114, 115
4:21	115
5–6	115
5:1–13	151, 154
5:1–8	151
5:1–2	34
5:1	90, 91
5:5–8	56
5:6–8	138
5:6	147
5:7–8	91, 146
5:9	xviii, 90
5:11	xviii, 53, 90
6	78
6:1–11	63, 71, 74, 77
6:1–8	78, 151
6:1	74, 78
6:2	74, 75, 78, 147
6:3	74, 147
6:5–8	76–77
6:5–6	54
6:5	74, 78

6:6	74, 78, 91	10:25	138
6:7–11	78	10:27–30	138
6:7–10	74	11–14	195
6:7	77	11:1	52, 114
6:8–11	74	11:2—14:40	151
6:8	54, 78	11:2–16	52
6:9–20	151	11:17–34	71, 79, 81, 82, 186, 198
6:9–10	78	11:17	79, 82
6:9	74, 78, 147	11:18–19	56
6:12–20	138, 142, 152, 164	11:18	79, 199
6:12	152	11:20–22	57, 79
6:15	147, 164	11:20–21	79
6:16	147	11:20	79, 85
6:18	154	11:21	80
6:19–20	8, 10	11:22	52
6:19	139, 140, 141, 142, 143, 147, 151, 152	11:24–25	85
		11:26	85
7	126, 151	11:27–32	83
7:1–16	52	11:28	85
7:12–16	94, 152	11:29–30	85
7:12–15	91	11:29	83, 85
7:12	54	11:33–34	57, 83
7:14	53, 54	11:33	79, 82
7:15	52	11:34	79
8–10	138, 151	12–14	62, 159, 161
8:1–11	146	12	159, 163, 173, 174, 176
8:1	53	12:1	58, 159
8:6	52	12:2	91
8:7–11	138	12:4–31	180
8:11–13	54, 56	12:10	159
8:11	57, 63	12:12–27	163, 173, 178
8:12	53, 164	12:12–26	138
8:13	57	12:12	xv, 164, 180
9	130	12:13	186, 198
9:1–14	138	12:14–26	162
9:5	52	12:14–25	176
9:13	146, 147	12:14–18	4
9:16–23	131, 132	12:14–16	165, 166
9:16–17	132	12:17	165
9:17	94, 130	12:21–22	200
9:18	132	12:22–26	181
9:19	132	12:22–24	165, 174, 183
9:24–27	4	12:22	165, 178, 181
9:24	147	12:23	181
10:14–22	138	12:24–26	165
10:14–17	138	12:24	181
10:17	79, 180	12:25	184, 199
10:18	146	12:26	185

1 Corinthians (continued)

12:27	xv, 198
12:28	159
12:30	159, 161
13	159
13:1	159, 160, 161
13:8	159, 161
13:13	161
14	159, 161
14:1–21	161
14:1	162
14:2–19	160
14:2	159
14:3–5	162
14:4	159
14:5–6	160
14:5	161
14:6	58, 159
14:9	159
14:12	160, 162
14:13	159
14:16–19	160
14:18–19	162, 184
14:18	159
14:22	159
14:23	160, 162
14:24–25	162
14:26	55, 58, 159
14:27–28	161, 162
14:27	160, 162
14:28	162
14:33	200
14:40	200
14:39	55, 159, 160, 162
15	151
15:1–8	127
15:8	94, 127
15:9	129
15:10	129
15:24	52
15:31	53
15:34	78
15:58	53, 55, 58
16:1–4	71, 87, 198
16:2	xvii
16:5	xvii, 52

2 Corinthians

1:2–3	52
1:15–16	xvii
1:23—2:11	xviii
1:23	xvii
2:1	xvii
2:3	xvii
2:14–16	138
2:17	132
3:1–3	4
5:1–5	143
5:11–21	116
6:1–10	116
6:11—7:1	153
6:11–13	94, 116
6:11–12	157
6:11	153
6:12	116
6:13	52, 119
6:14—7:2	144
6:14—7:1	142, 156
6:14	142, 156
6:15	156
6:16—7:1	143
6:16–18	52, 154
6:16	139, 140, 142, 153
6:17–18	154
6:17	154
7:1	154, 157
7:2–4	117
7:2	157
7:5–16	xviii
8–9	58, 71, 86, 87, 198
8	88
8:1–5	34, 73, 87
8:1	58, 86, 87
8:2	88
8:6	87
8:7	88
8:9	87, 88–89, 132
8:11–15	89
8:15	88
8:16—9:5	90
8:18	58, 86, 90
8:22	58, 86, 90
9:1–5	89
9:3	58, 86, 90
9:5	58, 86, 90

9:6–15	89	5:22—6:9	95
9:8	89	5:23	163
9:11	89	5:29–30	163
10–13	119		
10:1—11:6	117	**Philippians**	
10:10	34, 125	2:6–11	132
10:14b	111	2:22	112
11:2	94, 117	4:15	153
11:5	117		
11:7–15	118	**Colossians**	
11:9	55, 58, 86, 89	1:8	163
11:26	91	1:28	111
11:31	52	2:19	163
12:14	71, 94, 120	3:1–17	44
12:15	52	3:8	44
12:14–15	118	3:9	44
12:14b–15a	118	3:10	44
12:14	xvii, 118	3:12	44
12:15a	118	3:15	163
12:15b	118	3:16	111
12:20–21	xvii, 154	3:18—4:1	95
12:21	xvii	4:16	73
13:1–2	xvii		
13:10	94, 119	**1 Thessalonians**	
13:11	58	2:7	122
		2:14	45
Galatians		4:3–8	61
1–2	71	4:9–12	61, 63
1:15	122	5:3	122
2:4	91	5:12–15	61
2:20	89	5:12	111
3:1	153	5:14	111
3:27–28	186		
3:29	180	**2 Thessalonians**	
4:19	122	3:15	111
5:13—6:10	90		
		1 Timothy	
Ephesians		2:8–15	95
1:15–23	163	3:15	143
1:22–23	163	6:1–2	95
2	163		
2:16	163	**Titus**	
2:20–22	143	1:12	34
3:6	163	2:1–10	95
4:1–16	180		
4:4–16	163	**Philemon**	
4:13	163	2	52
4:14–15	163	10	112, 122
		12	112

Hebrews

5:12–14	120, 121

1 Peter

2:2	120, 121
2:18—3:7	95
4:17	143

DEAD SEA SCROLLS

1QH 15.20–22	122

GRECO-ROMAN WRITINGS

Aelius Aristides

Orationes

17.9	169
23.31	169
24.16	179
24.18	169, 179
24.38–39	169
26.43	169

Apuleius

Metamorphoses

9.33	76

Aristotle

Ethica nicomachea

8.7.7	107
8.12.1–6	64
8.12.3	107
8.12.5	107
9.2.8	107
1165a	109

De generatione anamalium

4.5.18	128

Physiognomonica

806b	124
807a–b	124

Poetica

21.7	9

21.8–16	9–10
22.16–17	12

Rhetorica

3.2.6–15	12
3.2.6–7	12
3.2.8–9	12
3.2.9–10	13
3.2.10	13
3.2.12	14
3.2.13	12
3.3.3–4	12
3.3.4	13–14
3.4.1	12, 14
3.10.6	12
3.10.2	12
3.10.7	12, 13
3.11.15	13

Aulus Gellius

Noctes atticae

10.3.17	104

Cicero

Divinatio in Caecilium

61–62	109

De legibus

1.9.26	124
3.8.19	128

De natura deorum

2.33.86	172

De officiis

1.17.54–55	64
1.17.58	108
1.45.160	107–8
3.5.22–23	167
3.5.22	168, 172
3.6.26–27	167

De oratore

3.152–55	15
3.155	15
3.156	15
3.157	15
3.159	15, 16

3.160–61	15–16
3.161	16
3.162–66	16

De republica

1.64	109

Epistulae ad familiares

9.25.3	77
13.10.1	109

In Pisonem

1	124–25
3.6	110

Pro Caecina

73	76

Pro Ligario

30	110

Topica

6.30	167

Demetrius

De elocutione

2.78–90	14, 15
2.78	14
2.82	14
2.86–87	21

Dio Chrysostom

Orationes

3.104–7	167
3.108–9	185
8.9	76
9:2	167
10.23	160
11.22	160
17.9	167
33.10	126
33.16	167, 171
33.34	167
34.17	179
34.20	175, 179
34.22	179
34.32	167
38.12	179
38.14	179
39.5	167, 169–70
40.21	167
41.9	167
50.3	167

Dionysius of Halicarnassus

Antiquitates romanae

6.68.1–5	167–68
6.86.4	167
7.66.5	70

Epictetus

Diatribai

1.15.6–8	69
2.5.28	171, 172
2.10.4–5	167
2.10.8	68
2.10.12–14	67
2.16.18	121
2.16.39	120, 121
2.16.44	121
3.24.9	120
4.7.33–47	69

Enchiridion

43	69

Galen

On Hippocrates' On the Nature of Man

128–30	178

Hesiod

Opera et dies

331–332	109

Hippocrates

De natura hominis

2.11–15	177
2.15–20	177
4.1–4	177
10.1–10	177–78

Horace

Satirae

1.4.105–6	104
1.4.120–21	105

Irenaeus

Adversus haereses

5.6.1	160

Isocrates

De pace

109	179

Panegyricus

4.43	83

Josephus

Against Apion

2.119	140

Jewish War

3.52	148
3.102–5	170
4.406–7	167
5.207	140
5.278–79	170

Juvenal

Satirae

7.2.10	105

Livy

History of Rome

1.16.3	109
1.55.5–6	148, 150
2.7.4	109
2.32.7—33.1	166, 168
2.60.3	109

Pausanias

Graeciae descriptio

II	137
10.6.3	148

Philo

Allegorical Interpretation

1.76	128

On Agriculture

9	120

On Dreams

2.10	120

On the Decalogue

150	175

On the Life of Moses

2.245	118

On the Migration of Abraham

29	120

On the Preliminary Studies

19	120

On the Special Laws

3.131	167

On Rewards and Punishments

125	182

That Every Good Person Is Free

160	120

Plato

Leges

IV.717B–718A	108, 109
IV.717C–D	108
IV.781A	108
IV.913C	108
IV.931E–932A	108, 109

Philebus

29D–E	172

Respublica

370A–B	167

Timaeus

44D	182
69C	172
92C	172

Plautus

Mostellaria

743–50	106

Poenulus

1137	100

Pliny the Younger

Epistulae

10.65–66	100
5.15	109

Plutarch

De cupiditate divitiarum

526a	118

De fraterno amore

478B–C	69
478C–D	70
478C	64
478D	64–65, 172
479A	65
479B	65
479C	66
479D	66, 67
480A	66
480B–C	66
480D	69
481A	70
481B	69
481C–E	70
481C–D	67
481C	69
481D	69
482A–C	69
482D–E	70
483A–E	70
483D	70, 77
483E–484F	70
484D	68
485F–486A	172
485C	67, 68
486F–487A	68
487B	68
487F	68
488A	69, 77
489C–D	69
490D	68
490E	67
491A–B	67
491B	67

De liberis educandis

3C–F	126
3C	107
3D–E	107
3E	103
4A–B	103
4C	103
5E	102
6A	102
6B–8B	103
7D	103
7E–F	103
8F	103
9A	105
9D	106
10A–F	103
12C	103
12D	103, 113
13A	103, 113
13C	113
14A–B	106, 113
479F	108
480A	108

Marcius Coriolanus

6	172
6.1–4	168
6.2	169

Praecepta gerendae rei publicae

823A	185

Quomodo adulator ab amico internoscatur

69C	126

Quintilian

Institutio oratoria

1.3.13	104–5
8.3.38	17
8.6.1	16
8.6.4	16
8.6.5–6	17

Institutio oratoria (continued)

8.6.5	16–17
8.6.9–10	17
8.6.11	17
8.6.14	17
8.6.16	17
8.6.17	17
8.6.19	17
8.8.18	17
11.1.3	124

Res gestae divi Augusti

35	110

Rhetorica ad Herennium

2.19	102

Seneca (The Elder)

Controversiae

10.1.2	76
10.1.7	76

Seneca (The Younger)

De beneficiis

3.1.5	108
6.23.5	108

De clementia

1.3.5—5.3	169
1.14.1	105

De ira

1.15	128
2.13.7	167
2.21	105
2.31.7	170

De prouidentia

2.5	107, 108

De sonstantia sapientis

12.3	105

Epistulae morales

122.7	124

Stobaeus

4.27.20	65, 69, 172

Strabo

Geography

5.3.9	43
6.4.2	110
8.6.20C	149
8.6.21B	149

Suetonius

Divus Augustus

58	110

Terrance

Heauton timorumenos

356	106

Phormio

220–21	106

Tacitus

Historiae

3.72	148, 150

Xenophon

Memorabilia

2.3.18–19	172
2.4.7	172
2.13.18	168

EARLY CHRISTIAN WRITINGS

1 Clement

1:1	200
2:4	200
3:2–3	199
4:6–8	200
13:1	200
14:1	200
20:11	200
21:6–8	201
31:4	200
33:1	200
35:8	200
37:1–5	200
37:1	200

37:5	200	62:1	200
38:1–5	200	63:2	200
38:3	200	65:1	200
41:1	200		
41:2	200	John Chrysostom	
41:4	200	*Homiliae in epistulam i ad*	
43:4	200	*Corinthios*	
44:3–6	200	31.425–426	174
45:1	200		
45:6	200		
46:5–7	200	**GREEK PAPYRI**	
46:6	200	*BGU* VIII 1974	70
46:7	200	*POxy* IV 744	100
46:9	200	*POxy* VII 2148	70
47:6	200	*POxy* XLII 3057	70
48:1	200	*SB* V 7661	70
51:1	200	*SB* XIV 11644	70
60:4	200	Select Papyri I/94	109
61:1	200		

www.ingramcontent.com/pod-product-compliance
Lightning Source LLC
Chambersburg PA
CBHW050347230426
43663CB00010B/2028